Dimensions of Mind

A SYMPOSIUM

EDITED BY SIDNEY HOOK

COLLIER BOOKS *New York*

COLLIER-MACMILLAN LTD *London*

The contents of this volume comprise the proceedings
of the third annual New York University Institute of Philosophy,
held at Washington Square, New York, May 15-16, 1959.

Preface

AMONG THE PERSISTENT problems of philosophy few, if any, are as complex and difficult as that of the relation between the human mind and human body, of which the relation between mind and brain is a special case. This problem was involved in the issues considered at the two previous meetings of the New York University Institute of Philosophy. It was a natural development of these discussions to make the mind-body problem the focal theme for the third meeting of the Institute, the proceedings of which are contained in this book. The theme was all the more appropriate because it bore directly upon the theoretical and practical concerns of several different disciplines and permitted fruitful collaboration among inquirers from diverse fields. It is one of the aims of the Institute to foster this interchange of ideas.

No matter what their approach to man, most scientists as well as philosophers find it necessary to take note of or refer in some way to "the unity of the human being." Whether this unity is described as a unity of action or of behavior, of experience or of life-career, all intend by it something common. This is the view that however we distinguish among the different aspects or functions of a person they are not separate from each other but are distinctions within an encompassing whole or ongoing process. Emphasis upon the unity of the human being is usually a protest against taking the word "and," when we speak of "mind and body," as if it were not only a grammatical conjunction but a term designating an existential conjunction. The fact that this unity seems to dissolve when we focus upon it, that, so to speak, we become unfamiliar to ourselves when we seek to make it an object of close scrutiny or attention, suggests that it is not itself a distinct element of experience, such as a pain, or something that can be observed, such as a bruise. It is a relation or organization of some sort.

The character of the relation between mind and body is what this volume explores. Any adequate theory of the relation between mind and body must do justice to at least three kinds of consideration. Even if we forego the use of terms like "experience" or "mental events" and speak only of behavior, there are felt qualities, or what the late E. C. Tolman called "raw feels," which cannot be banished from the world by calling them illusory or private. Any theory which leaves them out or makes them mysterious cannot but give us a truncated account of the unity of the human being. The second order of consideration is our traditional language habits, which are frankly dualistic. Many puzzles about things are created by the peculiar way we speak about them. The question here is whether a theory of the relation between mind and body can be so formulated that any linguistic paradoxes to which it leads may be resolved without intellectual violence to rules of what makes good sense—good sense judged not by antecedently-held doctrines about meaning but by the necessities of fruitful communication among men. The third order of consideration derives from the well-attested results of modern brain physiology, psychology, and cybernetics. No theory is acceptable that ignores or makes inexplicable their findings, and that does not provide a place for them in its scheme of explanation.

The way of modern philosophy, it has been said, is to solve its problems by dissolving them rather than by resolving them. They are dissolved, according to some, by semantic or linguistic analysis (without reference to the specific results of the sciences), assording to others, by showing (on the basis of the findings of modern science) that they are illegitimately formulated. There are still others who contend that, whatever may be the case with other philosophical problems, the problems considered in this book are primarily problems of empirical science rather than of linguistic analysis, and that they can only be solved, if at all, by the winning of new knowledge.

The cluster of problems connected with the concept of mind constitutes a crucial test of all these claims, which also throw some light on the selection of topics. For purposes of publication it was deemed desirable to alter the order of the topics from that in which they were discussed in the proceedings of the Institute.

Sidney Hook

Contents

PART I. *THE MIND-BODY PROBLEM*

Contents

PART II. *THE BRAIN AND THE MACHINE*

PART III. *CONCEPT-FORMATION*

PART ONE

The Mind-Body Problem

Chapter 1

The Mind-Body Problem

Wolfgang Köhler, *Dartmouth College*

AMONG THE PROBLEMS with which philosophy and the various sciences have to deal, the mind-body problem is still the most intriguing. No completely convincing solution has so far been offered. I do not claim that I have found such a solution. Recent advances in philosophical thinking and in experimental research have made the problem even more challenging than it was, say, thirty years ago. For now we have begun to realize that almost any imaginable solution is likely to affect our interpretation of what we call the physical world. I will try to explain this statement in the following paragraphs.

In present discussions we do not assume, as the philosophers of the past did, that the mind and the body are two substances. In the first place, we have the very best reasons for regarding the bodies of animals and men as processes or, more specifically, as approximately steady states, which maintain their shapes and other characteristics by self-regulating activities. Biologists know that the material of all organs of the body is continuously being eliminated, and at the same time replaced, in the course of metabolic events. Similarly, there is no evidence that mental functions represent the activities of a mental substance. What we call, in a purely empirical sense, the *self* is not a permanent entity with constant characteristics—although, among the various states through which this important part of the mental scene passes, there is a great deal of coherence. The relative constancy of a person's self is likely to be basically of the same kind as the relative constancy of his heart, his muscles, his brain, and so forth— that is, a constancy of a state of affairs.

All this does not alter the fact that the events which occur in our organisms appear to us to be of one kind, and those that we call "mental" events to be of another kind. It is this prima facie dualism which makes us speak of a mind-body problem.

We are less and less inclined to believe that the dualistic view can be accepted as final. For one thing, we prefer unitary

15

knowledge to the view that certain groups of facts will never become parts of one cognitive system. Secondly, numerous observations, particularly in medicine, tend to show that, however different from processes in nature the mental phenomena may seem to be, they only occur when certain conditions are fulfilled in a particular part of nature, the brain. Causal relations between processes in the brain and mental facts are, of course, readily recognized by the dualists. But mental facts depend upon biological conditions in a much more radical fashion. I need not mention details. One example will suffice. When the oxygen supply to the human brain is lowered beyond a certain crucial level, the mental world of the person in question disappears entirely—until the oxygen level rises again, and sufficiently. We do not usually speak of interaction when the presence or absence of one of the allegedly interacting entities or events depends upon variations in the state of the other. This and similar arguments against the dualists' thesis may not be fully convincing, but they have made most of us feel that the solution of the mind-body problem must lie in another direction. Meanwhile, the dualists have not yet surrendered. Some philosophers and also some biologists remain convinced that certain achievements of the mental world will never be explained in terms of natural science. On the contrary, such authors sometimes add, even the most important activities of the *organism* cannot be understood in such terms, for these activities exhibit the same characteristics as do the irreducible mental processes. Although the more extreme form of this thesis, namely vitalism, has so far proved to be singularly unproductive, the dualists' factual arguments may at least serve as warnings. To be sure, those who claim that certain mental processes have no counterparts among the facts of the physical world often offer examples for which people more familiar with natural science will find physical partners without the slightest difficulty. In other instances, however, no such simple answers to the dualists' arguments are available. This ought to prevent their opponents from proceeding too rashly. The tremendous store of knowledge which natural science has accumulated in the past may sometimes make them overconfident. There is a risk that, when now approaching the mental world, they will inadvertently crush rather than recognize some outstanding facts of this world or (what would be just as bad) that they will simply ignore such parts of the less familiar field as do not immediately yield to the impatient demands of the conquerors. Some geneticists and evolutionists have actually proceeded in this fashion. But can we be interested in a unity of knowledge that only destruction or partial omission of the evidence makes possible?

We wish to compare psychological facts with the facts of natural science. We must, therefore, make sure that we know the characteristics of these facts as such. For our present purposes, an inspection of some psychological evidence and a consideration of a major biological issue will suffice. We may regard ourselves as fairly well acquainted with the behavior of inanimate nature, but we do not always have sufficiently clear concepts in psychology and biology.

I begin with psychology. Here, early behaviorism made an error, the consequences of which still disturb the psychologist's work. It is quite true that, in natural science, all observation of systems is observation "from the outside." But does it follow that, when the psychologist deals with human subjects, he must always use the same procedure? Must he also restrict his observations to behavior as watched from the outside? Why should he not be interested in mental life as *experienced* by himself or others? If a certain scientific enterprise which we admire has unfortunately only one kind of access to its material, why should psychology, which has two, refuse to make use of both? In the meantime, the behaviorists themselves have discovered that, when a physicist observes his systems from the outside, the content of his observations as such consists of certain perceptual facts, mostly in his visual field, and that the same holds for the behaviorists' own observations of animals and of men. But perceptual facts belong to the mental world, the world of experienced phenomena, and it therefore follows that such phenomena play a decisive role in any scientific enterprise. Hence, modern behaviorists no longer maintain that the phenomenal world has been invented by the metaphysicians. What is left, however, is their preference for observation from the outside, which under the right conditions yields clear quantitative results, in contrast to phenomenological procedures which in this respect are generally inferior. In this methodological sense, most American psychologists now seem to be behaviorists. Under the circumstances, not only details but also impressive aspects of the phenomenal scene are often ignored in the psychologists' work. Their admiration of method, of precision, prevents them from paying attention to phenomenological evidence even when this evidence could hardly escape the very simplest observation. Naturally, the psychologists' sin of omission makes them incapable of contributing to the solution of the mind-body problem in its most serious form, in which it refers to the relation between the *phenomenal* scene and the characteristics of events in nature. Once more, one cannot study the relation between two groups of facts without knowing the facts in each group *per se*.

I have just implied that, when trying to solve the mind-body problem, we actually have to answer more than one question. The reason is that the expression "mental processes" is sometimes given one and sometimes another meaning. But so abstract are many discussions of the problem that, at a given moment, it may be almost impossible to decide whether the term is being used in one sense or the other.

In its first meaning, the term refers to all facts which are directly accessible to a person, the facts which are phenomenally given. I have repeatedly been asked to indicate more clearly what I mean when I refer to "phenomenally given facts." It seems quite possible that in this case no actual definition can be given and that, if the attempt is made, one undefinable word is merely substituted for another. But I also doubt whether such a definition is really needed. Everybody will recognize the meaning of the expression if I tell him that objects as felt, sounds as heard, colors and shapes as seen, and movement perceived in any fashion are all phenomenal facts. To avoid misunderstandings, I should have to include a person's hilarious or dejected moods, the direction of his attention, his awareness of relations, and the values, both positive and negative, with which objects or ideas seem to him to be imbued, and which thus establish his motivations. It is the task of phenomenological psychology to study these facts; and, in its first form, the mind-body problem refers to the relations between the characteristics of such facts and those of facts in nature.

The psychologist's work is not restricted to the study of the phenomenal scene, he investigates other facts besides, which often are also called "mental." The phenomenal facts as such do not constitute a functionally complete material. There is a coherence among the phenomenal experiences of a person which transcends these experiences themselves. A person may suddenly have a new idea, which he has begun to elaborate when circumstances arise which force him to do other things first, and only after they have been done is that idea, with the reasoning which it had barely started, likely to emerge again as an experienced fact—whereupon the reasoning may be continued. This is memory in the strictest sense of the term. In the present case, it makes temporally separated stages of the phenomenal flux coherent in spite of an interruption. Most probably, if a person's mental life was crowded with phenomenal experiences, but deprived of the coherence established by memory, this life would be of very little value. Memory is generally regarded as a fact which the psychologist has to study, and so are its gradually developing *defects* which we call forgetting. But neither retention in memory *per se* nor forgetting *per se* are generally experienced in the sense in which we experience the emergence of a new idea and, afterwards, its recall. Retention, often for considerable periods, and gradual forgetting are facts which do not belong to the phenomenal scene. This holds also for memory in its more general sense, in which the word refers to our habits and to our cognitive, motivational, or emotional dispositions. Habits and dispositions as such are not parts of the phenomenal, the experienced, world. Only their temporary *effects* will generally be experienced—although not necessarily *as* effects of the underlying more permanent entities, the habits and dispositions themselves. But again, if all our habits and dispositions were suddenly to disappear forever, our mental life would probably no longer deserve its name.

Even though the effects of memory in all its meanings are so closely related, and so necessary to most mental processes in the phenomenal sense, it is perhaps not wise to refer to retention in memory, to our habits, and to our dispositions as "mental facts." After all, the existence of retention in memory, of habits, and of dispositions can only be inferred from certain achievements within the phenomenal field, which they make possible. And, from the point of view of epistemology, this means a fundamental difference between these products of the past and the experienced facts, however much these may owe to such hidden entities. Consequently, when dealing with the mind-body problem, we must try to keep two comparisons separate: that of the phenomenal world with the facts of natural science, and that of memory, and so forth, with the same facts.

All merely inferred "mental" states seem to have much in common with certain facts in nature. For instance, memory as a mere retention, as an aftereffect of events which have taken place in the past, is by no means a rare fact in physical nature. It has therefore been suggested that memory in psychology simply *consists* of more or less permanent physical states which earlier events have established in the brain. Thus, the comparison of merely inferred "psychological" facts with certain facts in the physical world may perhaps be expected to yield positive results. But, when we compare phenomenal situations with the various facts which occur in nature, we have reasons for being far less optimistic.

Some difficulties arise only when particular classes of phenomena are being considered. It would, for instance, not be easy to find in nature anything like Dilthey's *"verständliche Zusammenhänge."* What, in the physical world as such, would be comparable to such *understandable,* as distinct from merely *factual,* relations? And also, what physical fact would be capable of what we call "understanding"? But, far more generally, present epistemology refuses to attribute *any* phenomenal characteristics to *any* fact in nature—whatever these characteristics may be. It seems to follow that, in this respect, not a single part of the phenomenal world fits the premises on which the system of natural science rests, and that therefore the dualists are right.

If we do not wish to accept this radical conclusion, we must obviously examine the thesis from which it is derived. How did it happen that the epistemologists excluded all phenomenal characteristics from our picture of nature? There is, I believe, no question that, as children, we have all been "naïve realists." The rocks, trees, houses, and so forth, which are perceived were at this stage regarded as permanent entities which happened to be thus accessible at the time, but were not at all dependent upon our presence. When we were absent, they continued to exist, and still had characteristics of the same kind as they had in our presence. These characteristics were, of course, phenomenal characteristics. Obviously, we had no difficulty in ascribing such characteristics to objects outside the field of actual awareness. In less sophisticated populations, adults share this view with their children. This we can safely say because even the most sophisticated physicists and epistemologists among *us* still think in the same fashion whenever they do not happen to remember the arguments against this simple view of the world. We are all naïve realists most of the time. It will not be necessary to mention the observations which gradually destroyed naïve realism in the thinking of scientists *as* scientists, and eventually made it necessary to distinguish, as a matter of principle, between all facts of phenomenal experience and an independent physical world. So gradual was this development—its final stages occurred during the nineteenth century—that even now a physicist may think of the behavior of molecules in a gas in concrete phenomenal terms, as though he were considering a *visual* scene and *visual* events. It is this behavior which obscures to us the consequences of a more consistent discrimination between all phenomenal facts and all facts in nature. I repeat, according to the epistemologists of our time, not a single phenomenal datum is, as such, a characteristic also of situations in the physical world. The content of all statements about this world is only a matter of inferences, of a construction in thought—although some simple perceptual facts used in actual observation are supposed to have somehow comparable partners in nature, and thus to control the direction in which the construction can proceed. From this point of view, what ingredients, what building materials, are being used in the construction? So far as I can see, only one material is available. Although we have been told that we must sharply distinguish between the characteristics of nature and those of the phenomenal world, the contents of this world remain the only stuff at our disposal when we do the constructing. What else could we use? To be sure, as scientists we are free to select such particular characteristics of the phenomenal scene as seem to us most adequate for our purposes; and, being parsimonious people, we do the constructing with a *minimum* of concepts taken from the phenomenal world. Thus, the various sensory qualities are never used, nor are our feelings, our experiences of value, and our motivations. As a consequence, the resulting picture of nature is, of course, a most colorless affair when compared with the world of which we are directly aware. Even so, any concept actually used in the process must contain one or several components which are known to us from phenomenal experience. If something in nature were totally different from *all* phenomenal facts, then this part of nature would forever remain inaccessible to us.

How well the process of construction has so far worked we all know. However, I have not yet been able to overcome a certain difficulty. I said that, in constructing the physical world, we have to equip it throughout with attributes directly known to us only as properties of the phenomenal scene. But we are also told that no state or event in nature has any phenomenal characteristics. It seems to follow that when, for example, the term "intensity" (the meaning of which is derived from certain experiences) is used as it is nowadays in physics, it is deprived of all phenomenal content and yet remains a term with a meaning. What exactly is left under these circumstances? Suppose we were told that "intensity" in nature must be understood in a far more abstract sense than it is when the term is applied to a phenomenal fact; that, in nature, the meaning of "intensity" is reduced to a system of mere *relations*. If this were said, I should be inclined to ask from what sources anybody derives his knowledge of such *relations;* and the answer would be that *their* meanings, too, must stem from relations experienced in the phenomenal world—whereupon the same difficulty would once more arise. Obviously, there would be no such difficulty if, contrary to present convictions, states and events in nature actually had phenomenal characteristics. It is a curious fact that a physicist as advanced as Galileo still regarded the behavior of the planets as partly determined by values. This is a strange situation. Epistemologists may, of course, be able to clarify the present issue entirely. I can only repeat that, as I see it, all parts of recognizable nature must more or less resemble *some* aspects of the phenomenal world. If this is a true statement, it may sooner or later have to be remembered in discussions of the mind-body problem.

I now turn to a fundamental issue in biology, namely, to certain consequences of the theory of evolution. Unavoidably, the following discussion will be concerned with problems in natural science with which few philosophers are accustomed to deal.

Until recently, one part of the theory had remained disappointingly obscure. We were unable to explain the *beginning* of life on this planet. We knew that, in the absence of large organic molecules, there could be no living cells. But we also knew that, in present organisms, these molecules are built up in the cells. Where, then, did such molecules come from when cells did not exist? Thanks to Oparin in Russia, and to Urey and Miller in Chicago, a great step forward has now been made at this point. The early atmosphere of our planet contained no oxygen. Could not organic molecules, which cannot survive in the present atmosphere, originate and survive under such conditions? Miller found that, in the absence of oxygen, a mixture of exceedingly simple molecules did produce several amino acids, if energy such as that of electric sparks was supplied to the original material. Amino acids are, of course, organic compounds—in fact, some such acids are essential components of protein molecules. To be sure, their molecular weight is still comparatively small, but the very procedure used by Miller may have prevented the formation of much larger molecules. At any rate, we can safely say that what used to be the weakest part of evolutionary thinking has now become a matter of precise experimentation.

If the theory of evolution wishes to unite inanimate nature with the various manifestations of life, then the theory cannot permit itself to introduce principles of action at *higher* levels that never operate on *lower* levels. From this point of view, the theory of *emergent* evoluton can hardly be called a theory of evolution. For emergent evolution is said to mean that, when systems become more and more complicated, entirely new forms of action are added at certain crucial levels to those which are valid on lower levels. An evolution in which such things happened would involve discontinuities which the scientist could not understand. Emergent evolutionists may not always realize that their theory is incompatible with physics as applied to inanimate systems. When the physicist formulates the general principles according to which his systems operate, he does not refer to degrees of complication beyond which these principles would no longer permit him to predict what the systems will do. But the theory of emergent evolution clearly implies that, in this respect, the physicist is mistaken, because he fails to realize that the validity of his laws depends upon the simplicity of the systems to which they are being applied. Only as a result of this error would he have given his laws their present *general* form. Emergent evolution, therefore, cannot be defended without attacking physics at the same time. On the other hand, if the physicist is right, no place is left for new principles which suddenly take over when systems become particularly complicated. The concept of emergent evolution in the present sense does not appeal to the scientific mind. We shall later see, however, that most attempts to deal with the mind-body problem tacitly accept *other* forms of emergence. For the moment, we will reutrn to evolution as the term is now most generally understood.

It is obvious that the theory of evolution tries to give us an explanation of amazing *changes*. But, if nothing is added to this statement, it is practically bound to cause grave errors. What has to be added to prevent such errors is a statement of this kind: While evolution took place, the basic forces, the elementary processes, and the general principles of action remained the same as they had always been, and still are, in inanimate nature. As soon as any new force, any new elementary process, or any new principle of action were discovered in some organism, the concept of evolution in its strict sense would become inapplicable. *This is the postulate of invariance in evolution.* Similar statements are generally made on the first pages of books on evolution, but they are seldom mentioned thereafter, and the remaining pages are filled with discussions of evolution only as a matter of changes. Many discussions of this kind are plausible contributions to science. Occasionally, however, an author makes asumptions which are, obviously without his being aware of it, incompatible with the postulate of invariance. The fundamental concepts of physics have seldom played an important role in evolutionary thinking. The factors which make for change—namely, accidental variations of germ cells or, in more recent thought, mutations of genes, the selective action of this or that environment, and so forth—tend to occupy evolutionary thinking to such an extent that the postulate of invariance and its consequences are not always given sufficient attention. This is a dangerous situation. According to the postulate, a tremendous number of physical and chemical processes occurs in all organisms, although often in combinations hardly ever found outside these living systems. The postulate claims that these processes follow the laws of physics and chemistry, including such principles as govern the combination of more elementary events. At every step, evolution must have come to terms with this store of invariant physical facts which has, therefore, been just as relevant to the tremendous development as have been gene mutations and environmental influences. For instance, not every characteristic of a given organism need be the result of an "adaptation." Some such characteristics may simply be physical or chemical consequences of the conditions which, at a certain time, prevailed in that living system. And yet, in well-known evolutionary explanations, the postulate of invariance has been completely ignored. I will mention only a few examples.

We remember that natural science proceeds in a most parsimonious fashion and that, when developing its picture of nature, it strictly excludes some forms of action which play a most important part in our lives. As examples, consider value and motivation. If value and motivation were suddenly removed from human life, not much of this life would be left—nobody would take trains any longer, nobody would read a book, no man would be interested in any woman (or vice versa), in fact, nobody would move from one room to the next, and so forth. For we generally do such things because, in doing them, we approach valued objects or goals we have in mind, some only mildly, but others intensely, important to us. Nothing of the kind, the physicist tells us, ever happens in inanimate nature. There are no values in this realm. Events in nature are supposed to occur as mere matters of fact. But what have we often read in books on evolution? Not a few authors have claimed that human values originated when, in the genes of our ancestors, certain mutations followed one another. In the history of evolutionary thinking, there have been times when no part of this thinking was so popular, and so widely accepted, as precisely this curious invention. And yet, it should have been obvious that the invention is incompatible with the basic premise of the theory of evolution—that is, the postulate of invariance. If, as a matter of principle, no event in inanimate nature has anything to do with value, then no mutations, however great their number, can have brought values into the life of man. For, according to the postulate, action in organisms still follows the basic rules which are valid in inanimate systems.

But the fact that evolutionary thinking sometimes ignores the supposedly invariant aspects of nature has caused a further most disturbing mistake. Biologists, psychologists, and laymen alike now seem to take it for granted that individual human achievements in perception, in thinking, and so forth, are either inherited or are products of learning. This alternative is unacceptable. It is only a minor point that given human activities may depend on inherited gifts and *also* be influenced by learning. The worst part of the alternative is that it leaves a most important third factor unmentioned. I said that countless processes which occur in organisms are merely repetitions of well-known events in inanimate nature, or combinations of such events. For instance, diffusion, electric currents, and a host of fairly simple chemical reactions are the same processes in living systems as they are elsewhere. When, in organisms, they assume more complicated forms, such complications are still supposed to be in line with the principles of natural science as applied to one histological condition or another. Under such circumstances, do they follow such principles because our genes are of a particular kind? In other words, are the rules of their behavior prescribed in inheritance? If the postulate of invariance is accepted, these rules must be independent of what has happened in evolution. On the other hand, are those processes or their laws products of learning? Clearly no learning is involved, if electric currents and chemical reactions follow the same laws in organisms as they do in outside nature. All these facts are obviously being ignored when we say that events in living systems are brought about *either* by inherited conditions *or* by learning. Actually, when trying to explain the achievements of animals or human beings, we must, of course, always consider *three* classes of facts. In part, such achievements are made possible by inherited conditions; they are often, in part, products of learning; but, in each case, they must also exhibit the characteristics of processes which, as such, neither evolution nor learning have affected. According to the postulate of invariance, there cannot be a single action in living systems to which this third statement does not apply.

Since the present discussion is relevant to our thinking about the mind-body problem, I had better add the following remarks. If evolution could not introduce new basic forces or events, and also could not alter the principles of physical and chemical dynamics, what *could* it change? For our present purposes, a very short answer will suffice. The course taken by a physical process depends not only on its own nature but also on properties of the medium in which it takes place. An electric current, for instance, may spread in a medium of high or of low conductivity. Moreover, the conductivity of the medium may be the same throughout, or it may vary from one place to another. In both cases, the intensity of the flow as a whole depends on such conditions and, in the second case, its particular spatial distribution is determined by the inhomogeneity of the medium. More specifically, a current may be forced to follow a linear conductor because this conductor is surrounded by an insulating medium. In this situation, the insulator plays the part of a "constraint," a term originally applied to analogous conditions in mechanics. It goes without saying that the current obeys the general laws of electric currents which spread in conductors, whatever the particular characteristics of these conductors may be. Such laws contain terms that refer to such properties of the medium. Similar considerations apply to the distribution of *fluids* moving in conducting arrangements of one kind or another, and to many other processes in nature.

While evolution could not affect the basic forces, processes, and laws of physical nature, it was free to establish or to modify the conditions under which these invariant factors of nature operate in organisms. In actual fact, a great deal of what we call an organism simply *consists* of special configurations of cells, by which events are given particular directions, distributions, localizations, and so forth. I need hardly give examples. Everybody knows about the role of the bones in constraining the movements of animals, of the blood vessels in prescribing the flow of the blood, and of the fibers of nerve cells in determining the direction in which nerve impulses are propagated. No fact of this kind is at odds with the postulate of invariance, if the processes which gave the tissues their forms and their other characteristics followed the laws of physics and chemistry. It might be argued that, in the organism, we cannot sharply distinguish between *action* and the *conditions* to which it is subjected, because the conditioning tissues themselves are not objects in the usual sense but, rather, steady states, and hence also processes. Such a statement would be slightly misleading for two reasons. First, the steady states in question are generally so stable that they do serve as conditions which prescribe the course of what we usually call functions. Secondly, far from weakening the thesis that invariant dynamics plays a decisive role in living systems, the statement actually emphasizes that this is true. For it rightly insists that even the most stable-looking anatomical entities are maintained by processes which are not creations of evolution.

In passing, I should like to remark that events in organisms cannot be properly understood unless we realize that organisms are *open* systems, that is, systems which absorb energy from the outside. Under these conditions, the direction of events in living systems need not be the same as it is in closed systems, no difficulties arise at this point.

We can now turn to the mind-body problem itself. Since what I have just tried to explain applies to all processes in animals and man, it also applies to the processes which occur in brains—whether or not these processes are directly related to psychological facts. No actual *event* in a brain can be a product of evolution. All action in brains must, as a particular kind of process, be known to natural science; and, if a brain process is a new combination of such known events, then the behavior of the combination must be derivable from the general principles which *other* combinations follow in *in*animate nature. For, if this were not the case, we should be forced to discard the postulate of invariance and, with it, the theory of evolution in its strict form. Naturally, the characteristics of the brain as a medium, and special histological conditions within this medium, are bound to influence the course of brain action, just as certain histological facts influence action in other parts of the organism. But, this fact cannot affect the following general conclusion. It is not quite correct to speak of "those unknown processes in brains which are related to psychological facts." Whatever we may mean by "related to," these processes (or their components) must belong to that well-known class: the basic events studied by the physicists and the chemists. In this class we must find the processes directly related to perceptual facts, to our feelings, our motivations, our thinking, and, of course, all forms of memory and recall. What remains to be done is the selection of such *special* members of the class as actually occur when those psychological events take place. Professor Feigl has rightly pointed out that the mind-body problem is to a large extent a problem of empirical science. Philosophical analysis alone cannot discover the right solution. At least the selection of those processes will have to be based on physiological evidence, which we shall then have to compare with the corresponding psychological facts. Only after such comparisons shall we be able to tell what exactly the expression "directly related to" means, that is, whether the dualist's or the monist's or the parallelist's views are to be accepted. For instance, if the comparison were to show that, say, in perception, brain processes with a certain functional structure give rise to psychological facts with a *different* structure, such a discrepancy would prove that the mental world reacts to those brain processes as a realm with properties of its own—and this would mean dualism.

At this point, it becomes necessary to consider concrete situations rather than psychological facts and their possible physiological partners in general. Unfortunately, so long as available physiological evidence is not yet conclusive, speculation must play a certain part in such considerations. As a simple example, I will discuss a problem in visual perception. I hope to show, first, that an apparently clear answer to a question in this field cannot be regarded as satisfactory and, secondly, in what direction a better answer may be found.

From the eyes to the visual cortex of the human brain, nerve impulses travel along separate fibers. So far as we know, the points of origin of these fibers in the eyes determine the particular places in the visual cortex at which the equally separate neural messages arrive—although it is actually a *sequence* of neurons with their fibers in which the propagation occurs. In one hemisphere, topological relations among the arriving messages are apparently the same as those of corresponding stimulated points on the retinae. The separation of the messages and the preservation of their topological order are undoubtedly important facts. But can we go farther, and assume that these facts explain the spatial order in which points or objects appear in the visual field? If it is always *processes* which are related to phenomenal data, then the merely geometrical distribution of functionally unrelated events in the brain cannot, as such, be responsible for any visual characteristics. And, at the present time, few will be inclined to believe that the human mind fabricates visual distances, directions, and shapes after having inspected a purely geometrical arrangement of separate events in the cortex. But, if it is a process which underlies our experience, say, of a certain visual distance between two points, then this process must arise after the local messages corresponding to the two points have arrived, and must now translate their merely *geometrical* relation into an aspect of its own spatial distribution as a *function*. A physicist will be inclined to assume that the process in question is a "field" which relates those points across their distance, and in doing so expresses this distance in functional terms.

There is a further fact which points in this direction. If it were true that local brain processes are functionally separate events, we could not expect visual objects to show symptoms of *interaction*. But, as a matter of fact, such interactions occur all the time. The color seen in one part of the field is affected by the colors of other parts. Under certain conditions, the place of a visual object is strikingly changed by the appearance or disappearance of another object. Both attractions and repulsions may be demonstrated under such circumstances. Again, it is perfectly easy to change the size, the shape, or the orientation of an object by showing properly chosen other objects in its neighborhood. There is no evidence that interactions of this kind take place within the phenomenal field as such. Only their *results* are phenomenally represented. Hence we are again forced to assume that, far from consisting of functionally separate local actions, the physiological processes related to the visual scene spread as fields, and so cause interactions. There seems to be little doubt as to the more specific nature of these processes. Some interactions in the brain occur across considerable distances, and yet very fast. In the brain, only one kind of process can operate so fast, namely, the electric field and the current which it establishes. It has therefore been suggested that parts of the brain which are affected by afferent neural messages are sources of electric currents, and that the spatial characteristics of visual facts depend upon the distribution of these currents in the tissue as a continuous volume conductor. Physiological evidence that active brains *are* pervaded by such currents has been offered by several investigators.

It would take too much time if I were to tell you how currents would cause interactions between parts of the brain. From the point of view of neurophysiology, the explanation is fairly simple, and sooner or later such matters will have to be studied by the philosophers. For, to repeat, in the near future discussions of the mind-body problem in a general and abstract sense will no longer satisfy us. Presently we shall be forced to consider questions which refer to particular psychological and physiological situations.

In the meantime, philosophers may wish to hear of any conclusions, however tentative, which follow from our present discussions. I will, therefore, add the following brief remarks.

1. We have distinguished between phenomenal facts and psychological facts in a wider sense, such as retention in memory, our various dispositions and our habits. Since more or less persistent states of this kind have no phenomenal attributes, their interpretation in terms of natural science may not be too difficult.

2. When dealing with the relation between any *phenomenal* facts and events in brains, we always seem to be confronted with a problem of *emergence*.

A. Take the dualist's interpretation of that relation. Nobody who has studied physics would predict that, when physical processes occur in brains, they will affect events in an entirely different realm, the mental world, and that, in turn, they will be affected by such mental events. The laws of inanimate nature are formulated in a way which seems to exclude this possibility. Surely, no such causal traffic across the boundaries of nature is envisaged when the physicist refers to the conservation of energy. If, nevertheless, brain processes and phenomenal events *were* causally related, this fact would argue against the scientists' laws as now interpreted. From the point of view of science, causal relations of this kind would have to be regarded as instances of an incomprehensible emergence.

B. Parallelists do not assume that phenomenal facts and brain events are causally related. None the less, their view also implies that what happens in the brain when we perceive, feel, think, and so forth, is a *novum* from the standpoint of natural science. No processes in inanimate nature are said to be "accompanied" by phenomenal facts. And yet, according to the parallelists, certain physical and chemical processes in brains *have* such companions. Even if it is not assumed that new laws of *physical* action are involved, this once more means emergence. And, like other forms of emergence, this form would again suggest that the scientists do not give us an adequate picture of nature. If their picture were entirely adequate, they would have foreseen what *now* appears as the unexpected emergence of phenomenal facts as partners of brain processes.

C. The thesis of Isomorphism as introduced by the Gestalt psychologists modifies the parallelists' view by saying that the structural characteristics of brain processes and of related phenomenal events are likely to be the same. If this should prove to be true, it would be an important fact under all circumstances. But, so long as phenomenal events are still said to "accompany" structurally similar partners in the brain, the Gestalt psychologists would find themselves in the same situation as the parallelists: structurally similar or not, those phenomenal events would appear as partners of physical facts only in brains. And this would mean emergence.

D. Professor Feigl defends the view that phenomenal facts are *identical* with certain events which occur in brains. He derives this view from the consideration of a cognitive network in which both phenomenal facts and corresponding brain events must find a logical location. It turns out that the location of both is the same. Mr. Feigl realizes that we do not generally identify facts unless they have the same characteristics, but I doubt whether he convinces his readers that such an identity as to content has been made plausible in the present case. Quite apart from such questions, his view again implies a form of emergence. For he does not claim that *all* physical and chemical events are identical with some phenomenal facts. On the contrary, he assures us that this holds only for certain particularly complicated processes in brains. If this were true, and if the postulate of invariance were accepted at the same time, we should be led to the following conclusion: At a certain level of complication, physical and chemical events which have shown no such tendency when investigated on simpler levels unexpectedly become identical with phenomenal facts, and therefore assume the characteristics of such facts. This would seem to me to be a clear case of emergence. If it were not emergence, that is, if the possibility of such a change were foreshadowed on simpler levels of physics and chemistry, then we should once more have to criticize the men in natural science who did not suspect that their materials contained such capacities for a radical change.

3. The difficulties inherent in the concept of emergence would, of course, disappear if we were to take a particularly bold step. Suppose that *all* events in nature have phenomenal characteristics of a more or less primitive kind. On this premise, it would simply follow that this holds also for the processes which occur in brains. But, if this were true, it would again show that the scientists have not given us an adequate description of nature. In fact, their error would be greater than it was in the various instances of apparent emergence. Bertrand Russell would be prepared to make the radical assumption which I just mentioned. This assumption would also answer a certain question in epistemology to which I referred in the beginning. Professor Feigl could not seriously object for this reason: let us assume that, in the not too distant future, physiologists will be able to study some brain processes which, according to Mr. Feigl, are identical with certain phenomenal facts. But, being accustomed to studying physiological events "from the outside," and not having heard of Mr. Feigl's thesis, their description of such events would be given in terms of potentials, chemical reactions, and so on. It would never occur to them to mention any *phenomenal* facts when describing their observations. Why, then, should we expect natural science to discover phenomenal facts when it studies the behavior of systems in *in*animate nature? Obviously, natural science would not be aware of them even if they were present.

In this situation, I prefer to reserve judgment. Even a causal inspection of phenomenal facts, on the one hand, and facts in nature, on the other hand, leads to questions which defenders of the present assumption could not easily answer. I am not a skeptic. But much may have to happen in natural science and in psychology before we can seriously approach such questions.

Chapter 2

Mind-Body, Not a Pseudoproblem

Herbert Feigl, *University of Minnesota*

ANY SERIOUS EFFORT toward a consistent, coherent, and synoptic account of the place of mind in nature is fraught with
embarrassing perplexities. Philosophical temperaments notoriously differ in how they react to these perplexities. Some
thinkers apparently like to wallow in them and finally declare
the mind-body problem unsolvable: *"Ignoramus et ignorabi-
mus."* Perhaps this is an expression of intellectual masochism,
or a rationalization of intellectual impotence. It may of course
also be an expression of genuine humility. Others, imbued
with greater confidence in the powers of philosophical insight
or in the promises of scientific progress, offer dogmatic solutions of the old puzzle. And still others, recognizing the speculative and precarious character of metaphysical solutions, and
deeply irritated by the many bafflements, try to undercut the
whole issue and declare it an imaginary problem. But the perplexities persist and provoke further efforts—often only minor
variants of older ones—toward removing this perennial bone
of contention from the disputes of philosophers and scientists.
Wittgenstein, who tried to "dissolve" the problem, admitted
candidly (*Philosophical Investigations,* §412): "The feeling of
an unbridgeable gulf between consciousness and brain-process.
. . . This idea of a difference in kind is accompanied by slight
giddiness," but he added quickly "which occurs when we are
performing a piece of logical sleight-of-hand."

As I see it, Wittgenstein's casuistic treatment of the problem
is merely one of the more recent in a long line of positivistic
(ametaphysical, if not anti-metaphysical) attempts to show
that the mind-body problem arises out of conceptual confusions, and that proper attention to the way in which we use
mental and physical terms in ordinary language will relieve us
of the vexatious problem. Gilbert Ryle, B. F. Skinner, and,
anticipating all of them, R. Carnap, have tried to obviate the
problem in a similar way: The use of mental or "subjective"
terms is acquired by learning the language we all speak in

References in this paper are to the Bibliography that begins on page 43.

everyday life; this language, serving as a medium of communication among human beings, is by its very nature *intersubjective;* it is on the basis of publicly accessible cues that, for example, the mother tells the child "you feel tired," "now you are glad," "you have a headache," etc., and that the child learns to use such phrases as "feeling tired," "being glad," "having a headache" as applied not only to others, but also to himself when he is in the sort of condition which originally manifested itself in the cues (symptoms, behavior situations and sequences, test conditions and results, etc.) observable by others. But here is the rub. Even if we *learn* the use of subjective terms in the way indicated, once we have them in our vocabulary we *apply* them to states or conditions to which we, as individual subjects, have a "privileged access." If I report moods, feelings, emotions, sentiments, thoughts, images, dreams, etc., that I experience, I am *not referring* to my *behavior,* be it actually accurring or likely to occur under specified conditions. I am referring to those states or processes of my direct experience which I live through (enjoy or suffer), to the "raw feels" of my awareness. These "raw feels" are accessible to other persons only indirectly by inference— but it is *myself* who *has* them.

I do not wish to deny that ordinary language serves many purposes quite adequate. As I see it, ordinary language unhesitatingly combines mental (phenomenal) and physical (behavioral) terms in many descriptions and explanations of human and animal conduct or behavior. "Eagerness was written all over his face"; "He was trembling with anxiety"; "No doubt his gastric ulcer is due to his suppressed hostility"; "An attack of the flu left him in a discouraged and depressed mood for several days"; "A resolute decision finally enabled him to overcome his addiction." As these few illustrations indicate, ordinary language clearly reflects an interactionistic view of the relations of the mental and the physical. As long as we are not too particular about squaring our accounts with the facts established, or at least strongly suggested, by the advances of psychophysiology, we can manage to keep out of logical troubles. Some philosophers, such as Ryle, Strawson, Hampshire, and other practitioners of the ordinary-language approach, have most persuasively shown that we can talk about the mental life of *"persons,"* i.e., about episodes, dispositions, actions, intentions, motives, purposes, skills, and traits, without getting bogged down in the mind-body puzzles. But, notoriously, there is in this approach scarcely any reference to the facts and regularities of neurophysiology. More-over, not all is well logically with these neobehavioristic analyses. "Persons" remains a term insufficiently explicated, and what I could glean from Strawson's analysis (13) is that he defines "person" as a sort of synthetically glued-together unity of a living body and its mental states. Strawson accounts for introspection in terms of "self-ascription." While this is helpful, it cannot be the whole story about mental states: infants, idiots, and at least some of the higher animals un-doubtedly have "raw feels," but are not "self-ascribers." If highly learned men nowadays express (philosophical) doubts about *other minds,* and debate seriously as to whether or not very complex robots have direct experiences, then obviously a better philosophical clarification of the relations of the mental to the physical is urgently needed.

The crucial and central puzzle of the mind-body problem, at least since Descartes, has consisted in the challenge to render an adequate account of the relation of the "raw feels," as well as of other mental facts (intentions, thoughts, voli-tions, desires, etc.) to the corresponding neurophysiological processes. The problems may fairly clearly be divided into scientific and philosophical components. The scientific task is pursued by psychophysiology, i.e., an exploration of the empirically ascertainable correlations of "raw feels," phe-nomenal patterns, etc., with the events and processes in the organism, especially in its central nervous system (if not in the cerebral cortex alone). The philosophical task consists in a logical and epistemological clarification of the concepts by means of which we may formulate and/or interpret those correlations.

Scientifically, the most plausible view to date is that of a one-one (or at least a one-many) correspondence of mental states to neurophysiological process-patterns. The investiga-tions of Wolfgang Köhler, E. D. Adrian, W. Penfield, D. O. Hebb, W. S. McCulloch, *et al.,* strongly confirm such a cor-respondence in the form of an isomorphism of the patterns in the phenomenal fields with the simultaneous patterns of neural processes in various areas of the brain. The philosopher must of course regard this isomorphism as empirically establishable or refutable, and hence as *logically* contingent. It is conceiv-able that further empirical evidence may lead the psycho-physiologists to abandon or to modify this view which on the whole has served so well at least as a fruitful working hypoth-esis. It is conceivable that some of the as yet more obscure psychosomatic phenomena or possibly the still extremely problematic and controversial "facts" of parapsychology will require emergentist or even interactionistic explanations. (As an empiricist I must at least go through the motions of an "open mind" in these regards!) But tentatively assuming isomorphism of some sort, a hypothesis which is favored by many "naturalistic" philosophers, are we then to interpret it philosophically along the lines of traditional epiphenomenalism? Although Professor Köhler (9) does not commit himself explicitly to this view, I am practically certain that this is the general outlook within which he operates. If the basic physical laws of the universe should be sufficient for the derivation of biological and neurophysiological regularities, if the occurrence of neural patterns (physical *Gestalten*) is not a case of genuine emergent novelty but a matter of the combination of more elementary physical configurations, and if, finally, the experimental patterns correspond in some way isomorphically to neural process patterns, then this *is* epiphenomenalism in modern dress.

It will be best here not to use the somewhat ambiguous label "parallelism." Psychophysiological parallelism, as held by some thinkers in an earlier period, allowed for a "mental causality" to correspond to "physical (i.e., neurophysiological) causality." Sometimes it even connoted an all-pervasive correspondence of mental and physical attributes (in the manner of Spinoza), and thus amounted to a form of panpsychism. But the favored outlook of modern psychophysiology amounts to postulating causal relations, i.e., dynamic functional dependencies only on the physical side, and then to connect the neural process patterns merely by laws of (simultaneous) coexistence or co-occurrence with the corresponding mental states. Only a small subset of neural processes is thus accompanied by mental processes.

Traditionally the most prominent objection to epiphenomenalism has been the argument from the "efficacy of consciousness." We seem to know from our direct experience that moods, pleasure, displeasure, pain, attention, vigilance, intention, deliberation, choice, etc., make a difference in the ensuing behavior. But, of course, this subjective impression of the causal relevance and efficacy of mental states can easily be explained by the epiphenomenalist: Since, *ex hypothesi*, some dynamically relevant physical conditions are invariably accompanied by mental states, there is, then, also a regular occurrence of certain types of behavior (or of intra-organismic events) consequent upon mental states. For empiricists holding an essentially Humean conception of causality, it is then quite permissible in this sense to speak of the causal efficacy of mental states. There are, it should be noted, countless highly "teleological" processes that occur in our organism evidently without the benefit of any mental influence, guidance, or instigation. For example, the kinds of regenerations and restitutions that are involved in recoveries from many types of physical injury or disease appear as if they were most cleverly "designed," yet for many of the phenomena purely physiological (and perhaps ultimately physicochemical) explanations are available. Yet according to the epiphenomenalistic doctrine such explanations are sufficient also for behavior which we ordinarily consider instigated, regulated, or modulated by mental factors. If an effort of concentration facilitates learning algebra, piano playing, or the like, then consciousness cannot be regarded as a causally irrelevant or superfluous "luxury." I don't think we need to apologize for arguments of this sort. It is true, radical Materialists and Behaviorists reject such arguments as "tender minded," but then radical Materialism or Behaviorism typically *repress* or *evade* the mind-body problem. They do not offer a genuine solution. Epiphenomenalism, while not evading the problem, offers a very queer solution. It accepts two fundamentally different sorts of laws —the usual causal laws and laws of psychophysiological correspondence. The physical (causal) laws connect the events in the physical world in the manner of a complex network, while the correspondence laws involve relations of physical events with purely mental "danglers." These correspondence laws are peculiar in that they may be said to postulate "effects" (mental states as dependent variables) which by themselves do not function, or at least do not seem to be needed, as "causes" (independent variables) for any observable behavior.

Laws of concomitance in the physical world could usually be accounted for in terms of underlying *identical* structures. Thus, for example, the correspondence of certain optical, electrical, and magnetic properties of various substances, as expressed in simple functional relations between the refraction index, the dielectric constant, and the magnetic permeability, is explainable on the basis of the atom structure of those substances. Or, to take a slightly different example, it is in terms of a theory of *one* (unitary) electric current that we explain the thermal, chemical, magnetic, and optical effects which may severally or jointly be used in an "operational definition" of the intensity of the current. Similarly, it is at least a partially successful working program of psychophysiology to reduce certain correlated macrobehavioral features to underlying identical neurophysiological structures and processes. It should be emphasized, however, that a further step is needed if we are to overcome the dualism in the epiphenomenalist interpretation of the correlation of subjective mental states with brain states.

The classical attempts in the direction of such unification or of a monistic solution are well known: double-aspect, double-knowledge, twofold-access, or double-language doctrines have been proposed in various forms. The trouble with most of these is that they rely on vague metaphors or analogies and that it is extremely difficult to translate them into straightforward language. I can here only briefly indicate the lines along which I think the "world knot"—to use Schopenhauer's striking designation for the mind-body puzzles—may be disentangled. The indispensable step consists in a critical reflection upon the meanings of the terms "mental" and "physical," and along with this a thorough clarification of such traditional philosophical terms as "private" and "public," and "subjective" and "objective," "psychological space(s)" and "physical space," "intentionality," "purposiveness," etc. The solution that appears most plausible to me, and that is entirely consistent with a thoroughgoing naturalism, is an *identity theory* of the mental and the physical, as follows: Certain neurophysiological terms denote (refer to) the very same events that are also denoted (referred to) by certain phenomenal terms. The identification of the objects of this twofold reference is of course logically contingent, although it constitutes a very fundamental feature of our world as we have come to conceive it in the modern scientific outlook. Utilizing Frege's distinction between *Sinn* ("meaning," "sense," "intension") and *Bedeutung* ("referent," "denotatum," "extension"), we may say that neurophysiological terms and the corresponding phenomenal terms, though widely differing in *sense,* and hence in the modes of confirmation of statements containing them, do have identical *referents*. I take these referents to be the immediately experienced qualities, or their configurations in the various phenomenal fields.

Well-intentioned critics have tried to tell me that this is essentially the metaphysics of panpsychism. To this I can only reply: (1) If this be metaphysics, make the least of it!;

(2) It is not panpsychism at all—either the "pan" or the "psyche" has to be deleted in the formulation. By way of very brief and unavoidably crude and sketchy comments let me explain my view a little further. The transition from the Logical Positivism of the Vienna Circle to the currently prevalent form of Logical Empiricism, as I interpret it, involved a complete emancipation from radical phenomenalism, behaviorism, operationism and their all-too-restrictive criteria of factual meaningfulness. Parallel with the critique of philosophical doubt by the Neo-Wittgensteinians, Logical Empiricists nowadays have no patience with skeptical questions regarding the existence of physical objects or of other minds. "Skeptical doubts" of these sorts are illegitimate not because the beliefs in question are incapable of confirmation or disconfirmation, but because doubts of this pervasive character would call into question the very principles of confirmation and disconfirmation that underlie all empirical inquiry—both on the level of commonsense and on that of science. There can be no question that assertions of the existence of stars and atoms, or of the occurrence of conscious and unconscious mental processes, are subject to the normal procedures of inductive, analogical, or hypothetico-deductive confirmation or disconfirmation. It is preposterous (not to say philosophically perverse or naughty) to deny that we have well-confirmed knowledge concerning imperceptible physical objects or concerning the mental states of other human beings. A mature epistemology can make explicit the principles of such, often highly indirect, confirmations or disconfirmations. And along with this a liberalized meaning-criterion can be formulated, broad enough to include whatever is needed by way of commonsense or scientific hypotheses, and yet sufficiently restrictive to exclude transcendent metaphysical (pseudo-) beliefs. Freed from the torments of philosophical doubt and from the associated reductive tendencies and fallacies of phenomenalism as well as of radical behaviorism, we can now with a good intellectual conscience embrace a genuinely critical and empirical realism.

Once this position is attained, a mind-body-identity theory of the kind sketched above appears as the most adequate interpretation of all the relevant facts and considerations. This is not panpsychism for the simple reason that nothing in the least like a psyche is ascribed to lifeless matter, and certainly at most something very much less than a psyche is ascribed to plants or lower animals. The panpsychists claimed to reason by analogy, but this is precisely what they did not do in fact. The difference between the nervous system of, say, an earthworm and of a human being is so tremendous that we should in all consistency assume a correspondingly large difference in their respective mental states. And even on the human level there is no need whatever for the assumption of a psyche in the traditional sense of a soul that could act upon the brain, let alone be separable from it. One may, of course, doubt whether a purely Humean conception of the *self* (as a bundle and succession of direct data) will be sufficient for an adequate psychology. Nevertheless no substantial entity is required. Events, processes, and their properly defined organization and integration, should be perfectly sufficient. Professor Stephen C. Pepper suggested to me in conversation that my view might be labeled "pan-quality-ism." While this locution is not pleasant to the ear, it does come much closer to a correct characterization than "panpsychism." But since Paul E. Meehl (10) who understands my view at least as thoroughly as does Professor Pepper, has designated me a "materialist," perhaps one last word of elucidation may be in order.

I am indeed in agreement with one main line of traditional materialism in that I assume, as does Professor Köhler, that the basic *laws* of the universe are the *physical* ones. But (and this is so brief and crude a formulation that I fear I shall be misunderstood again) this does not commit me in the least as to the nature of the *reality* whose regularities are formulated in the physical laws. This reality is known to us by acquaintance only in the case of our direct experience which, according to my view, is the referent also of certain neurophysiological concepts. And if we are realists in regard to the physical world, we must assume that the concepts of theoretical physics, to the extent that they are instantiated in particulars, are not merely calculational devices for the prediction of observational data, but that they denote realities which are unknown by acquaintance, but which may in some way nevertheless be not entirely discontinuous with the qualities of direct experience. But—"whereof we cannot speak, thereof we must be silent." If this is metaphysics, it seems to me entirely innocuous. I have little sympathy with the mysticism of Eddington or the psychovitalism of Bergson. I reject the former because there is literally nothing that can be responsibly said in a phenomenal language about qualities that do not fall within the scope of acquaintance. Extrapolation will carry us at most to the concepts of unconscious wishes, urges or conflicts as postulated by such "depth-psychologies" as psychoanalysis. And even here, future scientific developments may be expected to couch these concepts much more fruitfully in the language of neurophysiology and endocrinology. And I reject psychovitalism because it involves dualistic interaction. At the very best "intuition" (empathetic imagination) may be heuristically helpful in that it can suggest scientific hypotheses in psychology (possibly even in biology), but these suggestions are extremely precarious, and hence must always be relentlessly scrutinized in the light of objective evidence (7).

Does the identity theory simplify our conception of the world? I think it does. Instead of conceiving of two realms or two concomitant types of events, we have only one reality which is represented in two different conceptual systems—on the one hand, that of physics and, on the other hand, where applicable (in my opinion only to an extremely small part of the world) that of phenomenological psychology. I realize fully that the simplification thus achieved is a matter of *philosophical* interpretation. For a synoptic, coherent account of the relevant facts of perception, introspection, and psychosomatics, and of the logic of theory construction in the physical sciences, I think that the identity view is preferable to any other proposed solution of the mind-body problem. Call my view metaphysical if you must; I would rather call it *metascientific,* in the sense that it is the result of a comprehensive reflection on the *results* of science as well as on the logic and epistemology of scientific *method.* But I admit that for the ordinary purposes of psychology, psychophysiology, and psychiatry an epiphenomenalist position is entirely adequate, if only the traditional, picturesque but highly misleading locutions (e.g., "substantial material reality and its shadowy mental accompaniments") are carefully avoided.

I conclude that the mind-body problem is not a pseudoproblem. There are, first, a great many genuine but unanswered questions in psychophysiology. And, secondly, there is plenty of work left for philosophers in the logical analysis of the intricate relations between phenomenal and physical terms. Problems of this complexity cannot be regulated to the limbo of nonsensical questions. I doubt quite generally whether many issues in modern epistemology can be simply "dissolved" in the manner in which some artificially concocted pseudoproblems can be disposed of by a minimum of reflection on the proper use of terms. Questions like "How fast does Time flow?", "Do we really see physical objects?", "Why is the world the way it is?", etc., can indeed be very quickly shown to rest on elementary conceptual confusions. But the issues of perception, of reality, and of the mental and the physical require circumspect, perspicacious and painstaking analyses.

BIBLIOGRAPHY

In a long essay (4) written nearly three years ago I have attempted to do fuller justice to the complexities and the unresolved issues of the mind-body problem than I possibly could in the preceding brief comments. A very ample bibliography is appended to that essay. Since its publication I have found a welcome ally in J. J. C. Smart (11). Carnap's early article, "Psychologie in Physikalischer Sprache," which anticipated much of the neobehavioristic argument of Ryle, Skinner, and Wittgenstein is at last available in English translation (1). A brief but perhaps not sufficiently elaborate critical reply to the Wittgensteinian position on the problem of other minds is contained in my symposium article (a response to Norman Malcolm) listed below (5). An exposition and critical analysis of Carnap's physicalism is presented in (7). For a forthright but philosophically unsophisticated physicalistic solution of the mind-body problem, see (12). The brilliant psychologist and methodologist Paul E. Meehl has dealt with the mind-body problem and related issues in several chapters of a book (10) which despite its primarily theological and religious intent contains large parts of scientifically and logically important and incisive discussions.

1. Carnap, Rudolf. "Psychology in Physical Language" in A. J. Ayer (ed.) *Logical Positivism*, pp. 165-98. Glencoe (Ill.): The Free Press, 1959.
2. Carnap, Rudolf. "The Methodological Character of Theoretical Concepts," in *Minnesota Studies in the Philosophy of Science*, I, 38-76. Minneapolis: Univ. of Minnesota Press, 1956.
3. Carnap, Rudolf. "The Philosopher Replies," in P. A. Schilpp, *The Philosophy of Rudolf Carnap*. New York: Tudor Publishing Co. (forthcoming).
4. Feigl, Herbert. "The 'Mental' and the 'Physical,'" in H. Feigl, G. Maxwell and M. Scriven (eds.), *Concepts, Theories, and the Mind-Body Problem* (Minnesota Studies in the Philosophy of Science, Vol. II), pp. 370-497. Minneapolis: Univ. of Minnesota Press, 1958.
5. Feigl, Herbert. "Other Minds and the Egocentric Predicament," *Journal of Philosophy*, L, No. 23, 978-87, 1958.
6. Feigl, Herbert. "Philosophical Embarrassments of Psychology," *American Psychologist*, XIV, No. 3, 115-28, 1959.
7. Feigl, Herbert. "Critique of Intuition from the Point of View of Scientific Empiricism," *Philosophy East and West* (forthcoming).
8. Feigl, Herbert. "Physicalism, Unity of Science and the Foundations of Psychology," in P. A. Schilpp (ed.), *The Philosophy of Rudolf Carnap*. New York: Tudor Publishing Co. (forthcoming).

9. Köhler, Wolfgang. *The Place of Values in a World of Facts.* New York: Liveright, 1938.
10. Meehl, Paul E. (co-author). *What, Then, Is Man?* (Graduate Study Number III.) St. Louis: Concordia Publishing House, 1958.
11. Smart, J. J. C. "Sensations and Brain Processes," *Philosophical Review,* LXVIII, No. 2, 141-56, 1959.
12. Smith, Kendon. "The Naturalistic Conception of Life," *American Scientist,* XLVI, No. 4, 413-23, 1958.
13. Strawson, P. F. "Persons" in H. Feigl, G. Maxwell and M. Scriven (eds.), *Concepts, Theories, and the Mind-Body Problem* (Minnesota Studies in the Philosophy of Science, Vol. II), pp. 330-53. Minneapolis: Univ. of Minnesota Press, 1958. Reprinted (with some alterations) in P. F. Strawson, *Individuals, an Essay in Descriptive Metaphysics.* London: Methuen, 1959.

Chapter 3

A Neural-Identity Theory of Mind[1]

Stephen C. Pepper, *University of California, Berkeley*

IN A PREVIOUS study[2] surveying the contributions of the Occidental tradition toward the development of a comprehensive account of the cognitive relations of man to the world about him, it appeared to me that the most likely prospect for an adequate world hypothesis lay in a direction midway between the paths laid out by the mechanistic and the contextualistic categories. In a tentative way in this paper I shall try to make some extensions of thought along this direction.

I shall dwell particularly on a suggestion toward the solution of the mind-body problem, a problem which persists in breaking into the adequacy of the mechanistic categories. These categories (which assert a cognitive priority of the space time field and of configurations of matter qualifying this field) are widely prevalent today wherever a "physicalist" movement in philosophy may be detected. The Logical Positivist school and its physicalist outgrowths appear to have their roots in these mechanistic categories, however much the exponents of these schools cast aspersions on "metaphysics." There is no point in quarreling over a term, but most aspersions against "metaphysics" seem to be against modes of analysis different from those of a school which purports to present an empirical treatment of the world. For the empiricist's conviction usually is that if his methods and analyses were correct there would be no fictitious elements concealed in his statements of fact, no interpretive distortions of fact of which he was not taking cognizance. Being thus personally assured of the transparency of his empirical methods, he cannot, he imagines, be susceptible to fictitious "metaphysical" presuppositions.

The contributions of the physicalist movement are, to my mind, so much confirmation of the present day vitality of the mechanistic categories and the metaphysical world hypothesis these generate. And, as have most mechanists of the past,

Notes to this paper are on page 61.

this movement has been much concerned with a clarification of the methods of physics as the model empirical science. In this process the physicalist school ultimately has to come to terms with the observational data upon which physical theories as empirical theories must finally rest their case. And the question of the status of these ultimate statements of observed data in the total context of cognition brings us once more face to face with the typical mechanistic problem of the relation of the "private" sensations of the observer to the "public" system of physics—the modern version of the old mind-body problem.

As a practical procedure where mechanistic thinking is uncritically going on, it would seem that some form of psychophysical parallelism is usually taken for granted, or maybe a naïve realism, or occasionally, if a man has done some philosophical reading, a phenomenalism. Where there is a long tradition of fruitful experimental procedure, as in physics and chemistry, the problem is hardly felt. The data of observations are highly controlled, and mostly reduced to pointer readings where the sense quality of the experience has an almost negligible significance. The "private" quality can almost be discarded. But this becomes less and less possible as we pass into the more complex subject matter of the biological sciences and especially of psychology. The issue comes particularly to a head in psychology.

Watsonian Behaviorism was an attempt in mechanistic terms to physicalize psychology. It had a very short and stormy life. Subsequent Behaviorisms have been much more qualified and in men like Tolman took on a pragmatic operational aspect which tended to lift them out of the mechanistic categories and into those of pragmatism where the mind-body problem no longer comes up in the same way. But this operational solution of the mind-body problem does not bring permanent peace, for an operationalist has his particular problems with the evidences for invariance and stability of structure in the environment. Physics seems to give us too much reliable, predictable information about our environment for this to be dissolved into a succession of operational procedures. Specifically, the physiological organism seems to be too stable and predictable a physical structure to be reasonably reduced to a schema of operational procedures. Yet this is what a thoroughgoing pragmatic operationalism would apparently have to do to the physical body described in books of anatomy and physiology.

Now, in this paper I propose to accept the physicalist account of the physiological body as a functioning configuration of cells occupying a limited volume of the space-time field. This description, if accepted, has the advantage of binding all our physiological knowledge solidly in with that of chemistry and physics, not to mention astronomy and geology. The structure of the physical world can then be accepted in very much the way it is 'pictured' to us in the common narrative of the world we receive daily as our cosmic physical myth.

A consequence of this conception is the confinement of our personal qualitative experiences within the space-time volume of our bodies. At least, this is the interpretation that requires the least amount of interpretive juggling of the factors available to a mechanist in handling this problem. To put it another way: It is the most naïve solution of the situation, once a mechanist has had a chance to read Locke, Berkeley, and Hume. The present day physicalists seem to have taken this lesson to heart, and that is where the force of their statements about the 'privacy' of emotion and sensation comes from. I propose to accept this naïve solution.

But I do not propose to accept many of the inferences that are commonly made on the basis of this 'privacy' of sense immediacy. This 'privacy,' I shall seek to show, is provisional and not ultimate. Sense immediacy may, by observing its relations to certain accepted public facts, be rendered as public as many public facts. At least, I shall seek to show that this is a genuine theoretical possibility, which is all that is required in answer to the theory of the 'privacy' of sense immediacy as something exclusive of 'publicity,' since this latter is necessarily also only a theoretical possibility. That is to say, if the only immediate evidence for the 'privacy' of sense immediacy is a private experience, this by definition and by the tenets of the theory itself is not subject to public verification; it can only be proposed as a theoretical possibility to take care of the configuration of evidence available for the act of human cognition. Consequently, a theory indicating the publicity of sense immediacy on the same evidence is all that is required to counter the theory of the 'privacy' of sense immediacy.

On the face of it, the theory of an indissoluble privacy of sense immediacy seems unlikely in view of the fact that all the observational data on which the 'public' systems of science are based are some observer's data of sense immediacy.

The foregoing remarks are directed upon the doctrine of 'privacy' of sense immediacy as developed by men following the mechanistic categories. There is a somewhat parallel theory of the incommunicable quality of ultimate immediacy held by many who follow the contextualistic categories. Many contextualists make a sharp distinction between 'knowledge' which applies to relations found in experience, and 'having' which applies to the immediate qualia of experience. Through 'knowledge' we gain our practical control of the environment and communicate with one another. But the qualia 'had' in experience are unique for each experience and incommunicable. Roughly, the qualia of the contextualist correspond with the sense immediacies of the mechanist, but there is not the same insistence on 'privacy' because in the contextualistic categories there is no justification for a sharp cleavage between 'mental' and 'physical.'

If, accordingly, we can find a way of rendering the "privacy' of sense immediacy public, we shall probably also have found a way of making the qualia of experience knowable.

And incidentally the sharp distinction made by many contextualists between relations that are 'known' but not 'had' and qualia that are 'had' but not 'known,' seems an unlikely theoretical distinction. For if relations do not have their qualities in experience, how on the contextualistic view are they to be differentiated from one another in experience? This distinction is the more paradoxical in that the early contextualists made much of the qualitative feeling of relations—the feeling of 'and' and the feeling of 'but,' etc.—as something neglected by previous philosophical theories. The more promising contextualistic approach is to accord 'having' to all experience and to treat the operational procedures which yield 'knowledge' as a particular mode of qualitative experience in which the aim is not that of exploiting the individual quality of the experience (as it is in the fine arts) but that of controlling the environment. The experience is qualitative both in the aesthetic 'having' and in the practical and scientific 'knowing,' but the aims of the two modes of human activity are different.

Accordingly, by the same stroke that breaks down the partition between the "publicity" of physics and the "privacy" of sense immediacy as developed under mechanistic categories, we may perhaps expect the breaking down of the partition between 'knowledge' and 'having' developed by a number of writers working under the contextualistic categories.

What, then, is the stroke that may bring about this commingling of modes of cognition so long held apart? It is a suggestion that has probably frequently occurred to men dealing with these problems, and which has as frequently been put aside as too fantastic to be elaborated. I personally tried it out on one or two of my friends twelve or fifteen years ago, and dropped it because of the cool reception. But at the last meeting of the Pacific Division of the Philosophical Association, Herbert Feigl in a portion of the paper he read there broached what was essentially this suggestion. There were other issues in his paper to be argued, but what struck me was that no one picked up this suggestion as anything particularly surprising or fantastic. And the reason, I believe, is that Feigl presented the idea in a context of alternative languages for the handling of a set of data. Perhaps because of the flexibility of mind engendered in the contemporary philosopher by the prevalence of the language metaphor, there is now a climate of opinion that can more fairly contemplate the suggestion. The suggestion is a way of indicating an identity of cognitive reference for what we report as a qualitative experience of immediacy and what we describe as a physiological state of the brain.

Stated very briefly and in pictorial terms, the idea is this: Supposing we know the neural activity correlated with an immediately-sensed quality, then if the brain were exposed so that this neural activity could be seen by a man in a mirror, the man would be viewing in the mirror in visual perception exactly the same activity he was feeling introspectively as a qualitative immediacy. On first thought this seems an utterly fantastic idea, and obviously based on a confusion of thinking. But I believe the confusions of thinking arise on the part of those who find the hypothesis fantastic, and this with certain ramifications consonant with the theory is what I shall seek to exhibit in the present paper.

To begin with, the data which have led to the widely-held working hypothesis of psychophysical parallelism are essential as the initial evidence for the development of this theory. It is not essential that we know exactly the neural processes correlated with the qualitative feelings indicated in introspective reports. It is not even necessary that the correlation should be restricted to areas of strict localization. One area of the brain could take over the function of another area of the brain that has been injured. All that is necessary is that some sort of definite correlation hold between configurations of neural or other physical activity and introspective data. If the data in support of psychophysical parallelism are denied, then the argument must begin with consideration of these data.

The chief difficulty in the acceptance of the data, however, seems to be with the theory of psychophysical parallelism and its unpalatable consequences rather than with the data themselves. The paradoxes induced by the theory throw some doubt back upon the soundness of the data that give rise to it. Since an alternative hypothesis is being suggested here, that particular difficulty can be discounted. The data for psychophysical parallelism will, consequently, be taken for granted.

What, then, are the unpalatable consequences of psychophysical parallelism? They boil down to what R. B. Perry called the "egocentric predicament." The only data of which a man is immediately aware are his introspective data. If these are correlated with neural processes going on in his body, these are encapsulated for each man within his body. No man, then, has direct cognizance of anything outside his body. Moreover, since the properties ascribed to physical objects in a man's environment and including his nervous system are physical properties qualitatively different from the data of his immediate introspective awareness, it follows that his descriptions of these properties are hypothetical constructions qualitatively divorced from the data of immediacy, which later are the only ultimate data available to the human observer.

From this point on, a man can work along several lines generating the various typical mechanistic hypotheses to take care of the situation, none of them very satisfactory. He may accept a dualism of mind and matter and give up trying to connect the two except by this queer sort of correlation in which only *one* of the correlated terms is a datum of immediacy, whereas simultaneously the only ultimate evidence for the other (the physical) term in the correlation is immediate data of a qualitative sort that this physical term cannot be. Leibnitz' "pre-established harmony," and Descartes's faith that God would not deceive a rational man are in this dilemma not excessively extravagant devices for the bridging of this extraordinary gap. Or a mechanist may throw out the introspective datum bodily, as the Watsonian Behaviorist and the unqualified materialist did. But then he loses his data of perceptual observation. Or he may keep his immediate data and throw out the physical correlate, except as a conventionalistic hypothesis for the convenience of ordering the data, as the phenomenalists do. None of these is a very satisfactory solution, and the first is probably the best and the most commonly resorted-to in spite of its anomalous cosmic correlation of matter and mind.

Therefore, a hypothesis that could start with the data of

psychophysical parallelism and institute a contact of neural processes with data of immediacy, should be welcome.

Our hypothesis, accepting the data, institutes this contact. The neural processes as the objects of the physiologist's observations and descriptions are in our hypothesis identical with the qualitative immediacies which are the object of the subject's introspective reports. As we were somewhat strikingly expressing the situation earlier, a man in the role of a physiologist observing his brain processes in a mirror could at the same moment in the role of an introspective psychologist report on the immediate quality of these processes as he feels them in his personal experience.

Feigl, in his paper, referred to the situation as that of a man describing the same event in two different languages—for a physiologist, in the language of the physical world, and for an introspectionist in the language of sense immediacy. If the language metaphor will obtain an understanding reception of the theory, I am agreeable to it. But for the theory to bite into the situation and offer a genuine solution, the "language of immediacy" cannot be finally accepted as a language except in a Pickwickian sense. The reports of immediacy, which are our only instruments of communication, are indeed couched in symbols and are a language. But the immediacies felt by the introspecting observer are the immediate qualitative data themselves devoid of linguistic convention.

However, let us approach the hypothesis by way of the language metaphor. For convenience of exposition let us initially assume a simple localization theory of brain function. Let us assume that the immediate qualitative feeling of the sound of Middle C is correlated with the activation of a definite set of neurons in the temporal lobe of the brain. Whenever this set of neutrons is activated, whether by normal stimulation through the ear, by central stimulation through 'associational' processes, or by artificial electrical stimulation of the exposed brain, the subject reports the feeling of the sound Middle C. Here is then a psychophysical correlation between the introspective report of immediacy for an auditory quality and a physical report of physical changes observed in a limited set of neurons. Again, for convenience of exposition let us say that the observed physical changes are movements of the neurons.

Now clearly movements of neurons are qualitatively different from an auditory sensation. The movements are visually observed and appear in the physiologist's reports as visual data. How, then, can anyone seriously conceive of an identity between the physiologist's report of a visual occurrence and the introspective observer's report of an auditory feeling? This is fantastic!

Here is where the language metaphor will help. Both the physiologist's report and the introspectionist's report are symbolic statements. The peculiarity of these statements is that both are referring to an identical event. Different as the two statements are as reports, they are about exactly the same thing. The symbolic elements in the two reports are entirely different, but the event referred to is an identical event.

In language we are daily familiar with such diversity of statement respecting an identical situation. In two different languages the identical event can be truly described in two qualitatively quite different sentences. "This cat is black," and "Le chat est noir" describe the same fact with equal precision. But the two reports are qualitatively different statements, as different as English is from French. Analogously, the physiologist's report describing the event in physical language is qualitatively different from the introspectionist's report describing the event in the language of immediacy. Both are equally true statements about the event. The qualitative difference between them arises from qualitative differences in the languages in terms of which they are presented.

The psychophysical correlation can now be interpreted as a correlation of two reports expressed in terms of two different languages about an identical event. Moreover, the correlation is no longer a cosmic mystery; it is fully explained by an identity of reference of two linguistic statements to the same event. Just as we should expect a report of a laboratory experiment written by a student in French to correspond, statement for statement, with a report of the same experiment written by a student in English, so with the reports of this brain experiment, one written in physical language and the other in the language of immediacy. The correlation (the psychophysical parallelism) between the two reports is guaranteed by the fact that they are both reports of the same identical event. What are correlated and parallel are the two languages. What necessitates the correlation is the identity of reference of the two reports.

But many readers I am sure will feel that there is something incomplete about this analogy. Is this actually just a question of two languages and a common reference? Isn't some crucial element overlooked? And isn't it that this analogy conceals the fact that the physiologist's data of observation are just as genuinely immediate as those of the introspective observer, and the physiologist's data are visual? How can one conceive an identity of visual data with an auditory datum? The physiologist reports an observation of gray shapes in movement (according to our assumption for convenience that the neural event is motions of the neurons); the introspective observer reports an auditory sensation of Middle C. However can the twain meet in any identity? These appear to be two separate reports about data of immediacy. There is in addition, then, the rather remarkable fact, it seems, of a close correlation between these two sets of immediate data, such that whenever these movements occur, the auditory sensation also occurs.

This is indeed where I think the linguistic analogy breaks down. But I believe it is half true. So, let us keep hold of it, and work out from it to see if a more careful scrutiny of the situation will not point out a modification of the linguistic approach which will leave the identity theory still intact.

First, observe that the visual data of the physiologist on the psychophysical parallelism evidences which we are accepting for this paper, are not in any sense identifiable with the neural event which the physiologist is observing in the introspectionist's brain. The visual data of immediacy which enter into the physiologist's report are, on the psychophysical evidences we are assuming, correlated only with certain neural activities in the *physiologist's* brain. On the evidences assumed, these visual immediacies correlated with neural activities in the physiologist's brain are in no sense to be ascribed to the event going on in the introspectionist's brain.

The situation for the physiologist is this: Certain events going on in the instrospectionist's brain are exposed to the physiologist's visual field, whence light rays are reflected to his eye, activating the retina, the optic nerve, and a set of neurons in his occipital lobe (again assuming, for convenience, simple localization), whereupon he experiences certain data of visual immediacy which he reports as movements of grayish objects. The physiologist from his observation does not, of course, assert a parallelism between his visual data of immediacy correlated with events in his occipital lobe and auditory data of immediacy in the temporal lobe of the introspectionist. Never has psychophysical parallelism suggested that mental events occurring in one man's mind are correlated with physical events occurring in another man's brain. The hypothesis suggests the correlation of mental events occurring in one man's mind with physical events occurring in the same man's brain. The immediate visual data of the physiologist are not, then, in any sense being offered as the neural correlates of the introspectionist's auditory experience.

What then is the character of the physical description of the brain activities reported by the physiologist? Clearly now, we can see, it is a symbolic expression in terms of carefully selected physical units controlled by physical procedures referring to a certain localized event in the spatio-temporal field. Physical units are generally expressed in visual terms, but this is not essential and results only from the properties of visual perception which favor the requirements of precise physical observation. The visual qualities entering into the physiologist's report of a neural event are as irrelevant to the structural relations described as the visual qualities of the pointer readings of a galvanometer are to a description of an electric current. A physical description is in relational terms, and its truth depends upon its relational structure, and qualities of perceptual immediacy only enter in at pivotal points of contact where physical theory becomes verified in perceptual experience. A visual pointer reading is an *effect* of a physical structure predicted by the descriptive hypothesis regarding the nature of that structure. The visual quality of the pointer reading is not considered as a *quality* of the structure described.

This distinction between the visual quality of the *observed data suporting* a description of a physical structure or event and the *description itself* of the physical structure or event, is very celar in the description, for instance, of the subatomic structure of atoms or of the atomic structure of chemical substances where the structures described are far below the threshold of visual perception. A confusion arises only when a molar event is being described in visual terms when the details are open to so-called 'direct' visual observation—as in a physiologist's description of a synapse on the basis of microscopic observations. If, however, we accept (as we are doing in this paper) a neural-response theory of perception and not a theory of direct realism, which latter attempts to locate a sensory quality on the surface of a stimulus object instead of locating it within the nervous system, then we note that all sensory qualities referred to external objects referential and symbolic in function and not revelatory of the qualities of those objects. According to the neural-response theory, for instance, the sound of Middle C is correlated with a neural activity of the brain, not with the vibration of the violin string which is the external generating stimulus and the source to which the sound is referentially referred. An organism *learns* to 'attribute' the sound perceptually to the vibration of the string. But that does not require that the vibration of the string is in quality the auditory quality Middle C. If a bow were drawn across the string by a deaf person, the vibration would occur but there would be no occurrence of the quality Middle C—on the neural-response theory assumed in this paper, and following a strict interpretation of the evidences ordinarily presented for psychophysical parallelism. For the physical event directly correlated with the mental occurrence is held to be a neural activity, not an external event in the organism's environment. Similarly, a color in visual perception is correlated with a neural activity within the organism and referred symbolically, through conditioning, to the surface of some environmental object. Consequently, on this theory al distance perception, whether auditory or visual, is in the nature of a symbolic description of an environmental object. The cognitive status of the visual perception of an apple, for instance, as a shaded, red, spherical object is exactly the same as that of a verbal description of it. Both are symbolic, referential, descriptive, and subject to error.

Accordingly, the physiologist's visual perception of the neural activity in the introspectionist's brain is as much a symbolic description of that activity as that expressed in verbal symbols and set down in his notebook. So we should agree with the assertion that the physiologist's references to the introspectionist's brain event are all literally descriptions of it. The physiologist has two descriptions of it: (1) the technical verbal description in physical language, and (2) the visual description in terms of the data of visual perception, which may now be called, if we wish, a visual-perception language. The verbal description in verbal language is based on the visual description in the language of visual perception.

Neither of these two languages of the physiologist, however, can be identified with the introspectionist's report of an immediate felt quality of Middle C, which on our evidence is directly correlated with a neural event referred to by the physiologist's two descriptions.

Now, to be sure, any report that is verbally expressed is symbolic. A report of immediacy is likewise so, since it is expressed in language. It is, therefore, proper to speak of the introspectionist's *report* as in introspectionist language. But the quality of immediacy reported upon in this introspective report is not itself symbolic or linguistic at all. It is, on the present hypothesis, an immediate quality directly felt and not subject to error. Error may enter into the *report,* so that the report may not veridically describe the immediate quality. A report of immediacy cannot, therefore, be identical with the immediate experience itself. The immediate qualitative experience itself is just what it is and the introspectionist presumably reports on this immediate qualitative experience as truly as he can.

Now compare the two things the introspectionist's report brings out with the two things the physiologist's description brings out. The introspectionist has (A) an immediate felt quality and (B) an introspective verbal report about it. The physiologist has (A^1) a visual perception of a neural event and (B^1) a verbal physical description of it. These two pairs are not parallel. (A^1) and (B^1) are *both* referential and symbolic, and subject to error, one in the language of visual perception, the other in physical language. With (A) and (B), however, the first is immediate and nonreferential and so not couched in any language; only the second is symbolic and properly regarded as in the language of introspection.

Notice that (A^1) and (B^1) refer to an identical event—a neural activity in the introspectionist's brain. (B) refers to (A), and according to psychophysical parallelism (A) is directly correlated with the neural event referred to by (A^1) and (B^1). (A) is the only one of these items that is an immediately intuited occurrence. The other three are all descriptions of an occurrence. (B) is a description of the occurrence (A). (A^1) and (B^1) are descriptions of an otherwise unidentified occurrence to which they refer. And, as we have just stated, the occurrence (A) is directly correlated with this otherwise unidentified occurrence referred to by (A^1) and (B^1). An inference thrusts itself out of this situation. What if the otherwise unidentified occurrence referred to by (A^1) and (B^1) were (A), which is also referred to by (B)? This is exactly the hypothesis of the present paper.

The qualitative difference between the introspective immediacy of (A) and the symbolic descriptions of (A^1) and (B^1) of (A) is now no objection but is precisely the difference to be expected between the character of an event and the character of the descriptive vehicles symbolically describing an event. Just as we would not expect the verbal introspective report of (A) to be qualitatively identical with the event (A) iself, so we should not expect the visual report of it (A¹) nor the physical report of it (B¹) to be qualitatively identical with the sound quality he introspectively senses the brain

Thus in the dramatic example suggested of the observer seeing his own brain activity in a mirror which he correlates with the sound quality he introspectively senses, the brain activity correlated with the hound he hears is going on in his temporal lobe stimulated by air vibrations in his environment. The brain activity correlated with the sight of the neurons in the mirror is going on in his occipital lobe. But these visual qualities correlated with the neural activity of the occipital lobe are, because of conditioning, referred descriptively to an environmental event and taken as a perceptual visual description of the occurrence in his own temporal lobe. He is thus obtaining a visual quality interpretation of an event which he is at the same moment introspectively feeling as the auditory quality of Middle C. This is just the qualitative difference to be expected between the visual vehicle of description correlated with neural activity in the occipital lobe and the quality of auditory sensation correlated with neural activity in the temporal lobe.

But now imagine the observer seeing in the mirror his neural activity correlated with the sensation red. Shouldn't he see a red quality in the mirror instead of the motions of gray neurons? Of course not. The sensation quality of red is stimulated by the surface of an environmental object selecting for reflection a limited range of electromagnetic vibrations with wavelengths of approximately .65 μ; whereas the surface of neurons as environmental objects seen in a mirror reflect a bundle of unselected waves yielding the sensation of a hueless gray. The neuron activity correlated with the introspective quality of gray will be different from that correlated with the quality red.[3]

To be sure, if the introspectionist sees in the mirror the neuron activity correlated with the quality gray, then by a predictable coincidence the quality of the visual perception will be identical with the quality of his introspective immediacy. But this is simply an interesting consequence of the theory—or, rather, if the theory is true, an interesting consequence of the actual situation. But this coincidental congruence of the two qualities—the congruence, that is, of the qualitative character of the vehicle of the perceptual symbols employed with the quality of the introspected immediacy—is the exceptional occurrence. It is not the pivotal evidence on which the hypothesis is based. In this one type of instance, the perceptual quality seen in the mirror by the observer in the role of physiologist is identical with the quality felt by the observer in the role of introspectionist. In all other instances, the expectation is that the quality of the visual perception of the neural activity will differ from the quality of the correlated introspective immediacy.

There is one other closely allied objection that can be raised to the hypothesis offered in this paper. And this is much the more serious objection. It may be pointed out that at least in certain instances—and the instance above is a case in point— the neural activity physiologically observed is complex whereas the introspected quality is simple. How can one reasonably suggest the identity of a complex event with a simple event? The physiological description of a neural event whether in verbal or perceptual visual terms is complex. Even if the correlate of the simple introspected quality red were the activation of a single neuron, still the correlate would be complex, for the neuron is not a simple physicochemical entity but a very complex chemical substance. And this neural-identity view is by implication embedding introspective qualities in the cosmic field. It is asserting that in physical language an event may be described in such-an-such symbolic terms, but in immediate qualitative experience this identical event is the quality red, or whatever it is intuited to be. Consequently, if the event referred to in physical language is indicated as complex, this cannot be literally identical with the event intuited as the simple quality red.

This is the point where some of the typical contextualistic categories come to the rescue.

First of all, on contextualistic grounds, it is questionable if there are any cosmically simple elements. This is not to question the value of analytical schemes for predictive control, but it is to suggest that actual events always occur in contexts of other events and that their character can never be completely isolated from the character of environing events. In actuality there is no such thing as a self-complete insulated atomic entity. The analysis of an event into elements is, accordingly, a descriptive linguistic device for operational convenience in formulating statements for the manipulation and control of events. An event is not literally composed of elements, even though it may be properly described as a configuration of discriminated analytical properties. The properties into which it is analyzed for any purpose have references to other events in the context of the event analytically described.

The stressing of this point would seem to foredoom the neural-identity theory offered in the present paper. But when taken in conjunction with another typical contextualistic category, it presents a solution. The other category is that of fusion. The qualiy of immediate experience 'had' in any event by a perceiving organism is described by contextualists as a fusion of the contextual properties of the event. Almost any event, however complex, may be intuited as the immediate fused character of its contextual properties. Such a total fusion appears as the simple quality of the event. An event, then, which may be analyzed as a complex configuration of properties may also be intuited as a simple fused quality. To offer just one example, a musical chord like the tonic triad may by a discriminating ear be heard analytically as the simultaneous occurrence in perception of three distinct tones. With a shift of attitude, it can also be heard as the fusion of these three tones in the unique single quality of the chord.

Applying these principles to our neural event and its introspected quality, we find: The neural description indicates an event of some complexity. The introspective report indicates an event of a single intuited quality of red. The solution suggested is that the intuited quality red is a fusion of the complex configuration of properties indicated by the physiological neural description.

It may be objected: If red is a fused quality like the quality of a chord, how does it happen we cannot discriminate in the analytical mood the qualities fused in it, as we can the component tones of a chord? I have, of course, designedly chosen the worst illustration for the neural-identity hypothesis here being presented. For all introspectively analyzable fusions, the answer (as with the chord) would be ready to hand. But I am assuming the existence of introspectively unanalyzable qualities such as the *hues* for color, simple *tones*, *sweetness*, *saltiness*, *sourness*, and *bitterness* for gustatory sensations, and the like.

The answer here, I think, is easily seen. There is a threshold of neural discrimination below which the organism cannot go. Just as the ear cannot discriminate a distinct pitch quality for every change of vibration frequency, so it cannot discriminate contributing qualities of neural activity below a certain level of complexity. These thresholds of discrimination for the various senses are biologically determined, and appear as hereditary limitations in an organism's capacities of response. Stimuli between which an organism cannot make a discriminating response will inevitably on contextualistic principles be registered as a single fused quality. By indirect means the complexity of the situation may be revealed to analytical description. But if the more refined discriminating apparatus is not present in the responding organism, the introspective report and the quality introspected cannot break up a fusion into elements below that threshold of discriminating response.

On the neural-identity theory, however, it would be permissible to infer the existence of qualities below the threshold of the simplest qualities of introspection, to correspond with the complexity indicated by the neural description of the introspectively-intuited qualitative event.

So by a combination of the mechanistic and contextualistic categories, I believe the neural-identity theory can hold up. If it can, it breaks through the wall of dualism between mind and matter that has pestered mechanistic naturalists from the time of Descartes. Contextualistic qualities then flow through the opening of neural correlations into the total space-time gravitational field of physics, and reciprocally the flabby texture of contextualistic experience are drawn up and given firmness and structure on the supporting framework of the mechanist's physical categories.

In respect to this particular problem both sets of categories profit from the amalgamation. The 'private' mental qualities of the mechanist can now, with the help of fusion, be publicly described in physicalist language. By the same stroke, the qualia of contextualism become embedded in the physical descriptions which give us our 'knowledge' of the world. Perhaps other problems will yield to the same co-operative action and a more adequate world hypothesis modifying and adjusting these sets of categories to one another may be in the making.

NOTES

1. This is the unpublished paper referred to as item ✗255 in the bibliography following Herbert Feigl's excellent article, "The 'Mental' and the 'Physical' " in Volume II of "Minnesota Studies in the Philosophy of Science," *Concepts, Theories, and the Mind-Body Problem.*

2. *World Hypotheses,* University of California Press, 1948.

3. This, and the paragraph following, furnishing the answer to the naïve criticism often made of the identity theory that it leads to the conclusion that a man observing the neural activity correlated with his red sensation will see a red neural activity. A fine example of the latter approach will be found in a recent review of Feigl's article on "The 'Mental' and the 'Physical.' " The reviewer says "Feigl doggedly finds nothing incongruous about the idea that we see, feel, smell, and taste the states of our brain" (Philos. Rev., V, LXVIII, No. 3, 395). This assumes that according to the identity theory on introspection is a visual, auditory, etc., *perception* of a quality on a brain state. Such a comment is as relevant to the identity hypothesis as Samuel Johnson's refutation of Idealism is to Berkeley's analysis. The identity theory is based on a causal theory of perception. The criticism assumes (rather confusedly, I fear) a direct realism theory of perception, postulating that the qualities of a perception are not located in the perceiver but somewhere external to the perceiver such as the "surface" of an environmental object.

Chapter 4

Doubts about the Identity Theory

Richard B. Brandt, *Swarthmore College*

I

IT IS USEFUL to stipulate the meaning of *"is a particular mental (phenomenal) fact"* as follows: *"F is a particular mental fact"* is to mean the same as *"F is temporal, and something is directly aware of F."* We can add, if we like, "And it is causally impossible for more than one thing to be directly aware of F." The concept of direct awareness may be taken to be sufficiently familiar. An example of a mental fact is that, if I thump the table, here and now there is a thumping sound. If a particular is wholly a constituent of a mental fact, we can call it a "mental particular," or a "mental event."

The phrase I suggest we may wish to add may need to be complicated if it is true that, in the case of split personalities, we must say that there are two things, both of which are directly aware of the same fact; conceivably, evidence for telepathy may lead in the same direction. For it is not true that, as some have thought, we can show that it is *logically* impossible for two persons to be directly aware of the same fact; the most we can say is that no one can demonstrate that he is directly aware of another person's mental events, as distinct from being directly aware of a numerically different fact, similar to and causally connected with the former.

Some would object to the foregoing proposal for the reason that it implies that some things—especially the look of physical objects—must be classified as mental, although ordinary language does not so classify them. Ordinary language calls "mental" only facts or things which we naturally regard as experiences or states or activities of ourselves—such events as thinking, remembering, noticing, attending, having an emotion, and being in pain. But the look of a tree would never be so-classified by ordinary language. Hence our definition is at best far too broad.

There is an adequate rejoinder to this objection. To begin, the expression "is a mental fact" is hardly a term of ordinary language, so we do not mislead if, for purposes of philosophy, we stipulate a meaning for it in any way that is useful. Further, there are good reasons for classifying things like the look of trees along with remembering, etc., as our definition proposes to do. For the look of trees is part of the subject-matter of the psychological theory of perception, not of the science of physics. It obeys certain psychological laws, such as size-constancy, and color-constancy. Moreover, the look of a tree is conditioned by the brain state of the observer, and is structured by his past experience; very probably nothing at all like it occurs except when a complex nervous system is present. So, although doubtless there are some reasons for refusing to classify the look of a tree with remembering, there are many reasons for doing so.

II

Let us now consider the things which qualify as mental facts or particulars. Among them are color patches, sounds, pains, thoughts, stabs of anxiety, memory images, and daydreams. We should notice, however, that it need not follow logically from the fact that something is a color patch, sound, pain, etc., that it is a mental fact in the above sense. We are apt to think of these kinds of things as "phenomenal qualities" and to speak of words which describe them as "phenomenal language." This way of thinking, however, is apt to be misleading. What is true is that we learn the use of such terms through being directly aware of what they designate, and we use them mostly to talk about situations of which at least someone is directly aware. But there is no formal contradiction in saying that there is a sound, or a pain, etc., which is not a mental event—is not observed by anybody—although, perhaps, in *some* sense it is meaningless to talk of such, since we know how to confirm the occurrence of such things only as they occur in the experience of persons. Philosophers who have supposed that colors are in inanimate nature, and that it is only an external relation for them sometimes to be objects of awarenes, were not contradicting themselves although doubtless they had only aesthetic preference as a reason for what they said.

III

Some philosophers have held that mental facts or particulars are *identical* with physical facts or particulars. What might this mean?

One thing that might be meant is this: Suppose we had a

description of some of these things, a true and complete description—perhaps, for instance, "There is a stabbing pain," or "There is a pinkish image in the center of this visual field"; suppose also we had the vocabulary of physics and chemistry —all the terms which are needed for giving a complete description of the inanimate world (presumably this vocabulary would consist of the basic terms of physics and chemistry, words like "velocity," "mass," "energy," "ion," "electron," and so forth); we might then hold that any description of a mental fact could be put in the vocabulary of physics and chemistry, in sentences *synonymous* with our "mental language" description. The claim that this is so may be called the logical-identity theory.

It would be agreed, I think, that the logical-identity theory is false. Given belief in Ps, a person who understood the language might doubt whether Ph; certainly he would not be contradicting himself if he asserted that Ps and denied Ph. One way of showing this is to point out that a blind man might well understand "Ph" but fail to understand "Ps" if "Ps" happened to be about visual facts; and it would not be merely that he could not be taught the meaning of "Ps" by ostensive means. He obviously would lack the *concept,* the *proposition,* which would not be the case if "Ph" were really synonymous with "Ps."

IV

Sophisticated contemporary advocates of an identity theory, such as Professor Feigl and Professor Köhler, do not support the logical-identity theory. In order to understand what they do advocate, let us first formulate what we may call the correspondence hypothesis. This hypothesis is the view that for every distinguishable class of mental fact or event, there is a distinct set (perhaps with only one member, if nature is simple) of types of brain state, such that if, and only if, there is a brain event of this set, there will be an associated mental fact of the corresponding kind. In other words, the occurrence of some one of a set of distinct types of brain state is a necessary and sufficient condition for a certain kind of associated mental fact. There are, of course, brain states which have no corresponding mental facts, e.g., those of a person who is sound asleep, or many microscopic events in the brain of a waking man (e.g., the pulsations in the blood vessels in the brain have no representation in experience).

A consequence of this view is that in a sense there can be

a physiological explanation of every mental event, provided brain states are instances of deterministic laws. That is, on this view brain states must be predictable on the basis of information only about their physical antecedents, and, given the predicted brain state, one can always predict the corresponding mental event by looking up, in a telephone-book-like directory, the kind of mental state which corresponds to the predicted type of brain state. One might question whether, on this theory, it "must" be that brain states can be predicted on the basis of information about physical antecedents only, given merely that they are instances of "deterministic laws." Thus, the interactionist theory might be proposed as an alternative, that we must have information about some prior mental events in order to predict the occurrence of at least some brain states—so that, while brain states may be instances of deterministic laws, they are not instances of purely physical laws. But this suggestion would be mistaken. For, according to the correspondence hypothesis, since some one physical state or disjunctive set of physical states always corresponds to a mental state, causal laws always *can* be formulated so that their antecedents refer only to brain states, and information about mental states is in principle unnecessary.

Do identity-theorists adopt the correspondence hypothesis? In a sense they do, except that they do not construe the hypothesis so as to imply that the facts or events which correspond are numerically different from one another. They hold that correspondence is the case because the corresponding entities are really identical. Note, incidentally, that they could not hold that some type of brain event is merely the *sufficient* condition of any given type of mental fact or event. For they hold that mental facts are identical with distinct and circumscribed facts about the brain, whereas one can include anything one wishes in the *sufficient* conditions of something. (If B is a sufficient condition of A, then B and C, where C is anything you please, is also a sufficient condition of A.)

V

The identity theory goes beyond the correspondence theory in asserting that every mental event is *identical* with some physical event, or more particularly, with some brain state. For instance, it holds that the fact that there is a stabbing pain now in A's experience is the *very same fact* as the fact that there is (let us suppose) an S-excitation in his thalamus (the corresponding physical fact). It holds that, although "is a stabbing pain" and "is an S-excitation in the thalamus" do not *mean the same,* nevertheless it so happens that they refer to the same thing. It is very like the fact that "This is garnet-colored" asserts the same fact as "This has the color of transparent almandite" although the two sentences do not *mean* the same. The same universal is named by the expression "garnet-colored" and identified by the description "the color of transparent almandite," and both statements say that something is an instance of that universal. The identity of reference, however, is an empirical fact which one must ascertain by observing transparent almandite. Similarly, it is an "S-excitation in the thalamus" refer to the same thing. There are, of course, differences between the two cases. There are simple tests which establish conclusively that a given object is transparent almandite; and direct inspection assures us that a sample of this stone has the color we designate by "garnet"—and that the same is true of all observed examples. On the other hand, we have at most only probabilistic observation indicators of an S-excitation in the thalamus, and we cannot inspect either our pain and note that it is an S-excitation in the thalamus, or our thalamus and note that some state of it is a stabbing pain.

Suppose a pesron, with these differences in view, tried to collect his thoughts about whether "There is a stabbing pain" and "There is an S-excitation in the thalamus" do refer to one and the same fact. What might he say? Let us suppose he means by "*x* is identical with *y*" that there is no property which *x* has which *y* has not, and vice versa; and let us suppose that he uses this expression in the same way, whether he is talking of individual things, or universal, or facts.

VI

Let us list some grounds for doubt.

(A) It is logically possible that interactionism is true—that we in principle need information about prior mental states in order to predict either brain states or mental states. If this is the case, the correspondence hypothesis, as we have seen, is false; and if the correspondence hypothesis is false, then *a fortiori* the identity theory is false. Now there is nothing absurd about interactionism in this sense, nor has it been shown to be mistaken.

(B) The identity theory is a stronger theory than the correspondence hypothesis. There is no empirical evidence for it beyond the evidence for the correspondence hypothesis.

Unless there are other advantages in the identity theory, we are in a better-entrenched position to support the correspondence theory and leave open questions of identity, refraining from commitment.

(C) The correspondence hypothesis, we saw, in theory makes mental events predictable, and in this sense explainable, by physical laws. That is, according to it brain states are predictable by physical laws, and since it is (*ex hypothesi*) a fact that certain physical states are correlated with the occurrence of certain mental states, the prediction of the brain state will also make possible the prediction of the correlated mental state. The apparatus for the prediction of mental states will then include (a) laws for predicting brain states, and (b) correlation laws, perhaps rather like a telephone book and quite unlike equations, connecting specific kinds of brain state with specific kinds of mental state.

What difference would it make if we adopted the identity theory? Only that in the correlation laws we should remove the signs of material equivalence ($\equiv$) and replace them by identity signs ($=$). There is no further theoretical gain. It is not as if the identity theory permitted compressing many correlation laws into one general law—as Newton's theory made possible for the description of motion—as compared with the correspondence hypothesis. If physical brain-theory enables us to predict that a certain time a person's brain state will be Ph, then, despite the identity theory, we must still consult our good old correlation rules to find out what the corresponding psychological state will be.

The theoretical gain in the identity theory, then, is trivial.

This conclusion may be disputed. It may be urged that the identity theory allows us to substitute, for the idea that a stabbing pain and an S-excitation of the thalamus are different but causally related, the much simpler idea that there is only one thing described or known in two ways. As a result, it may be suggested we can simplify our ontology, not only with respect to the number of different kinds of fact, but with respect to the number of laws of nature (since laws causally connecting these different things are no longer required).

But where is the simplification in ontology? There are still all the distinct types of property mentioned in books on physics and chemistry. Moreover, there are still things like pains, colors, sounds, smells, etc., they are what they are and cannot be made to disappear by any alchemy. The only simplification is the disappearance, as a property distinct from a stabbing pain, of the property of being an S-excitation of the thalamus (and so on for the particular physical properties correlated with other brain states). This is a very doubtful boon. Nor do any laws disappear. The physical laws which predict an S-excitation of the thalamus presumably are general laws needed elsewhere in physics or chemistry. Nor do we dispense with the correlation laws, for whereever previously we moved from some state K to an S-excitation of the thalamus and from there via a correlation law to a stabbing pain, now we must move from state K directly to a stabbing pain, and this law will be irreducible. One might suggest that at least we no longer have two widely separated kinds of substance on our hands, a mental and a physical. We need not dispute this, but we still have electrons and velocity and spatial position and mass and colors and smells and pains and emotions. There is nothing missing from the new list of kinds of thing that was present on the old list, unless it be the transcendental ego, but the transcendental ego is not an entity currently in dispute.

(D) What would it *mean* to say that the reference or designation of "is a stabbing pain" and "is an S-excitation in the thalamus" are one and the same? We may suppose there is no difficulty about the fact referred to by "is a stabbing pain"; we know how to pick out, in our own experience, just the fact that would fit this description, and to distinguish it from other facts of experience. But "is an S-excitation in the thalamus" is a theoretical term in science which is partly an *uninterpreted* term. It has no explicit definition in terms of observables. It gains whatever meaning it has from the fact that there are commitments in asserting that something has this porperty, because of the theoretical postulates of our system of science, and because of the "dictionary rules" which connect some of the predicates of our theoretical system with observation predicates. But while use of this theoretical predicate commits us in various directions, it is not explicitly definable in terms of these commitments see C. G. Hempel, "The Theoretician's Dilemma," *Univ. of Minnesota Studies in the Philosophy of Science,* II [1958], 84–85). In what sense, then, may we say that some fact in nature is designated or referred to by a partly uninterpreted predicate? And is there then a clear sense in which we can say that this uninterpreted term, and the observation predicate "is a stabbing pain" have the same reference?

(E) It may be argued that the foregoing objection carries purism to an extreme; the same argument, it may be said, would prove that the scientist ought never to identify a given temperature of a gas with a given mean kinetic energy of its constituent particles, that the scientist should never identify magnetism with certain micro-structures and processes involving electron spins, and that the scientist should not say that the disease of general paresis, formerly defined by certain symptoms, is the very same disease as that now identified by the presence of spirochetes. If the foregoing objection were correct, it may be said, science should in each case content itself with asserting a correlation. But in fact it has felt free to do more, to say that temperature really *is* just mean kinetic energy of molecules, and so on.

Is the parallel exact? Let us consider the parallel with temperature, even though there is some reason for rejecting the identification of temperature with mean kinetic molecular energy.

It is important to note that there is excellent reason for regarding all molar physical objects as aggregates of micro-objects, evidence all the way from observations of Brownian motion to the subtlest triumphs of atomic theory. We have reason, therefore, to suppose in advance that temperature is identical with some fact about molecular atomic behavior. Moreover, it can be successfully construed in this way. There is a micro-theory of the behavior of mercury in thermometers; there is a micro-theory of heat-conduction. The whole theoretical structure fits together to give a coherent account of heat-phenomena of great generality and fine predictive force. Moreover, it does not make sense to say there is merely a *correlation* of molar physical facts and this molecular theory. What it is for there to be a thermometer, according to the theory, is for there to be a certain structure of particles; there is no place in the world for two thermometers, the micro-thermometer and the macro-thermometer. The atomic theory is all-encompassing in the physical world; it leaves no room for micro-objects *and* correlated macro-objects; the whole point is that a macro-object is a complex micro-structure and nothing more. There *is*, of course, room for the *perception* of these objects, and that is a very different story.

There is not similar compulsion to identify stabbing pains with states of the brain. There is not even necessity to locate them in the brain at all: one can adopt conventions about location of mental events which have this result, or one can decide to say that an event is where its necessary and sufficient conditions are, but in either case there is not forceful *evidence* which supports the principle. Even if one does decide to locate them in the brain, it is possible to hold that the brain-volume contains *both* physical events *and* these other events, and to deny that they are one and the same thing. (One might say they are aspects of something else, a fundamental substance, but to say this is only to introduce more mysteries.) Moreover, in the case of stabbing pains, it is not possible to hold that the micro-picture is the real picture, that perceptual appearances are only a coarse duplication, for in this case we are dealing with the perceptual appearances themselves, which cannot very well be a coarse duplicate of themselves.

Furthermore, it seems likely that mental events have properties that are discrepant with the properties of the correlated physical processes, and hence cannot be the same. Suppose I am looking at the sky, and all I see is a homogeneous blue expanse. The identity theory, however, tells me that this homogeneous blue expanse is the very same fact as a vast pattern of electrical discharges between tiny wires, three dimensional in character, and perhaps occupying an ellipsoidal volume of the brain. Can this identication be accepted? Of course, one can hope to pick out a corresponding brain feature which has not got properties discrepant with those of the corresponding mental event. But one cannot go forever on hopes.

Chapter 5

The Mind-Brain Problem

Elmer Sprague, *Brooklyn College*

THE MIND-BRAIN PROBLEM is a puzzler, because we are uncertain of the point of view from which it is to be regarded. The mind-*body* problem afforded the philosopher certain comforts which we miss here. He could at least be sure that *he* had a mind and that *others* had bodies. Indeed, it is this certainty which enables Professor Gilbert Ryle to dissolve the mind-body problem. But when we turn to the mind-brain problem there is no prospect of dissolving it by translating mind questions into brain questions in the way that mind questions can be turned into body questions. I know that I have a mind (i.e., I can assess my own intelligence, appreciate jokes, see my hand before my face, feel pains, etc.), but I do not know my own brain. Of course, by supposing that the general laws of human physiology apply to me, I infer that I have a brain. But I do not know my brain in the way in which a physiologist can when he analyzes and measures the physical and chemical processes which take place in my brain cells. So how can I achieve a satisfying assimilation of my mental life to my brain processes? I just cannot "see" it, yet there are philosphers who feel that I ought to.

Should I try to think of my mental life as the electrochemical processes which the physiologists have discovered in the brain cells? I think not, and I shall try to show why not. We shall have to learn the limits of the usefulness of this latest report of the physiologists, in the same way that philosophers had to learn the limits of the usefulness of the physiologists' discoveries about vision. When physiologists dicovered that in seeing I have images on the retinas of my eyes, some philosophers wanted to insist that the word "see" could be used properly only in sentences on the order of "I see —————— images on the retinas of my eyes," in which the blank is to be filled with specifications of the kind of image. It has taken over 300 years to get away from this position, but I think that there are now few philosophers who would subscribe to it. They would agree that it is one thing to talk about what I am seeing and quite another thing to talk about the physiology of vision. References to images on the retinas of eyes certainly have a place in the latter but not in the former kind of talk. Knowledge of the physiology of vision is of great importance to the optometrist when he is testing my eyes for a pair of glasses. But the physiology of vision is beside the point, when I cannot se my collar button although I am looking straight at it. When my wife says to me: "You need a new pair of glasses," her remark is not a comment on the physiology of my vision, but rather an admonition to learn better habits of searching.

Now might this lesson, drawn from the meeting and mismating of philosophy and the physiology of vision, show the way through the mind-brain problem? We must not say that an electro-chemical process in the brain is but another aspect of some mental activity—joking, for example. Then we should be rightly smashed by Professor Herbert Feigl's question: "Two aspects of what?" We cannot say what the electro-chemical processes in my brain and my joke-making are two aspects of, for we cannot name a third thing for them to be aspects of. Should we then reduce one to the other? But clearly the processes are not my jokes, and vice versa. Are the processes necessary to my jokes? Yes. Without a brain, I could not make jokes. But we must not be overly impressed by this point. As my colleague Mr. Victor Balowitz has pointed out, if the physiologist did not have a mind, he would be incapable of practicing brain physiology. Are the electro-chemical processes in my brain the causes of my jokes? No. My sense of humor must be blamed for them. Then just where do these processes come into any account of my joke-making? The blunt answer is that they do not. Suppose that you wanted to teach a child to make jokes. Would you give him a lecture on the electro-chemical processes of the brain? I think not. In general you would alert him to the differences between the expected and the unexpected, between fulfillment and disappointment, between promise and performance. But at no time would it be essential to your teaching to say: "And all the time that you are seeing jokes, making jokes, and appreciating other people's jokes, the following electro-chemical processes are going on in your brain cells."

Is there a mind-brain problem? As with many problems of philosophy, only if philosophers make one. The mind-brain problem arises only when we suppose that a description of joking lacks something if we do not find room for the physiologists' account of the electro-chemical processes in the brain. But what the physiologist can tell us is not a part of a description of joking. It is another story altogether. And it would remain so, even if a physiologist might attach his apparatus to my brain, mutter about electrical discharges and chemical transformations, check his graphs and pointer readings, and then say: "You've been making a joke." Even if a physiologist could do this, while I should be both mystified and impressed by the way he found out, I should not be surprised by what he told me. After all, it was I who was making the joke. But what is crucial here is that if he wants me to improve my jokes he must talk about the theory and practice of humor, and not about his findings concerning my brain cells. Those, we must never forget, are part of another science.

Chapter 6

On Parapsychology and the Nature of Man

J. B. Rhine, *Duke University*

IN ANY INQUIRY as to how the human brain operates the entire range of related activities ought to be examined. The findings of parapsychology represent a part of that range.

It seems more profitable, however, to focus a review of that field on the thought-brain relation rather than on a brain-machine comparison. I shall turn, therefore, to the more fundamental scientific problem of what properties an organism must have to account for parapsychical (or *psi*) phenomena that are now established as valid.

The Field of Parapsychology

Parapsychology deals with experiences and behavior that fail to show regular relationships with time-space-mass and other criteria of *physical* lawfulness. It began with the study of spontaneous parapsychical experiences, and from this study hypotheses emerged that were brought to controlled test. Eventually, within a few university laboratories, an experimental science of parapsychology began slowly to develop with the usual accompaniments of periodicals, graduate degrees, professional organization, and the like.

It has now been established, by some of the most safe-guarded methods known in the sciences, that a person's relation with his environment need not be solely dependent on the sensorimotor system; an independent mode of interaction has been discovered that is reversible in operation, identified on the cognitive side as *extrasensory perception* (ESP) and on the other as psychokinesis (PK). This exchange with the world through ESP and PK appears to be a more direct one than sensorimotor interaction, inasmuch as no organs of contact are known. PK remains as yet undivided but ESP is dealt with under three headings: *telepathy,* ESP of the mental state of another person; *clairvoyance,* the ESP of objects; and *precognition,* the ESP of future events. The hypothesis is widely entertained that one basic common psi function is involved in both ESP and PK.

It would be wise at this point to review the present status of this highly controversial field, the degree to which criticism has been met, the extent of independent confirmation, and the degree to which the findings have made sense. But, for reasons of brevity, I shall have to be content with providing a list of references* instead and turn rather to an account of what is known about psi.

An Outline of the Findings of Parapsychology

Psychologically, psi is distinguished mainly by its differences from sensorimotor action. Not only are there no localized organs of contact, psi-receptors or effectors, but there is not even any conscious experience of psi functioning as such. Sensory experiences, of course, are generaly conscious and even motor response has sensory accompaniment. ESP, however, has to assume one of the familiar forms of conscious experience—mainly intuitions, hallucinations, dreams, and compulsions. But since these forms are not restricted to parapsychical usage, they do not identify a psi experience.

This lack of a conscious clue to its operation, while it allows a certain degree of motivational direction of the abilities (for example, orientation may be directed toward a consciously selected target), does not permit control of success by means of introspection in the exercise of ESP or PK ability. Accordingly, neither the demonstration of psi on demand nor the reliable application of it to practical problems is possible as yet.

The place of psi in the schema of personality, however, offers thus far no special difficulty. It has already been found to show some of the familiar characteristics of such cognitive abilities as memory and learning. It responds positively to motivation and conditions favoring concentration of effort. Favorable attitudes toward psi capacity, toward the experimenter and toward the test situation appear rather uniformly to improve the operation of psi. The position of a given trial in the test structure reflects much the same configurational principles and pattern effects found in more familiar cognitive behavior. For example, tests involving a column of targets are likely to show greater success at the beginning and end of the column.

Certain other consistent effects obtained in routine psi tests are explainable in terms of the unconsciousness of psi; for ex-

* The list will be found on page 78.

ample, some subjects will consistently displace to the adjoining target symbol ahead of or following the one they try to identify. Others will confuse one symbol with another throughout a long series of tests. Most subjects decline in scoring rate as they continue repeatedly through routine sets of trials in the tests. A number have, under the strain of excessive effort, unconsciously *avoided* the targets to a highly significant degree. Also, in certain studies of psi and personality correlates, one extreme of the personality scale was found correlated with positive scoring while the other end correlated with this avoidance reaction or psi-missing.

But, on the whole, the relationship of ESP scoring to attitudes, school grades, intelligence quotients, extroversion and the like, show sufficient consistency to give assurance that a natural function of the personality is involved. The absence of any association with neurotic tendency, maladjustment, or psychosis, along with the large normal population from which material has now been drawn, suggest that psi capacity is a part of the healthy endowment of the species. The indications already strongly suggest, though they do not conclusively prove, that certain animal species have ESP abilities.

There is, however, little yet to say on the *biological* relationship of parapsychology, though the two fields do have a common frontier. As I have stated, there is evidence to indicate a prehuman origin for psi capacity. The well-controlled experiments on ESP in animals confirming evidence from collections of spontaneous cases, taken together with the fact of the unconsciousness of psi functioning, suggest that psi is an acquisition of the animal organism that even predates the (conscious) sensory specializations. This hypothesis can probably be brought to test as comparisons of psi ability extend through the species. In general, we can say that biology already provides something of a natural setting for psi, although its place in the living system is only tentatively defined as yet.

It is, however, on its frontier with *physics* that parapsychology acquires its most distinctive feature, giving it both its radical aspect and its main present signifiance. Not only in all four of the categories of spontaneous cases but in the experimental verification of all four of these types of psi phenomena, physical explanation seems to be cleary excluded. No physical barrier or boundary has thus far been found to have reliable effect upon results. And altogether a remarkably consistent body of evidence has accumulated.

Since precognition is the most obviously nonphyscial type

of psi, I shall choose for brief illustration the latest work from twenty-five years of precognition experiments, this one but recently completed at the Duke Laboratory. In it Mrs. Elsie Gregory, a teacher in Wheaton, Illinois, administered the tests to her sixth-grade music class, presenting them in a fascinating, gamelike procedure designed with the help of Miss Margaret Anderson at Duke. The pupils were asked to fill in symbols on fifty numbered blanks spaces, trying to match a definite order of target symbols to be selected at the Laboratory at a later date by means of a complex random method. A similar test was given every fortnight through the year. When returned to the Laboratory the record sheets were handled with all the precautions of a two-experimenter system. The results were highly significant (see *Journal of Parapsychology*, September, 1959, pp. 149–57).

To those who accept scientific method, reinforced by its most advanced precautions and with its results adequately confirmed, this finding will, I think, against the background of preceding work, justify the conclusion that the operation of a capacity has been established that extends human perception extrasensorially not only over a long distance but over a period of time into the future. But we shall need a considerable extension of knowledge, general as well as parapsychological, before we may expect such a finding to be understood. Psi phenomena have already shown a great deal of rational consistency or lawfulness, but the rationale of their interaction with physical systems may be as slow in developing as has been that of conscious mental action.

Nonphysical Agency in Man

But even at this stage and according to current definitions (which are the only ones usable), the experimental results of these psi studies present phenomena from human life that *require* the rejection of the conception of man as a wholly physical system. This is simply to say that the acceptance of the occurrence of nonphysical operations in personal action as an established finding of parapsychology today is necessarily to abandon any view of human nature dependent wholly upon physical principles.

On the other hand, this distinction of nonphysicality is reasonably certain to prove to be a transient, even though a temporarily very important, point. It is important now as the essential negative boundary in the definition of parapsychology; it is necessary in order to call the attention of science to the existence of another domain of nature that is now measurably and experimentally demonstrable as a distinctive territory.

But already for decades at least one inquirer has been urging exploration also of the positive or *common ground of nature that makes a psychophysical border necessary;* this should in due time become a principal object of scientific study for those in the field of parapsychology.

Psi, then, is an integral part of the universal system, and its discovery adds to our knowledge of that system. Further relationships, as discovered, should provide increased understanding of man's place within it, a place that has long been a matter of speculation. But we can see even now that, to comprehend the role of human personality in the natural order, it is necessary to deal with certain properties and operations that are part of the personal living system although they are nonphysical in their character. Their description is the body of findings of the beginning science of parapsychology.

SELECT BIBLIOGRAPHY ON THE PRESENT STATUS OF PARAPSYCHOLOGY

Crumbaugh, J. C. "ESP and Flying Saucers," *Amer. Psychologist,* September, 1959, 604-606. A critique of ESP's nonrepeatability. Reply by J. B. Rhine follows in same issue under title: "How does one decide about ESP?"

Eysenck, H. J. *Sense and Nonsense in Psychology.* London: Penguin Books, 1957. See Chap. 3, "Telepathy and Clairvoyance" for appraisal.

Pratt, J. G. Rhine, J. B., Smith, B. M., Stuart, C. E., and Greenwood, J. A. *Extrasensory Perception after Sixty Years.* New York: Henry Holt Co., Inc., 1940. Summary of research and criticism to date of publication.

Price, G. R. "Science and the Supernatural," *Science,* CXXII (1955), 359-67. A critique of ESP. For replies by Soal, S. G., Rhine, J. B., Meehl, P. E., Scriven, M., and Bridgman, P. W., and counter-replies, see *Science,* CXXIII (1956), 9-19.

Rhine, J. B. and Pratt, J. B. *Parapsychology.* Springfield, Ill.: C. C. Thomas, 1957. Findings, methods, and research techniques.

Schmeidler, G. R. and McConnell, R. A. *ESP and Personality Patterns.* New Haven: Yale University Press, 1957. See especially Chap. 2, "Evidence That ESP Occurs."

Soal, S. G. and Bateman, F. *Modern Experiments in Telepathy.* New Haven: Yale University Press, 1954. Recommended for survey of Soal's own work.

Chapter 7

Some Objections to Behaviorism

H. H. Price, *Oxford University*

FIRST, LET ME SAY that I have no objections at all to the behavioristic *method*. There is no reason why there should not be a branch of scientific inquiry which confines itself strictly to investigating the publicly observable behavior of human beings and animals. And it has turned out in practice that there is a surprisingly large field of empirical facts which can be profitably studied in this way, especially facts about the behavior of animals. There *is* a science which might be called behavioristics, or the science of behavior, though one may well doubt whether this science should be called psychology. It seems rather to be only one part of psychology, namely that part which can be studied by methods approximating to those used in the physical sciences.

What I do object to is the behavioristic philosophy of mind, which is sometimes called "reductionist" behaviorism. This is the view that propositions about mental states and happenings of every kind are *reducible* to propositions about publicly observable behavior. On this view, statements containing such words as "seeing," "thinking," "consciousness," "feeling," and "wishing" are only meaningful if and so far as they can be translated into statements about publicly observable bodily happenings. That is the doctrine, or dogma, to which I object, and I do not think it becomes any less objectionable when the term "behavior" is widened so as to include tendencies of dispositions to behave in such-and-such ways.

The first objection I have is so simple that it may seem naïve. It seems to me to be a fact about human beings that they are *aware* of things, and I find it hard to rid myself of the conviction that at least some of the lower animals are aware of things too, at least sometimes. What I am trying to indicate by the phrase "aware of" is something which cannot be defined or analyzed. It is too fundamental, and if anyone says he cannot understand what I am talking about, I do not know how I can help him. All the same, I do not think he really needs any help. It seems to me that everyone already knows for himself what it is to be aware of something, because he himself is constantly being aware of things. And everyone knows for himself that being aware of something is totally different from any kind of bodily happening, though it may, of course, have all sorts of causal connections with bodily happenings.

My second objection is connected with this first one, and as it is a little more complicated, perhaps it may appear more convincing. It seems to me that there are some serious difficulties about the concept of the *publicly observable,* which I take to be the basic concept of behaviorism.

To begin with, what is observing if it is not a way of being aware of something? What does a behaviorist think he is himself doing when he *observes* a rat running about in a maze? Is he just receiving optical stimuli and responding to those by inscribing black marks in his notebook? If he has a colleague who is also observing the rat, he might perhaps try to maintain that this *is* all that is happening in his colleague. But can he possibly think that this is all that is happening in himself? On the contrary, he is being *aware of,* being *visually conscious of,* the movements of the rat, and the black marks he inscribes in his notebook are a record of what he is being aware. Bodily occurrences, of a pretty complicated kind, are certainly taking place in him. But surely it is obvious— obvious to him if not others—that this is not all that is taking place? He is also being aware of certain events in his environment, and moreover he is being aware of them in an intelligent or thoughtful manner, and is noticing the relevance they have to some hypothesis concerning rat-behavior.

So my first difficulty about the publicly observable is concerned simply with the notion of "observing" itself. Observing it itself and instance of being aware of something—in that fundamental and unanalyzable sense of the phrase "aware of" to which I drew attention before. My second difficulty about the concept of the publicly observable is concerned with the concept of "publicity." This difficulty too may be stated in a way which may seem naïve. When something, *X,* is described as public, *to whom* is it public?—Presumably to a number of human beings or persons, each of whom either is or can become *aware* of *X.* Lest this should appear too simple, I shall add another argument which is a little more complicated. The word "public" is what one might call a contrast-word. "Public" is contrasted with "private," and gets its whole meaning from that contrast. If nothing is private, nothing is public either. And if we go farther and say, as some behaviorists would, that the term "private" makes no sense, that such expressions as "private experience" or "private mental occurrences" are simply devoid of meaning, then the term "public" makes no sense either. To put it crudely: if everything is public, nothing is public, because the term "public" has lost all its meaning. (The same absurdity would result, of course, if one said that *everything* is private. By saying so, one would have abolished the antithesis from which the term "private" derives its meaning.) This is what is wrong with subjective idealism. Extremes meet, and the "reductive" behaviorist is more like the subjective idealist than one might think.

These remarks about privacy and publicity lead naturally to my final topic, which is introspection. When someone maintains, as I want to, that there is such a process as introspection, he is maintaining: (1) that there are private occurrences or experiences which are not accessible to public observation; (2) that such private occurrences can sometimes be attended to or scrutinized by the person who has them; (3) that such introspective scrutiny is a genuine source of information, a way of finding things out about one's own experiences; (4) that though the occurrences one finds out about are private ones, they are nonetheless publicly describable, since the information one gets by means of introspection can be imparted to others, who can *understand* one's introspective reports whether or not they believe them (it is not true that what is private is therefore incommunicable).

In connection with (2) and (3), a good deal of fuss has been made about the difficulty that the introspective scrutinizing of an experience cannot be simultaneous with the experience itself. I cannot see how this matters very much. Introspection may always be *restro*spection; it may always be form of short-range memory. But even if it is always "retro-," the point is that it *is* "intro-." The attention of scrutinizing may always be a scrutinizing of the recent past, not the present; but still what is scrutinized is an experience of one's own.

It is also argued that an experience is altered by the process of introspecting it: for example, that if one attends carefully to a feeling, the feeling thereupon becomes less intense, and may even disappear altogether. But supposing this to be a fact, how is the fact known? Surely it itself can only be ascertained by introspection? This anti-introspective argument only amounts to saying that introspection may be more carefully or less carefully conducted (which is, of course, true) and that the findings of careless or unguarded introspection can sometimes be corrected by introspecting more carefully.

Moreover, if it is also said that all introspection is retrospective, what meaning can we attach to the contention that a *past* experience can be altered by introspecting it? I suppose we should have to represent the situation thus: we should have to divide both the introspecting and the experiences introspected into successive temporal slices

$$I^1 \quad I^2 \quad I^3 \quad I^4$$
$$E^1 \quad E^2 \quad E^3 \quad E^4$$

and the contention should be that I^1, by having the earlier event E^1 for its object, causes the *contemporary* event E^2 to be different from what it would have been otherwise. And consequently I^2 has a different object from the one it would have had if I^1 had not preceded it. But then we must still ask the same question as before: Assuming this to be a fact, how is the fact known, if not by better and more careful introspection?

One must admit, of course, that there has been some excuse for the attacks which have been made on introspection, and even for the attempts which have been made to argue it out of existence. Extravagant claims have been made for introspection in the past, and they have naturally led to an equally extravagant reaction against it. It has sometimes been alleged that introspection is an infallible source of information, and this has led people to say that on the contrary it is not a source of information at all.

I certainly do not want to defend this claim to infallibility. Perhaps it arose from a confusion between the having or living-through of an experience on the one hand, and the introspective scrutiny on the other. (Both alike could be referred to rather loosely as "self-conscious.") Now if I have an experience I do have it. It is just something which happens, and no question of being mistaken arises. That question only arises when I attend to the experience and make judgments about it. The mere having of experiences—just living through them—is something to which the notion of fallibility does not apply. But it does not follow from this that the mere having of experiences is a kind of infallible cognition. It is not a form of cognition at all. It is neither knowing nor believing, neither correct nor erroneous.

Introspecting, on the other hand, the attentive scrutinizing of experiences and the attempt to make judgments about hem, to bring them under concepts and to distinguish between one type of experience and another—this certainly *is* a form of cognition, but it is not an infallible one at all. I find it hard to see why anyone should suppose that it is, if he has ever made a real effort to do some introspecting himself. We need only consider how very difficult introspection can be, what trouble one often has in classifying or describing an experience and disentangling the different elements, how doubtful one often is about the most appropriate words to use in describing one's experiences even to oneself, and still more when trying to describe them to others. Let us remember too that some people are masters of introspective description—William James is the greatest one I know—while others make a very poor job of it, and still others fall somewhere between the two extremes.

Introspection, in short, is something which requires skill and care (and honesty too). It can be done well, or moderately well, or badly, and up to a point one can train oneself to do it better.

So the claim that introspection is an infallible source of information must certainly be abandoned, and ought never to have been made. But this conclusion should not dismay the advocate of introspection. On the contrary, it should encourage him. One of the characteristic marks of a genuine procedure for obtaining information is that mistakes are possible when one uses it. When one can be wrong, one can also be right. And if someone alleges that there is a procedure in which mistakes are impossible one supposes that it is not really a way of obtaining information at all. When one cannot be wrong, one cannot be right either.

I suggest, then, that we must distinguish between having or living-through an experience and making introspective judgments about it. The first is not infallible, but might mistakenly be thought to be so, because it is something to which the notion of fallibiliy does not apply. The second, just because it is a genunie source of information, is perfectly capable of being mistaken on accasion, as other means of getting information are.

In this paper I have said nothing about the bearing of paranormal phenomena upon the behaviorist philosophy of mind. It appears to me that what the "reductive" behaviorist is primarily concerned to deny or to argue out of existence is a set of facts so "normal" and so obvious that everyone is familiar with them—for example, the fact that we are aware of things, that each of us has experiences, that each of us can attend to and make judgments about the experiences which he has. His error seems to me the philosophical error of denying the obvious, and not the scientific error of denying new and strange facts which fail to fit in with current scientific theories.

I do, however, find it very difficult to understand how even an epiphenomenalist or a parallelist, and a fortiori a behaviorist, can manage to reconcile the phenomena of paranormal cognition with his conception of human personality. If he were to make a serious attempt to do so, I think he would have to begin by revising his views of the natural world in a pretty radical way by postulating new types of matter and new types of physical energy which are certainly not parts of the publicly observable world as our sense-organs reveal it and as contemporary physics and biology conceive of it. He might find himself obliged to suppose that each of us has a "hyper-physical" organism in addition to the publicly observable physical organism which physiologists can experiment upon and anatomists can dissect, and that the publicly observable physical environment is sometimes interpenetrated by a "hyper-physical" environment obeying causal laws quite different from those which physicists have discovered. What began as a naturalistic theory of human nature would be transformed into a kind of occultism. A return to an old-fashioned dualistic theory would seem to be a more tolerable alternative.

Chapter 8

In Defense of Dualism

Curt Ducasse, *Brown University*

NEITHER IN THE section of this symposium on "The Mind-Body Problem" nor in that on "The Brain and the Machine" is much, if any, attention given to the dualist-interactionist conception of the relation between mind and brain. A summary presentation of the case for it and against its rivals may therefore be appropriate here.

The first point to which attention must be called is that, beyond question, there are things—events, substances, processes, relations, etc.—denominated "material," or "physical," that there are also certain others denominated instead "mental," or "psychical," and that no thing is denominated both "physical" and "psychical," or both "material" and "mental." Rocks, trees, water, air animal and human bodies, and the processes occurring among them or within them, are examples of the things called "material" or "physical"; emotions, desires, moods, sensations, cravings, images, thoughts, etc., are examples of the things called "mental" or "psychical."

To question whether the first *really* are physical or the second *really* are psychical would be absurd, as it would be absurd to question whether a certain boy whom his parents named "George" really was George. For just as "George" is a name, so "psysical" or "material," and "psychical" or "mental," are names; and a name is essentially a *pointer*, which does point at—designates, indicates, denotes, directs attention to—whatever it actually is employed to point at.

It is necessary, however, to ask what characteristic shared by all the things called "physical" or "material" determined their being all designated by one and the same name; and the same question arises with regard to those denominated instead "psychical" or "mental." Evidently, the characteristic concerned had to be an obvious, not a recondite one, since investigation of the recondite characteristics respectively of physical and of psysical things could begin only *after* one knew which things were the physical and which the psychical ones.

In the case of the things called "physical," the patent characteristic common to and peculiar to them, which determined their being all denoted by one and the same name, was simply that all of them were, or were capable of being, *perceptually public*—the same tree, the same thundercalp, the same wind, the same dog, the same man, etc., can be perceived by every member of a human public suitably located in space and in time. To be material or physical, then, *basically* means to be, or to be capable of being, perceptually public. And the unperceivable, recondite things physicists discover—electrons, protons, etc., and the processes that occur among them—only have title at all to be also called physical *derivatively*—in virtue, namely, (and *only* in virtue) of their being *constituents* of the things that are perceptually public.

On the other hand, the patent characteristic which functioned as a basis for the application of one identical name to all the things called "psychical" or "mental" was their *inherently private* character, attention to them, as distinguished from attention to what they may signify, being accordingly termed "introspection," not "perception."

The events called "psychical," it must be emphasized, are private in a sense radically different from that in which the events occurring inside the body are private. The latter are private only in the sense that visual, tactual, or other exteroceptive perception of them is *difficult*—indeed, even more difficult for the person whose body is concerned than for other persons—such perception of those events being possible, perhaps, only by means of special instruments, or perhaps only by anatomical "introspection"(!), i.e., by opening up the body surgically and looking at the processes going on inside it. The "privacy" of intra-somatic stimuli, including so-called "covert behavior, is thus purely adventitious. The privacy of psychical events, on the other hand, is *inherent and ultimate*.

It is sometimes alleged, of course, that their privacy too is only adventitious. But this allegation rests only on failure to distinguish between being *public* and being *published*. Psychical events can be more or less adequately published. That is, perceptually public forms of behavior correlated with occurrence of them can function as *signs* that they are occurring —but *only* as signs, for correlation is not identity. Indeed, correlation presupposes non-identity.

Psychical events *themselves* are never *public* and never can be made so. That, for example, I *now remember* having dreamed of a Siamese cat last night is something which I can *publish* by means of perceptually public words, spoken or written. Other persons are then *informed of it*. But to be informed *that I remember* having so dreamed is one thing, and to *remember* having so dreamed is altogether another thing, and one *inherently private*. The dreaming itself was not, and the remembering itself is not, a *public* event at all and cannot possibly be made so in the way in which my *statement* that I remember that I so dreamed is or can be made public.

How then does it happen that we have names understood by all for events of inherently private kinds? The answer is, of course, that we heard those names—e.g., "anger," "desire," "remembering," etc.,—uttered by other persons when they perceived us behaving in certain more or less stereotyped manners. But the point crucial here is that although each of us acquires his vocabulary for mental events in this way, the words of it, at the times when they are applied by others to *his* behavior, denote *from him* not primarily or perhaps at all his behavior, but the particular kind of inherently private event, i.e, of physical state, which *he* is experiencing at the time. It is only in "behaviorese," i.e., in the language of dogmatic behaviorism, that for example the word "anger," and the words "anger-behavior," both denote the same event, to wit, the event which ordinary language terms "behaving angrily."

There are several varieties of behaviorism, but they agree in that they attempt to account for the behavior of organisms wholly without invoking a psychical cause for any behavior—that is, wholly by reference to physical, perceptually public causes, present and/or past.

Dogmatic behaviorism is the pious belief that the causes of the behavior of organisms, including human organisms, *are never other than physical*. Nothing but this dogma dictates that even when no physical occurrences are actually found that would account for a given behavior, physical occurrences nevertheless *must* be assumed to have taken place.

Empirical or methodological behaviorism, on the other hand, is not thus fideistic. It is simply *a research program*, perfectly legitimate and often fruitful—the program, namely, of *seeking*, for all behavior, causes consisting of physical, i.e., of perceptually public stimulus events, present and past. Evidently, the fact that one undertakes to search for causes of this kind for all behavior leaves entirely open the possibility that, in many of the innumerable cases where no physical causes adequate to account for the given behavior can in fact be observed, the behavior had a psychical not a physical cause.

For, contrary to what is sometimes alleged, causation of a physical by a psychical event, or of a psychical event by stimulation of a physical sense organ, is not in the least paradoxical. The causality relation—whether defined in terms of regularity of succession, or (preferably) in terms of single antecedent difference—does not presuppose at all that its cause-term and its effect-term both belong to the same ontological category, but only that both of them be *events*.

Moreover, the objection that we cannot understand how a psychical event could cause a physical one (or vice versa) has no basis other than blindness to the fact that the "how" of causation is capable at all of being either mysterious or understood only in cases of *remote* causation, never in cases of *proximate* causation. For the question as to the "how" of causation of a given event by a given other event never has any other sense than *through what intermediary causal steps* does the one cause the other. Hence, to ask it in a case of proximate causation is to be guilty of what Professor Ryle has called a "category mistake"—a mistake, incidentally, of which he is himself guilty when he alleges that the "how" of psycho-physical causation would be mysterious.

Again, the objection to interactionism that causation, in either direction, as between psychical and physical events is precluded by the principle of the conservation of energy (or of energy-matter) is invalid for several reasons.

(A) One reason is that the conservation which that principle asserts is not something known to be true without exception, but is, as M. T. Keeton has pointed out, only a defining-postulate of the notion of a *wholly closed* physical world, so that the question whether psycho-physical or physico-psychical causation ever occurs is (but in different words) the question whether the physical world *is* wholly closed. And that question is not answered by dignifying as a "principle" the assumption that the physical world is wholly closed.

(B) Anyway, as C. D. Broad has pointed out, it might be the case that whenever a given amount of energy vanishes from, or emerges in, the physical world at one place, then an equal amount of energy respectively emerges in, or vanishes from, that world at another place.

(C) And thirdly, if "energy" is meant to designate something experimentally measurable, then "energy" is defined in terms of causality, *not* "causality" in terms of transfer of energy. That is, it is not known that *all* causation, or, in particular, causation as between psychical and physical events, involves transfer of energy.

These various objections to interactionism—which, let it be noted, would automatically be objections also to epiphenomenalism—are thus wholly without force.

Epiphenomenalism, however, is open to the charge of being *arbitrary* in asserting that psychical events are always effects of physical events but never themselves cause other psychical events nor cause any physical events. For the experimental evidence we have—that, for instance, decision to raise one's arm causes it to rise under normal circumstances—is of exactly the same form as the experimental evidence we have that, under normal circumstances, burning one's skin causes occurrence of pain.

Psychophysical "parallelism" has widely been adopted as supposedly an alternative escaping the difficulties which—mistakenly, as we have now seen—are alleged to stand in the way of interactionism. "Parallelism," however, is really the name not of a solution but of a problem. For the parallelism itself remains to be accounted for. And the "double-aspect" explanation, or would-be explanation, of it is but an empty figure of speech unless and until the "substance," of which mind and brain are alleged to be two "aspects," has first been shown to exist. And this never yet has been done.

Interactionism, then, as presented in what precedes, though not as presented by Descartes, is a perfectly tenable conception of the relation between some mental events and some brain events, allowing as it does also that some brain events have bodily causes, and that some mental events directly cause some other mental events. It conceives minds as consisting, like material substances, of sets of systematically interrelated dispositions, i.e., of capacities, abilities, powers, and susceptibilities, each of which can be analyzed as a causal connection, more or less enduring, between any event of some particular kind—*C,* occurring in a state of affairs of some particular kind—*S,* and a sequent event in it, of some particular kind—*E.* The series of *exercises* of the different dispositions (which together define the *nature* of a given mind) constitutes the *history* of that particular mind, i.e., its *existence* as distinguished from only its *description*.

Chapter 9

Some Comments on Dimensions of Mind

P. W. Bridgman, *Harvard University*

IN ALL THE DISCUSSION in the present symposium of the mind-brain problem, and of the possible similarities and differences bewteen brains and machines, one can sense an underlying problem, never explicitly formulated, but tacitly felt—sometimes with emotional overtones. With regard to the machine the problem seems to be whether it is possible to discover and formulate some method of functioning of the brain which is intrinsically impossible to a machine. With regard to the mind the implicit problem seems to be to discover and formulate some method of functioning of an organism which can be said to imply the possession of a "mind" and which cannot be completely explained in terms of any conceivable functioning of a brain. There is a wide range in the temperamental attitude of the discussants toward these questions. To some it is a matter of indiffrence whether such differences between machine, brain, and mind could be found, or indeed whether they exist, whereas others seem to feel an emotional need for the assurance that there are such differences. The emotional reaction seems tied up in some way with a feeling for human dignity. The general situation is somewhat like that with regard to the concept of "life." Some people regard it as of little or no interest whether it is possible to find or formulate a distinction between the living and the non-living, whereas others are greatly concerned about it.

I think a third attitude toward these questions is possible, one not embraced in the two extreme positions just described. This third attitude I have elaborated in my recent book *The Way Things Are*. It seems to me that many of the words of daily life have two recognizably different aspects, a public and an introspectional aspect, and that there is an operational dichotomy between these two aspects. The magnitude of this dichotomy is not usually appreciated. On the contrary, we usually try to assimilate both aspects into a single unitary point of view, corresponding to an underlying "reality." This, it seems to me, can result only in philosophic confusion. In some cases the difference between the public and the introspectional aspects is comparatively slight, but in other cases it is so important that it seems to me justifiable to practice a special verbal technique to emphasize the difference.

Perhaps the difference between the two aspects is greatest, and it is most important to emphasize the difference, in the case of the word "conscious." "Conscious" is both an introspectional word and a "relational" word, in the same sense that "I" is a relational word. In both cases the person using the word stands in a unique relation to it. In the same sense that there is only one "I" there is only one consciousness. In this sense, only *I* am "conscious." I would like to retain the word "conscious" for this unique introspectional sense, and not discard it entirely, as would some of the more extreme behaviorists. In discussion about the possibility of consciousness in machines the impulse to use "conscious" in a public sense is very common. Professor Wiener adumbrated the point I am trying to make here when he remarked that a person could justifiably say only of himself that he was conscious. But then he spoiled it by remarking that a person could say this only with a certain probability.

The third attitude alluded to above is one which recognizes the difference between the public and the introspectional aspects of many of our common words. The fundamental and inescapable dichotomy is not between brain and machine or between brain and mind, but between myself and all else. I believe that some of the implications of this dichotomy are uncritically and unconsciously carried over into the first and second attitudes above, and that this partly explains any emotional involvement. Thus the "consciousness" which many people find it so repugnant to concede to a machine is not the consciousness which can be defined in terms of overt observable behavior, but is the consciousness which only I can have. The question of the possession of this sort of consciousness by a machine (or by another organism, for that matter) simply does not arise when the issue is properly understood. The situation is similar with regard to "mind." "Mind" has strong relational introspectional components. I say of myself, when I am thinking that I am using my "mind," but I have no way of knowing whether you have a "mind" in the same sense, and the question is indeed meaningless. (By the same token, there is a sense in which it is only I who think, and the question whether a machine can "think" does not arise.) Since I have no awareness of my brain in introspection, the question of any connection between brain and "mind" cannot arise in this context.

A due recognition of the dual aspects of many of our words and concepts alters, I believe, our attitude toward the general significance of this symposium. It does not strike me as shocking or even particularly revolutionary to entertain the possibility that someday I or someone else might succeed in putting together a system with all the behavioral characteristics of my neighbor and which I could not distinguish from him. Nor would it bother me particularly, nor would I regard it as particularly important, if someday I succeeded in drawing up a formal definition of "machine" which might apply to myself. Such an achievement would in no way alter my firsthand experience, in terms of which I would continue to think of myself as a person and not as a "machine."

It seems to me that, back of the deliberations of this symposium and giving them point, the one truly important question is the highly specific and concrete question as to how to construct systems which should reproduce more faithfully than is now possible the known modes of functioning of the brain. The solution of this problem is of great importance, both because of the use to which such systems could be put in practical applications and because of the light it would throw on the way in which brains function.

Chapter 10

Theory-Categories in the Mind-Body Problem

Abraham Edel, *City College of New York*

PROFESSOR KÖHLER'S view that currents in the brain have
phenomenal attributes just as electric currents have magnetic
attributes provokes afresh the conflicts of interpretation in
the well-stocked tradition of mind-body problems. The pro-
cedural meaning of "having an attribute" is clear enough for
scientific work. But the philosopher cannot help responding
almost automatically: "Have we here a parallelism, an epiphenomenalism, a monistic identity, and emergent phenomenon,
or what?"

Considerable reassessment of these mind-body theory-categories has been taking place in contemporary philosophy—
for example, in Professor Feigl's recent defense of identity
approaches (Herbert Feigl, "The 'Mental' and the 'Physical,' "
Concepts, Theories, and the Mind-Body Problem, eds.
Herbert Feigl, Michael Scriven, and Grover Maxwell [Uni-
versity of Minnesota Press, 1958]). By far the greater part
of it is concerned legitimately with the logic of the relation
of terms, laws, and theories in different fields. The *analysanda*
are the existent systematized scientific results of the specific
mind-areas and body-areas. What we have then is the application of general logical and philosophy-of-science lessons to
the relation of different branches of physics, physiology, and
psychology. If we remain completely ("philosophically")
parsimonious, there is no need for differentiating theory-inter-
pretations where the same scientific evidence is appealed to
by the different ones. The most that, for example, an identity
theory could claim over a parallelistic theory in that case,
would be a greater protective function against the reintroduc-
tion of metaphysical dualism of substance. But, of course,
protective function depends on the source of attack, and an
identity theory might find itself saddled with a double-aspect
methodology that would be a handicap in meeting irrationalist
claims for direct inner knowledge in the sciences of the human
spirit. All this is familiar enough, so that perhaps the issue
I should like to raise may most expeditiously be put in *ad
hominem* form. After all the logical issues of correlation,
reference, logical and empirical identity, reduction of theories,

and so forth, have been explicated for given, relevant, several-science materials, what elso does Professor Feigl want or have a right to expect? Why should not these different mind-body theories be analyzed in terms of the problems in the historical relations of the sciences at different periods of their growth, when they functioned as competing heuristic principles pointing to possibly different paths of scientific extension—e.g., an autonomous psychology versus a physically reductive one? Perhaps the "cash-value" of the different theories is still to be found today in their heuristic role; some sense of these problems arises in specific areas—for example, in conflicting explanatory principles in psychosomatic medicine.

If this path of interpretation, while adequate, seems too restricted for the revivified philosophical mind-body theory, I should like to suggest what seems to me an avenue in which there are numerous logical questions of a non-formal sort, inadequately explored and analytically tempting. Let us try the path of consciously giving to our theory-categories a definite *empirical-descriptive* interpretation, not a purely logical one, though refined by the logical advances so as not to generate pseudo-problems. Perhaps the easiest category in which to illustrate this is *emergence*. If we ask whether the phenomenal field is an emergent, we need no longer be introducing vague vitalistic principles, nor do we need to avoid this by saying simply that emergence must be a relation only between theories, not between phenomena. We could instead press forward for that cluster of hypotheses which would arise if *emergence* were regarded as an empirically-descriptive concept. To talk of emergence then involves reference to *an emerging process*. We could thus ask: "What emerged over what period?"; "What were the forces that brought about the emergence?"; "Did what emerged emerge as a whole or bit-by-bit, and under what conditions over what period?", and so on. In such analysis the concept of emergence would itself be rendered explicit and more sharply delineated. What are its essential properties? For example, there would have to be a first temporal occurrence of a quality, its repeated occurrence, its establishment as a regular phenomenon. There might be different types, some involving own-level laws, others only lower-level lawful relations. All such properties might be cast as analytic of the concept of emergence, or else some as contextual conditions of its applicability if it is given a narrower "definition," or in several other logically possible ways. I think that *epiphenomenal* might be given an empirical-descriptive analysis of this type. It is an emergent quality with severe limitations on its causal properties, arising perhaps largely from non-formal restrictions in the analysis of *causality*. (It is a "helpless" phenomenon.)

Parallelism might try to resist such an approach because it has had such a comfortably ambiguous status. It kept the door open to metaphysical dualism while letting autonomous sciences develop. And in modern times it could seek modestly to equate itself with the scientific hypothesis of isomorphism, and claim the virtue of being a non-metaphysical description of the scientific results. But if we take it as a descriptive term we have to look for some actual *parallelizing process*—some modern substitute for the old process of setting the clocks to keep time together as well as the explanation of how they work so as to keep together. Deny the search for such a *process,* and we no longer have a parallelistic mind-body theory but merely a search for correlations, no more entitled to the eminence of a theory-status than any regular phenomenal-phenomenal correlation or physical-physical correlation.

Strikingly enough, *identity* theory, which so often prides itself on its parsimony, is likely to prove the most complex of these concepts. Thus if we say that the *phenomenal quale* Q is empirically identical with the *physical event* P (specific electrical brain state), we have as a minimum the correlation of the two distinguishable phenomena. I doubt whether the logical analysis of identity and of correlation will get us any further so long as we focus on Q and P in this isolated context. We do get further, as we know, by asking whether the theory within which Q is systematized is in general reducible to the theory in which P is systematized—in short, how far science has gone in integrating perceptual psychology within a system of physics. Perhaps this is what we mean when we say not merely that Q is correlated with P, but that Q is an *attribute* of P. But an additional possibility here suggested is that we can find that we have in mind a number of non-formal conditions which determine whether we regard Q as an attribute of P, or P as an attribute of Q, or both as parallel events. The kinds of conditions I am thinking of would be some such as the following:

(1) While Q and P coincide temporally, yet when Q is not present, there is still something of the P-family around, though not precisely P.

(2) (Perhaps a stronger form of [1].) When Q has been present and is not succeeded by something of the Q-family,

there will still be found something of the P-family, on some occasions differing only in degree or intensity from what it was when Q was present. In other words, there are degrees or intensities in brain phenomena whereby rises and falls (whether continuous or discontinuous) will occasion the phenomenal quality. (This shows who is "boss" or wields the "executive power.")

(3) Historically it will be found that the Q-family is an emergent from the P-family.

(4) For any descriptive meaning that can be found in ordinary use for the term "thing"—even where the defining properties of "thing" are themselves phenomenal—the physical (brain) will be found to possess them, whereas the phenomenal quality will not. Or if usage shows differences in degree rather than sharp thinglike and non-thinglike demarcations, then the phenomenal quality will be "farther removed" than the physical phenomenon. Thus if the electrical current is taken to be a "state of the brain," then the phenomenal quality will be a "state of a state of the brain." I am not too happy about this condition, but that is because attempts to analyze the phenomenal-physical configuration which is the referent of terms like "thing," "event," and "substance" have suffered from neglect through despising the material mode of speech.

There is little point here in attempting to refine these conditions or to seek out more satisfactory ones. My purpose is simply to illustrate the thesis that the surplus meaning in 'identity' as a mind-body theory involves some such material conditions, and that its vindication would have to proceed through such complex discoveries rather than come from a bare, parsimonious role.

I am not wholly assured that the avenue of exploration I am here suggesting will be a fruitful one for body-mind theory, but it does seem hopeful and should at least be worked through. In any case, we should remember that our theory-categories had a rich content in their origins, though it was a fusion of scientific, metaphysical, and, at many points, valuational material. In sorting out the problems in modern times we have made them bloodless categories. If we want to infuse new life into them, we should consider the possibility that they have a broad material content which involves some configuration of scientific knowledge cutting across many areas—in short, that they are concepts geared to the theoretical expression of material truths.

Chapter 11

Whitehead's Concept of Organism and the Mind-Body Problem

Howard W. Hintz, *Brooklyn College*

IN HIS DISCUSSION of "The Brain and the Machine," Dr. Norbert Wiener stresses some of the striking resemblances between the activity of the electronic brain and of the human brain as the latter's activity is reflected in recorded electrical impulses and wavelengths. It is not quite clear exactly what far-reaching inferences, if any, Dr. Wiener wishes to draw from these comparisons, or whether he intends to imply that the machine will ultimately be able to perform all of the functions of the human brain and perhaps perform them more efficiently. In any event, the subsequent comments of Mr. Scriven, Mr. Putnam, and others serve very helpfully to point up some significant differences between machine and brain activity which were presumably not accounted for in Dr. Wiener's experiments.

Dr. Köhler deals at considerable length with the same basic question, but his conclusions seem to be at variance with the implications, at least, of Wiener's findings. Köhler maintains that earlier assumptions regarding the existence of close parallels between electronic-brain and human-brain activity were greatly weakened if not altogether refuted by his own experiments in the observation of electrical impulses in the human brain induced by perceptual activity. He further suggested that if all mental phenomena were to be explained within the naturalistic-scientific framework, then parallels between mental phenomena and non-mental phenomena above and beyond any yet observed would at some time have to be discovered. The particular relevance of Köhler's comments to Wiener's arguments (however variant their special interests and areas of research may be) is at the point of their common interest in the relationship of human mental processes and other natural processes and phenomena. I do not regard the

Notes to this paper are on page 105.

implied differences in their observations about parallels and resemblances between mental and non-mental phenomena as particularly important. Obviously, the investigations of both men in this vast and complex field are too limited and tentative to have produced any conclusive evidence one way or the other. What is important, is the basic empirical-naturalistic assumption upon which both men proceed. Dr. Köhler, for instance, was quick to point out during the course of his paper, that he was in no sense implying the need for any metaphysical explanations of the mind-body problem. Yet at the same time he was rather sharply critical of certain tendencies of contemporary "scientism" and of the rigidity and bigotry of certain current scientific-naturalistic attitudes and practices.

It is my contention that the solution of the mind-body problem (to the extent that it *is* a "problem" and to the extent that it can be "solved") will never be reached if it is sought solely wihin the naturalistic-scientific framework and by the investigation of empirical data alone. It is my further contention that a much more fruitful approach to the problem, and one offering much greater promise of clarifying rather than confusing the issues is the approach suggested by Whitehead and his concept of "organism."

Before indicating more specifically the applications of Whitehead's theories to this problem I should like to suggest certain unique properties of "mind" as distinguished from "brain" which are of the utmost importance in any consideration of either mind-body or mind-machine relationship.

Briefly stated, the crucial question, then is this: Could any brain-machine or group of machines carry on the type of discussion which has produced the present book? This leads to a host of corollary questions involving feeling, volition, curiosity, aspiration, evaluation, etc. What would be the machines' purposes and desires? What would be their incentives and objective? What manner of *self-consciousness* would the machines possess which would enable them to attach value to or to derive satisfaction from their enterprises? In what sense would they *feel* a sense of frustration, success, failure, achievement, or self-satisfaction? And let it be remembered and emphasized that "thought" in relation to these "states of mind" is inseparable from feeling and that to this extent mind is inseparable from the body which *includes* the brain.

The underlying fallacy of the conventional and traditional "naturalistic" approach to the mind-body problem is indeed graphicaly exposed by the very introduction of the "brain-machine" issue into the discussion. I contend that the brain-machine has no relevance to the philosophical question confronting us and that the investigation and discovery of mechanical or physical parallels between brain activity and brain-machine activity can throw no significant light on the issue. For the problem, let it be remembered, is not and never has been the brain-body relationship, but the *mind-body* relationship. The machine does indeed bear striking and startling resemblances to the human brain in terms of certain types of processes, functions, and activities. But it bears little or no resemblance to the *mind*. At best and at most, the brain-machine is an extension, however ingeniously contrived, of the human brain. But it is not primarily a creation of the brain. It is essentially a creation of the human mind, which, having willed to create it, created it, and which, should it will to destroy it, can also destroy it. Study of machine-brain and human-brain resemblances might disclose information of importance to the physician or to the brain physiologist. It is extremely doubtful whether such study can reveal anything important to the psychologist, for his concerns are much more with the mind than with that physical organ known as the brain.

The point to be stressed, of course, is the uniqueness of those qualities of the human entity that are identified with mind and that, although they involve the brain, also involve many other parts and elements of the human organism and that have traditionally been associated with such etymologically-related and synonymous terms as "spirit and soul." Thus the non-rational forms of thought and behavior are as fully embraced by the concept of mind as are the rational forms. Therefore, as has been noted, feeling (even more than thought), and the unconscious and irrational activities of the *brain,* as well as the rational and conscious activities, are represented by the term "mind." Now it is precisely that kind of "thinking" which is most closely associated with feeling— with pain and sorrow, love, hate, aspiration, purpose, and above all valuing and evaluation—it is that kind of thinking which the machine-brain does not do. Hence we need not be at all concerned about that absurd fear expressed by Dr. Wiener that the brain-machine may some day control men. Here is the Frankenstein fantasy all over again, but this time on the part of a man who is strangely confusing the mechanical brains he has helped create with the "minds" which conceived them, built them, and must continue to operate or "prepare" them. Surely Dr. Wiener does not want to fall into the Cartesian error of believing that he can locate and install some "soul" object into the brain-machine, albeit an electronic or mechanical one! No one, I submit, who understands the true nature of the mind-body problem could possibly be misled by the false analogy between either the human mind and the brain-machine, or for that matter between the human brain and the machine-brain.

Observe what has now happened as a result of this confusion. The scientific-naturalist who is foremost among those who will admit of no separation of mind and body, now unwittingly makes that separation complete by endowing the non-human and hence disembodied machine with those attributes of mind that would presumably enable it to operate independently, not only of human minds, but of a biophysical body. Thus has the naturalist-physicist disembodied a mind and given it non-bodily existence. This, I suggest is indeed *meta*-physics in a new dimension, and in itself a complete refutation of the premise of mind-body inseparability. I submit further that if the inseparability premise negates the possibility of the separate and independent existence of "mind" in the traditional metaphysical or religious senses, it also negates it in every other sense. For either mind is separable from body or it is not. Whichever way it turns out, the *fact* will apply right down the line. If there cannot be disembodied minds invisibly floating about in the ether, there cannot be disembodied "minds" (or even "brains" except in a highly metaphorical sense) in the form of electronic monsters.

We return then to the essential *philosophical* problems on which the mechanical investigations, whether they take the form of noting resemblances between calculating machines and human brains or of measuring electrical brain impulses, have shed little or no light. In its traditional form, the problem can be simply stated. Are mind and body two separate and distinct entities? Can "soul," "spirit," "mind," exist independently of the physical body as we know it? Is reality monistic or is it dualistic, containing two separate life elements to be roughly designated as the physical and the spiritual, the "natural" and the "supernatural"?

The confusions about the issue revealed by scientists as noted above are indeed paralleled by similar confusions long prevalent among theologians and among philosophers of all stamps—metaphysicians and philosophers of science, empiricists *and* rationalists, naturalists and idealists. The confusion is, perhaps, inevitable, as Whitehead suggests, and due to a failure to understand the nature of the problem, or, to put it more precisely, the failure to recognize that it is not a real problem at all, but a pseudoproblem. Once reality is seen as "process" and nature as "organism," the problem disappears.

Keeping within the naturalistic-empirical restrictions of "evidence" (as Whitehead does), a few basic conclusions about the mind-body relationship can be drawn:

1. Mind, as far as we have any *direct* knowledge of this entity, is in its natural-human manifestations, inseparably associated with and dependent upon the physical organism known as body. If mind has any other form or kind of existence in a non-physical or non-corporeal realm we have no acceptable evidence to establish such existence.

2. We have no real knowledge of the source, cause, origin, or essential nature of those activities or phenomena (seemingly centered in the brain) which are most exclusively associated with mind, and especially with the human mind—namely, qualities of *feeling*, such as emotional states, moral and aesthetic evaluation, the search for meaning, etc. The activities of glands and other physical organs under the stimulation of emotional or mental states may be as much *effects* of these states as causes. (Does the adrenal secretion induce my fear or does my fear induce the secretion?) It is a mistake to say that fear or any other emotional state is ever either purely mental or purely physical. It is always, invariably and necessarily, both.

3. Mind and body are equally part of the natural order. In other words, mental phenomena of all types are as much a part of natural-physical phenomena as are earthquakes, floods, electromagnetism, gravitation, the color of grass, the web of the spider, and the birth and death of organisms.

4. All theoretical explanations of mental and spiritual phenomena which extend beyond the realm of the natural and empirically demonstrable are to the present moment untested and unproved. At best, they might be described as symbolic or poetic representations of natural reality. Whitehead, following Hume on this point, insists that scientific "explanations" like metaphysical ones, have never approached the determination of ultimate causality. "Causal nature," says Whitehead, "is a metaphysical chimera."

5. To sum up, nature cannot be "bifurcated" by making a

separation between the green which the mind perceives and the molecules which produce the green. We do not, maintains Whitehead, "explain" the natural phenomena by saying that they exist in the mind. They exist in the objects as well as in the mind.

The most satisfactory solution to the mind-body problem would seem to me to be found along the lines thus indicated by Whitehead. It is to be found in the concept of organism which removes the "problem" simply because it permits of no essential dichotomy in reality. Mind is as much a part of nature as is body. We cannot even legitimately refer to them as separate entities. They are types of phenomena resulting equally from the operation of molecules which meet in time and space. Indeed, the question of ultimate causation is beyond our reach, but the point too often missed is that so-called physical phenomena are as much beyond our reach in terms of ultimate causation or complete comprehension as are the so-called mental or spiritual phenomena.

In a germinal passage in *The Concept of Nature* Whitehead has this to say about the "bifurcation" fallacy:

"[The] theory which I am arguing against is to bifurcate nature into two divisions, namely into the nature apprehended in awareness and the nature which is the cause of awareness. The nature which is the fact apprehended in awareness holds within it the greenness of the trees, the song of the birds, the warmth of the sun, the hardness of the chairs, and the feel of the velvet. The nature which is the cause of awareness is the conjectured system of molecules and electrons which so affects the mind as to produce the awareness of apparent nature. The meeting point of these two natures is the mind. . . ."[1]

In another section Whitehead makes some observations particularly relevant to the type of approach to the mind-body relationship engaged in by empirical scientists in various disciplines.

"The modern account of nature is not, as it should be, merely an account of what the mind knows of nature; but it is also confused with an account of what nature does to the mind. *The result has been disastrous to both science and to philosophy, but chiefly to philosophy*. It has transformed the grand question of the relation between nature and mind into the petty form of the interaction between the human body and mind"[2] (my italics).

Why is this mistaken approach a disaster to science? Because it has led scientists to probe into realms beyond their legitimate scope and to speculate upon questions to which they do not and cannot have the tools for deriving precise and empirically-demonstrated answers. The error is in part due to the acceptance of unproved premises regarding the *limitations* of natural phenomena, and in part to the resultant confusion, already discussed at some length, about some presumed and hypothetical "bifurcation" between natural and mental phenomena—both of which may more likely be different aspects of the same fundamental natural reality and therefore not organically separable.

Another way of stating the issue is by suggesting that a basic fallacy may be involved in talking about mind and body, or about mind and external nature, as though they were separate entities or entailed separate kinds of realities. In the philosophy of organism, *all* of nature (not just the fraction of it which is animate) is infected with mind, just as all of mind is infected with body. Once we get rid of the stubborn and conventional notion that there is external reality on the one hand, and internal, perceptual reality on the other hand, as two different kinds of reality, the mind-body "problem" literally vanishes. In the concept of organism, all phenomena are of one piece. All *natural processes* are as well mental processes of a sort. To put it still another way, all "natural" or physical processes partake of mental events, and all mental processes involve physical events. If mind permeates the whole of reality the existence of it in animate objects does not differentiate these objects in kind from any other natural phenomena, but only in degree.

Why is this erroneous bifurcation a "disaster to philosophy"?—Because in Whitehead's words, it has transformed the "grand question" (by which he means the *philosophical* question) into the petty form of the "interaction between the *human body* and mind." This is the scientist's problem, properly narrow and essentially manageable in scope. But the philosophers have been deluded into believeing that this also constitutes the nature and limits of the philosophical problem. But note: the "grand question" is the relation between nature and mind—the mind in nature, and the nature in mind—which is a very different question from that which merely involves the interaction between individual human bodies and individual human minds.

One further significant aspect of the "disaster" to which Whitehead refers involves metaphysics. We are confronted with the paradoxical situation in which the scientists draw broad metaphysical inferences from their limited study of mind-body interactions, while the philosophers either accept these inferences without careful scrutiny of their foundations, or reject the inferences and refuse to engage in further metaphysical inquiries of their own. Whitehead states at one point: ". . . any metaphysical interpretation is an illegitimate importation into the philosophy of natural science. . . . [The Philosophy of Science] is the philosophy of the thing perceived and is not to be confused with the metaphysics of reality of which the scope embraces both perceiver and perceived." [3]

Thus the so-called "mind-body" problem as it continues to be posed and discussed implies and assumes not only that nature is somehow bifurcated but that reality as a whole is in some sense divided or separated as well. Those who refuse to accept this bifurcation on naturalistic or scientific grounds tend to eliminate the dualism by reducing reality to the physical and material, and by somehow rendering the mental or spiritual aspects of reality subservient to, or dependent upon, or derivative from, the physical-material. The reverse may just as likely be true. The philosophy of organism, however, would permit of no such discrimination, simply on the grounds that there is no empirical or rational evidence to support it. All reality as *process* partakes equally and interdependently of both phenomena.

Certain theologians, metaphysicians, and non-naturalistic philosophers, on the other hand, tend to resolve the supposed dilemma by rejecting altogether the depreciation and subjugation of the mental to the physical-material realm. They accept a metaphysical rather than a naturalistic bifurcation concept by returning to the ancient and traditional dichotomy between "Body" and "Soul" regarded as two separate entities or realities. And in returning to this solution they are of course laying themselves open to all of the traditional and familiar strictures of naturalism, empiricism, and logical analysis.

The philosophy of organism in denying the very validity of the dichotomy on strictly naturalistic and empirical, as well as on rationalistic grounds, removes the necessity for reducing all reality to physical and material entities. It also renders unnecessary, as an alternative, the acceptance of logically and empirically untenable dualisms. It simply removes the dilemma by revealing it not to have been a real dilemma in the first place. Moreover, it opens the way for potentially fruitful inquiries on the part of both scientists and philosophers into the nature of a reality which, while remaining wholly within the frame of naturalism, is as much Mind as it is Matter and in which neither can conceivably exist or operate without the other.

NOTES

1. A. N. Whitehead, "The Concept of Nature," *Whitehead Anthology,* ed. by Northrop and Gross (New York: 1953), p. 219.
2. *Ibid,* p. 217.
3. *Ibid,* pp. 217-18.

PART TWO

The Brain and The Machine

Chapter 12

The Brain and the Machine (Summary)

Norbert Wiener, *Massachusetts Institute of Technology*

THE PROBLEM I wish to discuss concerns the programming of programming, and machines that are of higher logical types according to Bertrand Russell's division of work-types. It has come to the practical attention of people constructing computing machines and automatic factories that the task of organizing the program of consecutive operations of such an instrument is by no means easy. There has been in many quarters an attempt to relegate at least a portion of this work to machine computation, which is what I call machine computation of a higher type. In this computation the elements to be determined, rather than numerical quantities, are logical steps to be taken in a definite order. A considerable amount of progress in this direction has already been made, and I have been shown some of the results of this work in, for instance, the detailed programming of an automatic milling machine and the mechanical results of this programming. This question of the programming of programming is most important, both as an indication of some of the problems which the brain has and as a source of a new conception of the possibilities and responsibilities of the machine. From the point of view of the brain, it represents an increasing mechanical understanding of what we can call the higher functions. Because we now have an application of mechanism not merely to the slavish following out of a program into which all the essential elements of human thought have been put in advance, but an actual aid to the lower stages of thought itself. It has been a common problem of those who emphasize the difference between the brain and the machine to say that the machine cannot do anything original but is merely an executory enlargement of the scope of the human beings who have made it. It has even been supposed that those who have made a machine must have automatically a full comprehension of all the possibilities of performance of the machine and that the dangers mentioned by Samuel Butler that the machines may

109

to some extent control humanity are absurd and empty. Now that the machines are stepping up one or more stages in their functions, this idea of the machine is already insufficient and the difficulties and dangers conceived by Samuel Butler assume a new actuality. I can illustrate this best by considering what is after all a minor function of the machine: that of playing games. One must realize that very considerable progress has been made in the construction of machines to play checkers. Chess-playing machines as of now will counter the moves of a master game with the moves recognized as right in the textbooks up to some point in the middle game. It is true that when they go wrong, they will go very wrong and commit absurdities. In checkers, the plays of the machine up to the very end game are already recognized to be better that the plays of a checker master. At the end game where the problem is not so much that of immediate captures as that of moving over an almost empty board into a good strategic position for later captures, the machine is not yet so totally satisfactory. On a nearly empty board one must look further ahead than when the board is reasonably occupied.

Now, let us consider the game-playing machine from the point of view of the opposing player. In order to eliminate the prejudices which this player will have on the basis of actually seeing a machine before him, let us suppose that the machine is being used to play correspondence chess, in which the opposing player receives his antagonist's moves in the familiar form of a postcard. In such a case the attitude of the opponent to the machine will initially be the same as that of the opponent to a person. It is impossible to play a game of high skill without getting an impression of the game personality of the antagonist. With a machine playing in accordance with an absolutely set program the opponent will get the impression of a game personality that is rigid and inflexible. This will not be the case if he is playing against a machine with a high-order programming. Such a machine will store up in its memory a mass of previously played games and to some extent will erase from its memory the results of games played a long time ago. Within limits, on the basis not only of its own plays but of the games played against it, it will determine a policy which is optimum not in the abstract but in view of the success or failure of earlier games and of earlier moves. As a consequence the tricks that its human opponent will have made at the beginning will cease in time to be as effective as they once were, and the machine will learn and benefit by the intelligence of its opponent. Such a machine will give a far less rigid impression of its playing personality and will gradually get on to the favorite tricks of the other player, which will thereby come to lose their effectiveness. It will not be at all easy for the human player to be sure that he is playing a machine and not a person.

In the case of such a machine, while the general policy will be put into the machine by a person, the detailed applications of this policy in particular instances may not and in general will not be known to those who have programmed it. There will be a strong unpredictable (or, at least unpredicted) element in its detailed plays. The problem of playing against it will be much more like the problem of playing against a human opponent than in the case of a machine of only first-order programming.

What can be done in the case of a game-playing machine can also be done in the case of a computing machine or an automatic factory. This gives rise to certain questions of a quasi-moral and a quasi-human nature. We have to face the fundamental paradox of slavery. I do not refer to the cruelty of slavery, which we can neglect entirely for the moment as I do not suppose that we shall feel any moral responsibility for the welfare of the machine; I refer to the contradictions besetting slavery as to its effectiveness. A slave is expected to have two qualities: intelligence, and subservience. These two qualities are by no means perfectly compatible. The more intelligent the slave is, the more he will insist on his own way of doing things in opposition to the way of doing things imposed on him by his owner. To this extent he will cease to be a slave. Similarly the machine with a higher-order programming will do things that we may not have foreseen in detail. The result is that in the employment of such a machine we are bound to find sooner or later that the purpose of the machine does not conform to the detailed mode of action which we have chosen for it. Indeed it is just because of such considerations that we have relegated to the machine its function of performance.

With a machine of this sort the dangers signalled by Butler become immediate. Where we do not fully understand we shall be under pressure to conform and to a certain extent the machine rather than ourselves will be the lord of such performance. This imposes upon us new obligations and new responsibilities. The machine will still be literal-minded on its highest level, and will do what we have told it to do rather than what we want it to do and what we imagine we have told it to do. Here we dig into the moral problems which earlier generations have faced on the level of magic. W. W. Jacob's story *The Monkey's Paw,* Goethe's poem *The Magician's Apprentice,* and the Arabian Nights legend of the fisherman and the genie call this matter to our attention. The Monkey's Paw gets its owner a small fortune at the cost of the mangling of his son in the machinery of the factory in which he works. The Magician's Apprentice has learned the words by which the broomstick was made to fetch water but has not yet learned the words to stop it. The genie in the bottle, once it had been released by the fisherman, has a will of its own which is bent on his destruction. These tales of imagination cease to be tales of imagination once we have actually made working agencies which go beyond the complete comprehension of those who have constructed them. There is nothing which will automatically make the automatic factory work for human good, unless we have determined this human good in advance and have so-constructed the factory as to contribute to it. If our sole orders to the factory are for an increase in production, without regard to the possible aspects of this new and vast productivity and without regard to the problems of unemployment and of the redistribution of human labor, there is no self-working principle of *laissez-faire* which will make those orders redound to our benefit and even prevent them from contributing to our own destruction. The responsibilities of automation are new, profound, and difficult.

Chapter 13

The Compleat Robot: A Prolegomena to Androidology

Michael Scriven, *Swarthmore College*

0. Introduction

THE DAY WAS when men sought to discover the secrets of the demigods, the elixirs, spells, and potions of the supernaturally endowed. Perhaps the day will yet come when we, having promoted ourselves to the leading role by discovering there is no one above us, will find ourselves in the role of the magician, the possessor of mysterious powers, and snapping at our heels will be the machines. The question in our mind, and on their tapes, will be: "What is the secret of consciousness?" If they are sufficiently well programmed in the language of mythology, ancient and contemporary, it is perhaps even conceivable that they will refer to their search as the Quest for the Thinking Man's Philtre. In this paper I shall consider what, if any, unique essence characterizes the human brain, what, if any, human property prevents a super-computer from saying 'Anything you can do, I can do better.'

1. The Meaning of "Machine"

There are many important terms in our language which cannot be explicitly defined, for various reasons, yet can be correctly applied in typical cases. One of these is "machine," another is "science," and there are others such as "truth" and "toothache." We can readily apply such terms in some cases, while in other cases it is hard to decide whether they apply, and there are likely to arise new cases of both sorts. It is possible to introduce some artificial definition—e.g., by requiring that a science be concerned with prediction or experimentation, which will be approximately correct and sometimes convenient. But when dealing with a logical problem, couched in terms which include these words, we can only employ a stipulative definition like this if we can prove in advance that we are not presupposing an answer to the question. For example, if we define "machine" as an inanimate artifactual device, we cannot go on to ask whether machines might one day be conscious. Yet it is not at all obvious that the answer *is* trivially negative in the usual sense of "machine." This definition has other drawbacks: to define a machine in such a way as to require that it be manufactured is both imprecise (why can't a human mother be regarded as manufacturing her offspring?) and too restrictive, since a spontaneously-generated adding machine, complete even to the Marchant label, would present a problem that might leave the physicist and the theologian at a loss for words but not the comptometer operator, who would not hesitate to call it a machine. Silimar criticisms apply to requirements about inorganic constituents (which would rule out aeroplanes and cranes with wooden pulley-blocks) and about predictable behavior (which would rule out roulette wheels or radium-driven randomisers).

I shall confine myself to enquiring whether something that *is* manufactured from the usual electronic and mechanical components found in a computer workshop, with possible future refinements and substitutes, must forever lack certain capacities possessed by the brain. I think we can safely say that this would be a machine, without having to commit ourselves to any dubious propositions about what would *not* be a machine. (Whenever possible, I shall try to make the points in terms of an even narrower kind of machine—e.g., contemporary computers.) And in these terms the phrase "thinking machine" is not a trivial contradiction. Incidentally, our answers will leave us uncommitted about the question of whether a biophysicist can produce living creatures from inorganic elements. Although at the moment this appears to be only a technical problem, it is certainly a different problem, since he has a narrower choice of materials and an easier goal than the roboticist in his task of duplicating the brain functions of higher vertebrates. We shall return to the problem of constituents in the next section.

2. & 3. Moving and Reproducing

A simple question arises immediately. May it not be true that the particular substances of which the brain is composed are enormously more efficient for its tasks than anything we could except to find in the inventory of a computer workshop? This might be true to a degree that would render machines with powers comparable to men so gigantic that they would be incapable of incorporation in a self-propelling unit comparable to that which the human brain inhabits.

Three comments are in order. First, this is not a very exciting point even if true, since there would be, under this hypothesis, few, if any, human tasks that could not be done by putting mechanical sensors and effectors where the human being would be, and using relays to fed data to and commands from the machine. Even if there are any such tasks, they are not ones that the human can do by virtue of his brain or mind, but by virtue of his body size. Second, there are no very strong reasons for thinking the point valid. Mechanical effectors and sensors can be made both smaller and better than human ones. For instance, they can be ultra-violet sensitive. The use of magnetic imprinting, crystal orientation, subminiaturization, and fail-safe circuitry, has already reduced or will reduce the required volume by several orders of magnitude and there seems no barrier except cost to further progress. Third, if we find that, for example, protein molecules provide the best storage medium, their employment would not necessarily mean we were no longer constructing a machine. Naturally, transplanting a human brain into a robot body is cheating, but the use of some of the same *substances*, either synthesized or extracted from dead tissue, is hardly enough to disqualify the product from being a machine. Our task is to see whether we can make a pseudo-brain—something with performance the same as or better than that of a human brain, but made in a different way, i.e., with largely different components and 'wiring.' There would still be considerable interest in the question of whether we can make a synthetic brain, no holds barred, but there would be less general agreement that it should be called a machine. (Would one call a synthetic flower a machine? A synthetic jellyfish?) I shall restrict our attention to the more difficult task of constructing a mechanical pseudo-brain, which utilizes at most some of the same substances or 'wiring' as the human brain, and thus retains a clearer title to the adjective "mechanical." There is a certain tension between the term "mechanical" and the term "living," so that the more inclined we are to call it alive because of the things it does, the less inclined we shall be to call it a machine. I shall continue to assume that these terms are logically marriageable, although they are uneasy bedfellows, but the substance of my points can be expressed in other ways if this assumption is not granted.

Having thus dealt with very simple behavioral and constitutional considerations, we may proceed to some of the traditionally more favored obstacles to the functional duplication of human mentality by mechanical means.

4. Predicting and Choosing

It is a standard sarcasm amongst computer technicians that, contrary to the popular opinion, they are dealing with some of the most unpredictable and unreliable entities known. There are serveral causes of this. First, there are the errors of inadequate programming, which cannot be dismissed as mere operator errors, since a program often involves tens of thousands of characters in the 'machine language,' not all the consequences of which can be foreseen by the programmer any more than Euclid foresaw all the consequences of his axioms. Secondly, there are mechanical breakdowns within the machine—by no means uncommon, though to some extent their seriousness can be overcome by duplication, fail-safe wiring, and alarm arrangements. Thirdly, there are variations due to uncertainty-principle effects in junctions, relays, thermionic valves, etc. The importance of these variations is commonly slight, but over a long haul they guarantee 'individuality' to a computer. Fourthly, there is the cumulative inaccuracy possible with analogue computers. Fifthly, these is the possibility of deliberately using a randomizer in the circuitry, important in learning circuits. Sixthly, there is the rapidity of operation that makes the fastest computer unpredictable in fact.

It is thus highly unsatisfactory to suggest that computer output behavior is predictable. Even if the addition of "in principle" will get you past some of these objections, it is such a slippery password that its users often find themselves in the wrong camp. Here, I think the only safe conclusion is that some computers are "in principle" unpredictable in a way essentially similar to the way human beings are.

The argument that "free-will" is (a) possessed by humans, and (b) implies a unique unpredictability different from that mentioned above, requires both clarification and substantiation, especially its second assertion. I would say it is now readily provable that the kind of free will required to make sense of the idea of responsibility and punishment is perfectly compatible with determinism and third-person predictability, and there is no evidence for any other kind. Hence, even if machines were predictable it would be possible for them to have free will. Since neither they nor human beings are in practice entirely predictable, the argument that only one of the two species has free will needs further grounds, several of which we shall examine under other headings, but none of which appears to provide insuperable differences.

The converse problem to the one just considered is also of relevance to the free-will issue, and serve to clarify the meaning of "predictable in principle." This is the problem of whether a computer can in principle predict everything. If, for the moment, one supposes that a computer can in principle be error-free, the answer is still negative, and thus a further element of similarity with the human being possessing free will is preserved—the limitation in the power *to* predict. The standard example is the computer with total data and unbounded speed which is connected to a photo-electric cell and phosphor lamp in a certain way and then programmed to predict whether the lamp will be alight five minutes later. The photo-electric cell is focused on the output tape and the lamp so connected that if the output tape reads "yes," the lamp switches off, and if it reads "no," the lamp switches on. The prediction is thus self-invalidating. The other standard case is the prediction of one computer's state by another which is trying to do the same to it; the necessity for a finite time-lag, however brief, between input and output can be shown to produce gross errors under suitable circumstances.

Now these cases have analogues in human experience. The realization that one can do 'just the opposite,' no matter what prediction is announced about one's choice, in trivial matters such as the closing of an eye is a powerful element in the support for free will. (It corresponds, as we shall see, to the first case just described.) One might say that all that is in fact shown by such feelings and freedom is that certain events are not *publicly* predictable. For the prediction can still be made as long as it is not announced to the individual to which it refers. But not only does this remark make less sense in the case of the computer, it also underestimates the importance of the point. For the possibility of falsifying any announced prediction does show that the feeling of free choice is not an "illusion" in any useful sense. "Illusions" can be dispelled, but dispelling a man's "illusion" that his choice is not yet made, that it is still "up to him," is often logically impossible since any announcement about his choice will immediately be falsified. But it is essential to remember that predictability does not eliminate freedom. A virtuous man is no less virtuous because we know he is and hence can guess what he'll do. We are not wrong to praise a man simply because we foresee his actions—we would be wrong only if they were actions over which he had no control (see D. M. MacKay, *On the Logical Indeterminacy of a Free Choice,*

Proceedings of the Twelfth International Congress of Philosophy [Venice: 1958]).

The predictability issue, taken either way, is deeply involved in philosophical puzzles of some interest, but it again provides no grounds for supposing the machine to be inferior to the brain, either because its powers of prediction are too great, or because they are too small.

5. Creating and Discovering

"Machines only do what we tell them to do. They are incapable of genuinely original thought." As in nearly all these claims, two importantly different points are run together here. These are what I shall call the "performatory" element and the "personality" element. The performatory problem here is whether a computer can produce results which, when translated, provide what would count as an original solution or proof *if it came from a man*. The personality problem is whether we are entitled to call such a result a solution or proof, despite the fact that it did *not* come from a man. The logical trap is this: no *one* performatory achievement will be enough to persuade us to apply the human-achievement vocabulary, but if we refuse to use this vocabulary in each case separately, on this ground, we will, perhaps wrongly, have committed ourselves to avoiding it even when *all* the achievements are simultaneously attained.* I shall, for convenience, use the human-achievement vocabulary, but without thereby prejudging the issue. If it transpires that there are *no* essential performatory differences at all, we shall then consider whether we are entitled to apply the terms in their full sense. No single simple property of an object suffices to guarantee that it is an apple, but several *sets* of such properties are sufficient.

The originality point has some sting when we are considering very simple computers, but the moment we have a learning circuit and/or a randomiser for generating trial-and-error runs, the picture is different. We will discuss the learning point in the next section, but I here wish to carry on with the consequences of the randomiser mentioned in the last section, which provides a simple kind of originality. For example, a computer using a randomiser may come up with a solution to a differential equation that no one else has been able to obtain. Is this to count as being original or not (observa-

---

* It is interesting to compare this with the view that none of the arguments for the existence of God are logically sound, but taken all together they are convincing.

tionally speaking—we ignore for the moment the fact that the result is mechanical in origin)? Certainly we 'built in' the instructions to use the randomiser, but this does not enable us to foretell what results will come out. This is another exercise in the trustworthiness of the "in principle" notion. I shall make only two comments.

First, the randomiser may be of two kinds. If it is a classical randomiser (i.e., of the 'roulette-wheel' type), there is some point to the remark that its outcome is in principle predictable, but none at all to the suggestion that we could ever in practice predict it. Now Euler was an original man, but was he original in any stronger sense than that no one did *in fact* think of his results before him? How could any further claim be supported? Even if it can, there is a stronger source of originality possible for a computer—the use of a quantum randomiser. And to argue that it is in principle possible to predict the outcome of a radium-driven randomiser is even less feasible, because, (a) taken at face value, it is denied by most contemporary physicists, (b) if it means that a deterministic theory might conceivably someday be found, then this is always true, and so the alleged distinction between the man and the machine, in terms of the "in principle" predictability of the latter, becomes vacuous, since one cannot rationally deny the *possibility* of an exact psychological predictive theory.

Of course, more is involved in producing solutions to equations than in producing random numbers, these must have been put through the test of satisfying the equation. But this involves only a routine calculation by the computer. There thus appears to be no reason why a computer cannot produce solutions to problems that are original in the sense of being (a) historically novel, and (b) in no useful sense predictable. Nevertheless, we feel that originality of this trial-and-error kind is relatively uninteresting. The important kind of originality is that which produces new theories, new conceptual schemes, new works of art. How could a machine possibly do this?

The key notion in the design of a creative machine would be the use of analogy. It has been argued by MacKay that in fact such a machine would have to be of the species referred to as analogue computers (as opposed to digital computers). I shall give some reasons for disagreeing with this in the section on understanding. But whatever type of computer is involved, there is no doubt that it must possess means for the *weighted comparison* of different descriptions. Thus, if it is fed data about the notion of a satellite around a planet, while on a theory-building program, it will register the formal similarity between this kind of motion and the motion of a body attached by a string to a fixed point and given a certain initial tangential velocity. It will, noting no better analogy, examine the consequences of the "theory" that an *invisible* connection exists between the planet and its satellite, the idea of invisibility being well-established in its data banks in connection with magnetic fields, sound waves, etc. Deduction of the consequences of such a hypothesis proves satisfactory for a certain value of the force in the invisible string, a value which depends on its 'length' in a simple way. The analogy with magnetic fields now registers strongly and the computer formulates and successfully tests the law of gravitational attraction.

The crucial difference from the trial-and-error method we first discussed lies not in the absence of trial and error, but in the origin of the candidates for trial; instead of randomly selected elements of a previously obvious class—e.g., the integers—it is necessary to provide a means for electing candidates from the indefinite class of possible hypotheses and then for improving them by adding modifications themselves selected in a similar way. The selection is no longer wholly random, because some candidates have better qualifications than others. What makes them better can be called their antecedent probability, but is perhaps better called the extent of the analogy between their known properties and those required in the situation under study. Any idea of an exact weighting of such analogies, which is perhaps suggested by referring to probabilities, is quite unjustified; the best one can expect is a partial ordering, and since this is all the human brain employs it is clearly adequate.

How would one go about giving the computer data of this kind? A simple beginning would be with curve-fitting problems where loose estimates of the importance of errors of a given magnitude, as against the value of simplicity for computation and theoretical fertility, can be given. The procedure can then be made more complicated in a way involving learning-circuits of the kind to be mentioned in the next section, enabling the computer to adjust the relative weighting of errors and complexity.

The procedure of *trial* is comparatively simple. The difinition of the problem (say, the proof of Goldbach's Hypothesis, or the production of an adequate theory for the behavior of liquid helium) itself gives the tests that the successful candidate must pass. The application of these tests is, in the sciences, perfectly routine. There is still the possible difficulty of dealing with cases where several candidates pass the test. Here selection of the best will involve a decision similar to that involved in selecting the best candidates for the tests. This will, for example, occur where ideas such as simplicity are involved, and these make us think of creativity in the arts, where it is clear that we do not have very precise standards for judging the merits of works of art. But the computer's memory banks can with ease be indoctrinated with the canons of free verse, iambic pentameters, or nursery rhymes, and instruction to exploit low-level analogies as if they were high-level ones, and to adjust the result in certain ways by reference to ease of comprehension, richness of associations, and onomatopoeic force, would provide poetry of any acceptable kind. There is no doubt that the subtlety of poetic metaphor and the emotive effect of various rhyme-schemes will not *easily* be compressed into a computer; but they are not easily learned by human beings, and human beings are remarkably disunited about the kind of scaling that would be correct in comparing these virtues (cf. simplicity and fertility of scientific theories). The net effect of these considerations is that there is much less chance that computer verse will be detectable by a literary critic than there was that paintings by chimpanzees would be identifiable by art-critics.

Summing up the discussion of originality, the simplest kind is readily obtainable by a machine and the more complicated kind is obtainable subject to the (feasible but difficult) development of analogy-assessing procedures. Connected with the assessment of analogies is the whole question of mechanical learning, to which we now turn.

6. Learning

The usual contemporary computer is essentially a complex instrument, a close relative to the comptometer, and the idea that it does only what we tell it to do is well founded. This idea is more precisely put by saying that it cannot modify its own programming, more loosely by saying it cannot learn by experience. But there are already a few computers, among them modified versions of the IBM 704 and 709, which are more advanced than this. Professor Wiener has referred to them as having "higher-order programming," i.e., as being programmed to modify their basic procedure in certain ways depending on the results obtained from earlier trials. Such machines are already capable of playing a good game of chess, proving theorems in geometry, and so on. The two special features of their design are the provision of assessment rules whereby they can judge the success of various procedures in various situations, and a special kind of instruction. In the chess case, we provide them with the set of possible moves by every chessman, they calculate the results of applying all applicable ones at a particular stage of the game and, using the assessment rules, decide which offers the best option.

A simple assessment rule, used during early stages of a game, would be one which gives greater credit for a position according to the number of pieces deployed, the 'openness' of the position, possibly measured by the number of squares covered. More complex, and more essential, rules will involve assessing a move in terms of its consequences in the light of possible moves by the opponent, the ideal being a move which can be inevitably (i.e., whatever the opponent does) converted into checkmate, less ideal ones resulting in the capture of favorable exchange of pieces. Thus we instruct the machine to proceed in such a way as to maximize the expectation of checkmate; and we provide certain suggestions as to reliable indicators of a good move, since no computer can actually compute all possible future outcomes of a given move except in some parts of the end game. So far, simple enough; but the special feature of the instructions is that we program the computer to continually reevaluate the suggested *indicators* in the light of its experience in using them to obtain checkmate. It is thus considering hypotheses at two levels. Within a game, it asks: "Is this a good move as far as my current standards of good moves go?"; and after each game, it asks whether a different weighting of the standards would have been more likely to produce success—and if so, it readjusts the weights for future use.

At this stage we have a model of learning by experience. Its application to a chess-playing machine is simpler than to a theory-building machine because the possible moves in chess are a precisely defined family, unlike possible theories. It is true that in computer design it is more difficult to achieve controlled imprecision than precision, whereas the converse might be said to be characteristic of adult humans; and it is the imprecise methods of analogy and suggestion that produce new theories. But the proper analogy to computer design is human education from infancy, not the generation of free associations in adults, and the learner, like the computer, finds it much simpler to follow the exact rules of the syllogism than to evaluate complex analogies. Despite the difficulties, there can be no grounds for radical pessimism about the possibility of combining the devices of originality with those of learning to produce a machine that is cognitively a match for the human being—so far as we have considered the differences between them.

7. Understanding and Interpreting

There is a special kind of cognitive barrier that we have not so far considered and which involves a novel difficulty. Naturally, we shall not speak of a machine as 'understanding' a theorem simply because it can type out a proof of it on command. What must it *do* in order to be doing what human beings do who are said to understand a theorem? (Even if it does this, it does not—as we have previously stressed—follow that we should say it understands, for apart from what it *does* there is the question of what it *is;* and it may be argued that such predicates as 'understanding' are inapplicable to machines. But we shall have removed one further *ground* for this argument.) It seems clear to me that the performatory element in the concept of understanding is the capacity to *relate* whatever is said to be understood to a variety of other material in the correct way. Understanding the special theory of relativity involves knowing the relation between its components, the relation of it to other theories, and the relation of it to its applications. Understanding is knowing, but it is knowing certain things. Knowing something is not *ipso facto* understanding something (one knows the date of one's birthday, or the composition of polyurethane, without understanding anything [except a language]). But there is a very large slice of personality in the concept of understanding; we are much more reluctant to apply it to a machine than such a term as "compute." About this slice we cannot dispute; we can only point out that the theory that understanding is a mental sensation, a theory which is heavily ingrained in us, no doubt contributes to our reluctance, but does so illicitly. The point is well, though briefly, discussed in Wittgenstein's *Philosophical Investigations.*

A special difficulty of the concept of understanding arises in connection with the idea of understanding the concept of an irrational number. We here run into the apparent obstacle of the Lowenheim-Skolem Theorem. According to this theorem, it is not possible to give a unique characterization of the reals and hence the irrationals, at least in the following sense: any attempted strict formalization of the real numbers can be shown to be ambiguous in that it can be given at least one interpretation in the rational numbers, i.e., every formalization we produce can be legitimately interpreted in a way contrary to that intended, a way that omits any reference to the irrationals. Now it seems plausible to say that the description of the reals that we give to a computer will be subject to the same irreducible ambiguity, and hence that we shall never be sure that it has actually 'grasped' the *proper* idea of real number, which includes the irrationals, rather than one of the other strictly permissible interpretations. A similar suggestion is made by Nagel and Newman in *Gödel's Proof* when they argue that the Gödel incompleteness theorem presents a serious obstacle to the construction of comprehensive theorem-proving computers; we shall return to this suggestion in a moment. The error in these arguments, as I see it, lies in the idea that the tests of understanding in mathematics are purely syntactical, that the intrasystemic transformations are the only defining properties of the concepts—of number, or proof, or truth. In fact, we can perfectly well regard it as a crucial test of comprehension of the concept of irrational number on the part of man or machine, that he or it immediately identify the square root of two, and π, and the base of natural logarithms as examples of irrational numbers. If this is required, then consideration of the formal properties will guarantee the correct field of entities (other simple requirements on the interpretaton oif the logical operators would also suffice).

It seems to me that the point is akin to the one arising when we ask whether a blind man can be said fully to understand the meaning of the word "red" when he has mastered (a) the syntactical rules governing color words, and (b) a device which correlates color-differences with musical tones so that he can indirectly differentiate (but not identify) colors reliably. This would *almost* locate the term "red" in the semantic space, but not completely; his interpretation would be invariant under transformations that did not offend current idioms or hue-separation. For example, he could get the color of a particular dahlia wrong although not the natural color of a ripe lemon. (There would be a *series* of tests—linked comparisons—which would uncover the dahlia's color, but he couldn't recognize it immediately.) We are somewhat undecided whether to say that his *comprehension* (of the term "red") is incomplete, or merely his *experience*. Certainly he is not capable of using the term properly in normal circumstances, but neither is a man who has lost his sight—yet the latter understand perfectly well what "red" means. Similarly, the axioms of a formal system provide much but not all of the meaning of "irrational number"; the clincher is the link with examples, the capacity to apply the language correctly in paradigm cases. In certain areas of mathematics, this is guaranteed by the formal rules, but in others the concepts are not merely formal shorthand, but refer to aspects of a complex construction that can readily be *perceived* but not exhaustively eliminated by substituting other, equivalent, concepts. (A related difficulty arises in trying to treat the Peano postulates as defining the integers.) In sum, then, I do not find the existence of a residual ambiguity in an axiomatization of mathematics a good reason for supposing that computers can never understand mathematical concepts.

Similarly, the limitations imposed by the Gödel incompleteness theorem on the formalization of mathematics are, so far as I can see, no more of an obstacle to a mechanical mathematician. As is well known, given any Gödel sentence G which is provably true but undecidable within a system S, it is easy to construct an S^1 within which it is derivable—the uninteresting way being to add G to the system S. Now, Nagel and Newman are struck by the fact that whatever axioms and rules of inference one might give a computer, there would apparently be mathematical truths, such as G, which it could never "reach" from these axioms by the use of these rules. This is true, but their assumption that we could suppose ourselves to have given the machine an adequate idea of mathematical truth when we gave it the axioms and rules of inference is not true. This would be to suppose the formalists were right, and they were shown by Gödel to be wrong. The Gödel theorem is no more an obstacle to a computer than to ourselves. One can only say that mathematics would have been easier if the formalists had been right, and it would in that case be comparatively easy to construct a mechanical mathematician. They weren't and it isn't. But just as we can recognize the truth of the unprovable formula by comparing what it says with what we know to be the case, so can a computer do the same.

It is appropriate here to mention another formal theorem,

one which an enthusiastic roboticist might think supports his cause. Craig's theorem has been invoked on occasions to support the view that theories, and hence the necessity for understanding theoretical terms, are dispensable. It does indeed demonstrate the eliminability of certain terms from a given vocabulary under certain conditions. If it is supposed that these conditions correspond to the relationship between theoretical terms and observational terms, the conclusion might follow. But one of the conditions is that there be an absolutely sharp separation between terms of these two kinds. Now, it seems clear that it is part of the nature of theoretical terms that they should sometimes—for example, by progress in techniques of observation—become observable. Another condition requires that the only logically interesting effects of theoretical terms lie in their deduced consequences in the observation vocabulary. Even if deduction were in fact the only vehicle for generating the consequences of theories, this would not be a satisfactory position. The reasons for this require support from a general theory of meaning, but they can be condensed into the comment that part of the meaning of a theory lies in its relation to other theories, and part in its internal logical structure, so that understanding a theory is by no means the same as understanding its empirical consequences. Finally, Craig's theorem has the awkward result that the elimination of theoretical terms is achieved only at the expense of adding an infinite number of axioms in the observation language.

8. Analyzing

At the practical level, some of the above considerations are already highly relevant. There is a great deal of work now proceeding on the mechanization of translation, abstraction, and indexing. A few words on each topic will perhaps serve to indicate the present situation and its consequences for our inquiry.

8.1 Translation

It is simple enough to build a mechanical *decoder* (or encoder) and they have been in use for many years. If translation were the same as decoding, there would be no special problem. Unfortunately, there are great differences. A code is a way of rendering portions of a single language obscure; decoding consists of applying the key in reverse. But French, except when used by certain people one knows, is not a way of rendering English obscure. It is a way of doing what English also does—describing, explaining, exhorting, ordering, promising, praising, and so on. Since they are both universal languages, and their relation is thus unlike that of mathematics to music, it is reasonable to expect that a *fairly* satisfactory equivalent exists in each for any natural unit in the other. Now, a word or a sentence is not what I have in mind when talking of a natural unit—a word or a sentence is a *phonetically,* or *calligraphically,* or *psychologically* convenient unit. A natural unit is a description, an explanation, an exhortation, etc., produced in a particular context. (Of course, a translation of this depends to some extent on a personal impression of the context, and the linguistic element usually does not fully describe the context.) If we were to suppose that the existence of workable translations of *natural units* implied the existence of workable translations of the *spoken or written* units (i.e., the words and sentences), then a mechanical translator would be a relatively simple problem for the programmer. The discovery that this supposition is unsound is, it seems to me, the chief ground for the present pessimism amongst workers in this area.

But there is no absolute barrier here. In the first place, there are actually many words or groups of words, especialy in Western languages, which allow a very general and straightforward translation into corresponding units in other such languages, partly because they are used in only one kind of context. This is especially true in the vital area of technical vocabularies. Secondly, although the language is not always descriptive of a context, it often affords clues to it, so that by taking large enough sections, a translation can be made highly accurate at least for informational purposes. But the translation of poetry is an example of the opposite extreme where a one-many relation holds between a context and associated language complexes. And it is a useful warning, since this is not altogether unlike the situation of theoretical propositions. Finally, provision once being made for the sensory equipment of a robot—a point shortly to be discussed—we would possess a system whose linguists would be of the same kind as our own, and whose translations would therefore be potentially better, their memory being better.

8.2 Abstracting

Mechanical abstractors have already been built in response to the desperate need for systematizing scientific work and publication. They operate on a word (or phrase) frequency count, retaining those words of four letters, or more, that occur most often. This is the most primitive possible device for abstraction and all one can say is that it is surprising how often it nearly does a fair job. (It is not very often.) There are really no short-cuts of this kind that are worth much trouble; we shall not be able to rely—and we need to be able to rely—on abstracting done by someone lacking a first-rate comprehension of the subject being treated. Unfortunately, using such rare individuals for such purposes is intellectually and economically inefficient. The natural solution is mechanization. It is less of a solution than might appear at first sight, since, although the comprehension is feasible as I have argued above, the difficulties are so formidable that the initial cost of such a device will enormously outweigh the cost of discovering and training extra humans for the task. We may indeed find that the super computers of the future will need human servants because they can't afford mechanical aides—a nice twist to the present argument for automation, although perhaps it ranges a little too far into the future to convince the unions today.

8.3 Indexing

Essentially similar problems arise over indexing. Under what headings should an article be referenced or a paragraph be indexed? A simple machine can index an article or passage under all the words in it, or under the most frequent. Both are clearly quite unsatisfactory. The crucial concepts here are those of *relevance* and *importance*. To know which topics an article is relevant to requires more than an understanding of the article—it requires knowledge of all potentially relevant fields. Worse, as our theories change, relevance changes and continual reindexing from scratch is necessary, i.e., all references must be scanned for deletion *and* amplification. It is a tall order to build a machine with the kind of knowledge and speed required for these tasks, but it is increasingly beyond the powers of man to perform such tasks himself, and an increasingly large amount of work is being 'lost' in the technical literature, or expensively duplicated because of the inefficiency of indexing (and cataloguing—a special case). There is really no satisfactory alternative to the machines and we shall have to try them, there being no reason for supposing we cannot succeed but every reason for supposing we shall find it very difficult. It may not be impossible "in principle," but we sometimes abandon our "in principles."

9. Deciding

In the indexing problem, that matter of relevance is crucial but only half the problem. A particular passage in the *American Journal of Physics* will be relevant to some degree to an uncountable number of topics. If an index is to be useful at all, a subset of these topics must suffice and a decision must be made by the indexer as to the most important of these. If this is to be done sensibly it requires some estimate of importance and some value for a "cutting score," i.e., a level of importance beyond which inclusion in the index is guaranteed and below which it is precluded. As we have suggested earlier, it is a mistake to suppose that a full arithmetization is possible, and partial ordering is all that we need. The issue is really the same as that associated with choosing likely hypotheses and raises no new difficulties for the programmer. The difficulties are bad enough even if not new. The procedure for governing the cutting score by estimates of the maximum permissible size of the index, the seriousness of errors of omission versus excessive bulk, corresponds to the procedure for deciding what hypotheses to consider in a given situation, or, in problem-solving, what maneuvers to try out, if any—e.g., which premises to try out as bases for a mathematical proof.

10. Perceiving

The performatory aspect of perception is differentiation of the responses to differentiated stimuli. This is the aim of good scientific instrument design and a computer with its own temperature-recording devices is easily made. The human brain, however, is rather good at detecting similarities and differences of a kind which it would be tremendously difficult to arrange to detect mechanically. For example, the visual recognition of a female acquaintance when she is wearing different clothes, is at varying distances, in varying light and from varying angles, wearing various expressions, hairstyles, and makeup, requires configurational comparisons of great sensitivity and complexity. It is clear enough how one would go about developing a machine with the capacity to perform such tasks, which we do so casually. Here again we would face the "degrees of similarity" problem, and "matching" problems probably best solved by the use of an optical comparator using rapidly varying magnification. A start will have to be made in connection with star-mapping programs using the photomultiplier tubes, and automatic navigation for unmanned interstellar rockets. The recognition of star patterns, regardless of orientation, should not prove too difficult, and the more complex gestalts may be attacked piecemeal.

10.1 Extrasensory Perceiving

Turing apparently thought that telepathy was the one impossibility for the machine. I am not clear whether he thought this because of scepticism about telepathy in humans or because of a 'direct-mental-contact' theory of telepathy, or for some other reason. Neither of the suggested reasons seems altogether satisfactory. The evidence for telepathy in humans is hard to dismiss fairly, but there is no ground for thinking it cannot be regarded as a brain function of a new kind, analogous to the generation of the alpha- and beta-rhythms. We are completely ignorant of the forms of energy or the physical features of the brain that are responsible for telepathy, although intensive work with the electroencephalograph is continuing at Duke and in London. In this respect, ESP represents a more difficult problem for the roboticist than any of the preceding ones, and forms a natural link to the problem of feeling. If it should transpire that no brain elements are responsible for ESP, then it will present a special philosophical problem; but until then, we must assume the contrary and continue the search. We are not at all clear how the memory works, but we do not doubt its existence. It is quite unreasonable to argue as some have done, that because the ESP function has not been localized in the brain, it follows that we should doubt its existence. What I have said about telepathy applies, a fortiori, to the less well-supported phenomena of precognition and psychokinesis.

11. Feeling

The most difficult problem of all those that face the roboticist trying to match human capacity is that of inducing the phenomena of sensation. The difficulty lies not with the outward signs—we have already indicated the way in which these can be achieved. It is the doubt whether there is any actual sensation associated with the wincing, gasping, sighing, and snapping that we succeed in building in for manifestation in 'appropriate' circumstances. A radical behaviorist will not of course be troubled by such doubts, but even the identity theorists would not share his equanimity. We all know what it is to feign feelings and we thus know what it is to behave as if one had a certain feeling although one lacks it—and we wonder if the robot is merely "going through the motions." (It is not, of course, correctly described as "feigning," since this entails an understanding of the nature of not feigning— and we are disputing even this possibility.)

Turing argued ("Computing Machinery and Intelligence," *MIND*, 1950) that if a robot could be so built that remote interrogation could not distinguish it from a human being we would have to agree that it had feelings. This is oversimple, not only because verbal stimuli are too limited for satisfactory proof, but because it seems to make perfectly good sense to say: "It says it is in love because we built to to say so—but is it? It says it is fond of A. E. Housman and thinks Keats is sickly, but does it really *enjoy* Housman?" In making these points in a reply to Turing ("The Mechanical Concept of Mind," *MIND*, 1953), I overlooked two points which now seem to me important and which improve the chances of a decision, although they do not support Turing's view.

In the first place, one must reject the 'argument from design' (androidological version), the argument that because the machine is designed to say it is in love it cannot be supposed that it is *really* in love. For the design may, and perhaps must, have achieved both ends. (To assume the opposite is to adopt a naïve interactionism.) Performatory evidence is not decisive (contra Turing), but neither is it negligible. It fulfills a necessary condition, in a sense which is amplified in my paper in the symposium on "Criteria" in the *Journal of Philosophy*, November 1959. What is a sufficient condition? The answer must be that there is no *logically* sufficient condition statable in terms that can be verified by an external observer. Even a telepath who declares that he directly perceives sensations in the robot exactly as in humans may merely be reacting to brain emanations that are similar. But there are conditions which make doubt profitless although not meaningless—e.g., doubts about the origin of the universe. These conditions are, for the most part, readily imaginable, consisting in the indefinitely sustained and effortles performance and description of emotional conditions, the development of new art forms, the prosecution of novel moral causes (Societies for the Prevention of Cruelty to Robots, etc.), in brief the maintenance and extrapolation of the role of a sensitive man, with dreams and feelings. However, I have thought of a less obvious further test which perhaps merits a separate section.

12. Lying

Remembering that, strictly speaking, to refer to an entity as lying commits one to the personality component as well as the performatory one, I shall use the term to refer to the performatory element for the moment. Now, the substance of my disagreement with Turing was that a machine *might* be made to duplicate sensation-behavior without having the sensation, i.e., the designer could fool the interrogator. But suppose our aim as a designer is not to pass the Turing test, since that is inconclusive, but actually to determine whether robots can be built that have feelings. I suggest that we construct a series of robots called R. George Washington I, II, II, etc. (using Asimov's convention of the R for "Robot" before name), with the following characteristics. They should be taught to use English in the strictest way. They would refer to human beings as being in pain under the usual circumstances, but under what appear to be corresponding circumstances with robots they would use behaviorist language, saying that R. Einstein XI had produced the words "I am in pain," etc. And they would use the same care when describing their own states, saying for example: "R. George Washington I has been subjected to overload current" or ". . . has received a potentially damaging stimulus of unknown origin"—it being the named robot speaking. In teaching them to speak in this way, we make it quite clear that other descriptions of themselves may also be appropriate, including those applied to human beings, but we do not assert that they do apply. We also introduce the robot to the concept of truth and falsity and explain that to lie is to utter a falsehood when the truth is known, a practice of value in some circumstances but usually undesirable. We then add a circuit to the robot, at a special ceremony at which we also christen it, which renders lying impossible regardless of conflict with other goals it has been told are important. This makes the robot unsuitable for use as a personal servant, advertising copywriter, or politician, but renders it capable of another service. Having equipped it with all the performatory abilities of humans, fed into its banks the complete works of great poets, novelists, philosophers, and psychologists, we now ask it whether it has feelings. And it tells us the truth since it can do no other. If the answer is "No," we construct further robots on different principles. If the answer is "Yes," we have answered our original question. To the objection that we cannot be sure it understands the question, it seems to me we can reply that we have every good reason for thinking that it does understand, as we have for thinking this of other *people*.

The logical structure of the argument thus consists in standing on a performatory analysis of understanding to reach a conclusion about the nonperformatory issue of sensations. If, with Brentano, one believes there is an irreducible non-behavioral element in such concepts as belief and understanding, and that these, rather than sensations, are the hallmark of mind, my maneuver will not be convincing because it does not refer to that element which his followers translate as intentionality. But one may accept the irreducibility thesis, as I do, and regard the missing element as a compound of the possession of sensations and the possession of personality. This element is not the only one responsible for the irreducibility which also derives from the complexity of the mental-activity concepts in the same way as that which renders theoretical terms not reducible to observational ones. Then we get half of the missing element from the first R. George Washington to say "Yes," and there remains only the question of personality.

13. Being

What is it to be a person? It can hardly be argued that it is to be human since there can clearly be extraterrestrials of equal or higher culture and intelligence who would qualify as people in much the same way as the peoples of Yucatan and Polynesia. Could an artifact be a person? It seems to me the answer is now clear; and the first R. George Washington to answer "Yes" will qualify. A robot might do many of the things we have discussed in this paper and not qualify. It could not do them all and be denied the accolade. We who must die salute him.

What about self-consciousness
reflection

Chapter 14

Comments on Key Issues

Satosi Watanabe, *International Business Machines Corporation*

Comments on Professor Wiener's presentation

PROFESSOR WIENER'S LECTURE consisted of three major parts:
(1) a description of new developments in the field of artificial intelligence; (2) a discussion of moral problems ensuing from further automation of production; (3) a description of the peculiar similarity of the brain waves of computing machines and brains.

(1) Professor Weiner characterized new developments in artificial intelligence by various descriptions, such as flexible programming, unexpected behavior, programming of programming, higher-order programming, a chess-playing program such that a human opponent feels as if he were playing with another human player, etc. In my opinion, the striking features of the newer programming of data-processing machines originates from the fact that the machine performs what may be called "pseudo-induction." This can be said of Samuel's checkers-playing machine, Gelerneter's geometry-problem solving machine and of many other similar attempts, aiming at intelligent behavior of a machine. Take the case of Samuel's checkers program; you might think that a machine with its tremendous speed of thinking and its large memory can explore every possible path leading to the end of the game and choose the best move at present. According to Samuel, such an exhaustive method will require 10^{21} centures with the fastest imaginable computing machine. What is done in Samuel's program is the selection of what is at present the best move according to evaluation of the board situations of the not-very-far future. There are thirty-eight criteria of evaluation of the board situation. Any linear combination of these criteria serves as a "hypothesis for winning." At the beginning all hypotheses are equally credible. But as the game proceeds, i.e., as the machine accumulates its experience, one particular hypothesis will emerge as the most credible hypothesis for a particular oponent, i.e., it will play the role of a "law for winning." This procedure fits in the pattern of "in-

ductive inference." This seems to me to be the secret of the amazing behavior of the newer programming. However, it should be noted that the machine does not, at present, at least, carry out the entire function of inductive inference. Usually, the difficulty of inductive inference stems from the fact that there are infinitely many possible hypotheses that are supported by experience. Limitation of these hypotheses to a smaller subset is often done by a vaguely conceived criterion, such as the principle of simplicity, or principle of elegance. The machine does not do this kind of subtle job. In the present "intelligent" machines, the hypotheses are already reduced to a very small number by a human agent, and only these selected ones are supplied to the machine. The machine only evaluates, or chooses from, this limited set of given hypotheses. That is the reason why I used the word "pseudo-induction." We should not be hasty in claiming that the machine can do something of the nature of induction, since induction is not a deductive-logical process such as the machines are primarily designed to perform. (I am at present writing a paper for *The IBM Journal* entitled "Information Theoretical Aspects of Deductive and Inductive Inference," in which my view on inductive inference will be explained. See also S. Watanabe, "Civilization and Science, Man and Machine," *Annals of Japan Assoc. for Philosophy of Science,* I, 4, p. 12.)

(2) On the moral level, everyone will agree with Professor Wiener. The real issue, however, is a political one. If the automation advances, the Fourth Class (*quatrième état,* or "workers") will lose its political power, because its members will be no longer the real agents of production. The solution of the problem will then be in the hands of what I call the Fifth Class (*cinquième état*), which is the class of people of creative intelligence, since they and they alone will be able in the future to produce real values, material and moral, including automated factories. This Fifth Class, being the sole productive power of the future, is bound to be vested with political power together with its moral obligations to build an equitable society in the age of atomic energy and automation. Today's problem is how to organize politically this Fifth Class (see S. Watanabe, "Manifesto of Fifth Class, 1948," *He Who Points to the Future,* [Tokyo: Chuokoron Publishing Co., 1949]).

(3) The particular curve derived from brain waves that Professor Wiener sketched on the blackboard is such an unusual one, that it may very well be an indication of the exist-

ence in the brain of a nonlinear coupling, resulting in a synchronization of many different oscillators. It is then quite plausible, as Professor Wiener maintained, that these oscillations "in phase" may perform a function somewhat similar to the "gating" circuits in the computing machines. However, this does not imply that the real mechanism of information-processing is the same in the brain and in the computing machines. Even if there is in the brain some part which functions on a principle similar to that of a computing machine, it can easily be expected that there are many other parts in the brain which function on an entirely different principle.

Comments on Professor Scriven's presentation

(1) The behavioristic method may or may not be able to detect the difference between presence and absence of consciousness. If not, it simply demonstrates that the behavioristic method is inadequate in discovering and describing the whole reality, since the existence of my consciousness is an undeniable *fact* to me.

(2) If a machine is made out of protein, then it may have consciousness, but a machine made out of vacuum tubes, diodes, and transistors cannot be expected to have consciousness. I do not here offer a proof for this statement, except that it is obvious according to well-disciplined common sense. A "conscious" machine made out of protein is no longer a machine, it is a man-made animal. I do not deny this possibility. On the other hand, let us not be carried away by a mechanical romanticism which takes a hidden animistic satisfaction in imagining a "soul" in electric robots, even if this romanticism is cloaked in cold logical arguments, and even if it is phrased as if it were trying to refute the concept of consciousness in general.

Comments on Professor Rhine's presentation

Both Professor Rhine and his critics seem to be taking the physical theories of today too seriously and too narrowly. The basic laws of physics are perfectly symmetrical with regard to the past and the future, but when we interpret them in connection with observation, we introduce an additional ingredient, namely the principle of causality in a particular sense: the future is determined (albeit probabilistically) by the past, but not conversely. This additional assumption suits very well our usual observational conditions, but it should not be taken as a universal rule. There may be some cases where the opposite assumption is valid. If a man has a memory of past events, why should he not have a memory of future events? Such a thing might be possible even without changing the basic physical laws.

Comments on Professor Köhler's presentation

(1) Objects of study in physics are almost always "emergent" properties or "environment-and-structure-sensitive" properties of matter. Even in the domain of physics of elementary particles, where the properties seem to be fundamental and irreducible, the modern view is that the elementary particles are gradually deprived of their essential attributes, until finally, I suspect, the object of physical theory becomes something like "nothingness." W. Heisenberg's recent idea of "Urstoff" is very close to this point of view. The values of "spin," "mass" and "electric charge" are at present considered as the given properties of the elementary particles, or building blocks of nature. But, in future theory, it can be expected that all these properties will be declared to be contingent properties determined by the situation (environment and structure), and the basic elementary building blocks by themselves have none of these properties. I do not see why Professor Köhler denies the "emergent" properties, as I understand them, in physics. Probably, I am ignorant about the historical connotation attached to the term "emergence."

(2) A dualism which I can envision, more or less in broad agreement with Professor Feigl, must be based on the principle of "complementarity," which was suggested by Niels Bohr and which still requires a great deal of refinement to withstand a philosopher's scrutiny. My version, at the present moment, of "complementarity" is as follows: Either we stick to one or the other of the two "phases" and keep the distributive law of Boolian logic, or we consider both "phases" simultaneously and replace the distributive law of logic by a less restrictive law such as a "modular law," as suggested by Birkoff and von Neumann. In the first case, the description is not comprehensive, and in the latter case, we have to give up the familiar logic. This seems to offer a model on which to build a philosophical dualism.

Chapter 15

Minds and Machines

Hilary Putnam, *Princeton University*

THE VARIOUS ISSUES and puzzles that make up the traditional mind-body problem are wholly linguistic and logical in character: whatever few empirical "facts" there may be in this area support one view as much as another. I do not hope to establish this contention in this paper, but I hope to do something toward rendering it more plausible. Specifically, I shall try to show that all of the issues arise in connection with any computing system capable of answering questions about its own structure, and have thus nothing to do with the unique nature (if it *is* unique) of human subjective experience.

To illustrate the sort of thing that is meant one kind of puzzle that is sometimes discussed in connection with the "mind-body problem" is the puzzle of *privacy*. The question "How do I know I have a pain?" is a *deviant* [1] ("logically odd") question. The question "How do I know Smith has a pain?" is not at all deviant. The difference can also be mirrored in impersonal questions: "How does anyone ever know he himself has a pain?" is deviant; "How does anyone ever know that someone else is in pain?" is non-deviant. I shall show that the difference in status between the last two questions is mirrored in the case of machines: if T is any *Turing machine* (see below), the question "How does T ascertain that it is in state A?" is, as we shall see, "logically odd" with a vengeance; but if T is capable of investigating its neighbor machine T' (say, T has electronic "sense-organs" which "scan" T'), the question "How does T ascertain that T' is in state A?" is not at all odd.

Another question connected with the "mind-body problem" is the question whether or not it is ever permissible to identify mental events and physical events. Of course, I do not claim that this question arises for Turing machines, but I do claim that it is possible to construct a logical analogue for this question that does arise, and that all of the arguments on both sides of the question of "mind-body identity" can be mirrored in terms of the analogue.

To obtain such an analogue, let us identify a scientific theory

Notes to this paper begin on page 161.

with a "partially-interpreted calculus" in the sense of Carnap.[2] Then we can perfectly well imagine a Turing machine which generates theories, tests them (assuming that it is possible to "mechanize" inductive logic to some degree), and "accepts" theories which satisfy certain criteria (e.g., predictive success). In particular, if the machine has electronic "sense organs" which enable it to "scan" itself while it is in operation, it may formulate theories concerning its own structure and subject them to test. Suppose the machine is in a given state (say, "state A") when, and only when, flip-flop 36 is on. Then this statement: "I am in state A when, and only when, flip-flop 36 is on," may be one of the theoretical principles concerning its own structure accepted by the machine. Here "I am in state A" is, of course, "observation language" for the machine, while "flip-flop 36 is on" is a "theoretical expression" which is partially interpreted in terms of "observables" (if the machine's "sense organs" report by printing symbols on the machine's input tape, the "observables" in terms of which the machine would give a partial operational definition of "flip-flop 36 being on" would be of the form "symbol # so-and-so appearing on the input tape"). Now all of the usual considerations for and against mind-body identification can be paralleled by considerations for and against saying that state A is in fact *identical* with flip-flop 36 being on.

Corresponding to Occamist arguments for "identify" in the one case are Occamist arguments for identity in the other. And the usual argument for dualism in the mind-body case can be paralleled in the other as follows: for the machine, "state A" is directly observable; on the other hand, "flip-flops" are something it knows about only via highly-sophisticated inferences—How *could* two things so different *possibly* be the same?

This last argument can be put into a form which makes it appear somewhat stronger. The proposition:

(1) I am in state A if, and only if, flip-flop 36 is on,

is clearly a "synthetic" proposition for the machine. For instance, the machine might be in state A and its sense organs might report that flip-flop 36 was *not* on. In such a case the machine would have to make a methodological "choice"— namely, to give up (1) or to conclude that it had made an "observational error" (just as a human scientist would be confronted with similar methodological choices in studying his own psychophysical correlations). And just as philosophers have argued from the synthetic nature of the proposition:

(2) I am in pain if, and only if, my C-fibers are stimulated, to the conclusion that the *properties* (or "states" or "events") being in pain, and having C-fibers stimulated, cannot possibly be the same [otherwise (2) would be analytic, or so the argument runs]; so one should be able to conclude from the fact that (1) is synthetic that the two properties (or "states" or "events")—being in state A and having flip-flop 36 on— cannot possibly be the same!

It is instructive to note that the traditional argument for dualism is not at all a conclusion from "the raw data of direct experience" (as is shown by the fact that it applies just as well to non-sentient machines), but a highly complicated bit of reasoning which depends on (A) the reification of universals [3] (e.g., "properties," "states," "events"); and on (B) a sharp analytic-synthetic distinction.

I may be accused of advocating a "mechanistic" world-view in pressing the present analogy. If this means that I am supposed to hold that machines think,[4] on the one hand, or that human beings are machines, on the other, the charge is false. If there is some version of mechanism sophisticated enough to avoid these errors, very likely the considerations in this paper support it.[5]

1. Turing Machines

The present paper will require the notion of a *Turing machine* [6] which will not be explained.

Briefly, a Turing machine is a device with a finite number of internal configurations, each of which involves the machine's being in one of a finite number of *states*,[7] and the machine's scanning a tape on which certain symbols appear.

The machine's tape is divided into separate squares, thus:

on each of which a symbol (from a fixed finite alphabet) may be printed. Also the machine has a "scanner" which "scans" one square of the tape at a time. Finally, the machine has a *printing mechanism* which may (A) *erase* the symbol which appears on the square being scanned, and (B) print some other symbol (from the machine's alphabet) on that square.

Any Turing machine is completely described by a *machine table,* which is constructed as follows: the rows of the table correspond to letters of the alphabet (including the "null" letter, i.e., blank space), while the columns correspond to states A,B,C, etc. In each square there appears an "instruction," e.g., "s_5L A", "s_7C B", "s_3R C". These instructions are read as follows: "s_5L A" means "print the symbol s_5 on the square you are now scanning (after erasing whatever symbol it now contains), and proceed to scan the square immediately to the left of the one you have just been scanning; also, shift into state A." The other instructions are similarly interpreted ("R" means "scan the square immediately to the *right*," while "C" means "center," i.e., continue scanning the *same* square). The following is a sample machine table:

		A	B	C	D
(s_1)	1	s_1RA	s_1LB	s_3LD	s_1CD
(s_2)	+				
(s_2)		s_1LB	s_2CD	s_2LD	s_2CD
	blank				
(s_3)	space	s_3CD	s_3RC	s_3LD	s_3CD

The machine described by this table is intended to function as follows: the machine is started in state A. On the tape there appears a "sum"(in unary notion) to be "worked out," e.g., "11 +111."

The machine is initially scanning the first "1." The machine proceeds to "work out" the sum (essentially be replacing the plus sign by a 1, and then going back and erasing the first 1). Thus if the "input" was 1111 + 11111 the machine would "print out" 111111111, and then go into the "rest state" (state D).

A "machine table" *describes* a machine if the machine has internal states corresponding to the columns of the table, and if it "obeys" the instructions in the table in the following sense: when it is scanning a square on which a symbol s_1 appears and it is in, say, state B, that it carries out the "instruction" in the appropriate row and column of the table (in this case, column B and row s_1). Any machine that is described by a machine table of the sort just exemplified is a Turing machine.

The notion of a Turing machine is also subject to generalization[8] in various ways—for example, one may suppose that the machine has a second tape (an "input tape") on which additional information may be printed by an operator in the course of a computation. In the sequel we shall make use of this generalization (with electronic "sense organs" taking the place of the "operator").

It should be remarked that Turing machines are able in principle to do anything that any computing machine (of whichever kind) can do.[9]

It has sometimes been contended (e.g., by Nagel and Newman in their book *"Gödel's Proof"*) that "the theorem [i.e., Gödel's theorem] does indicate that the structure and power of the human mind are far more complex and subtle than any non-living machine yet envisaged" (p. 10), and hence that a Turing machine cannot serve as a model for the human mind, but this is simply a mistake.

Let T be a Turing machine which "represents" me in the sense that T can prove just the mathematical statements I can prove. Then the argument (Nagel and Newman give no argument, but I assume they must have this one in mind) is that by using Gödel's technique I can discover a proposition that T cannot prove, and moreover *I* can prove this proposition. This refutes the assumption that T "represents" me, hence I am not a Turing machine. The fallacy is a misapplication of Gödel's theorem, pure and simple. Given an arbitrary machine T, all I can do is find a proposition U such that *I* can prove:

(3) If T is consistent, U is true,

where U is undecidable by T if T is in fact consistent. However, T can perfectly well prove (3) too! And the statement U, which T *cannot* prove (assuming consistency), *I* cannot prove either (unless I can prove that T is consistent, which is unlikely if T is very complicated)!

2. Privacy

Let us suppose that a Turing machine T is constructed to do the following. A number, say "3000," is printed on T's tape and T is started in T's "initial state." Thereupon T computes the 3000th. (or whatever the given number was) digit in the decimal expansion of π, prints this digit on its tape, and goes into the "rest state," (i.e., turns itself off). Clearly the question "How does T 'ascertain' [or 'compute,' or 'work out'] the 3000th. digit in the decimal expansion of π?" is a sensible question. And the answer might well be a complicated one. In fact, an answer would probably involve three distinguishable constituents:

(i) A description of the sequence of states through which T passed in arriving at the answer, and of the appearance of the tape at each stage in the computation.

(ii) A description of the *rules* under which T operated (these are given by the "machine table" for T).

(iii) An explanation of the *rationale* of the entire procedure.

Now let us suppose that someone voices the following objection: "In order to perform the computation just described, T must pass through states A,B,C, etc. But how can T ascertain that it is in states A,B,C, etc.?"

It is clear that this is a silly objection. But what makes it silly? For one thing, the "logical description" (machine table) of the machine describes the states only in terms of their *relations* to each other and to what appears on the tape. The "physical realization" of the machine is immaterial, so long as there *are* distinct states A,B,C, etc., and they succeed each other as specified in the machine table. Thus one can answer a question such as "How does T ascertain that X?" (or "compute X," etc.) only in the sense of describing the *sequence of states* through which T must pass in ascertaining that X (computing X, etc.), the rules obeyed, etc. But there is no "sequence of states" through which T must pass to be in a single state!

Indeed, suppose there were—suppose T could not *be* in state A without first *ascertaining* that it was in state A (by first passing through a sequence of other states). Clearly a vicious regress would be involved. And one "breaks" the regress simply by noting that the machine, in ascertaining the 3000th. digit in π, *passes through* its states—but it need not in any significant sense "ascertain" that it is passing through them.

Note the analogy to a fallacy in traditional epistemology: the fallacy of supposing that to know that p (where p is any proposition) one must first know that q_1, q_2, etc. (where q_1, q_2, etc., are appropriate *other* propositions). This leads either to an "infinite regress" or to the dubious move of inventing a special class of "protocol" propositions.

The resolution of the fallacy is also analogous to the machine case. Suppose that on the basis of sense experiences E_1, E_2, etc., I know that there is a chair in the room. It does not follow that I verbalized (or even *could* have verbalized) E_1, E_2, etc., nor that I remember E_1, E_2, etc., nor even that I "mentally classified" ("attended to," etc.) sense experiences E_1, E_2, etc., when I had them. In short, it is necessary to *have* sense experiences, but not to *know* (or even *notice*) what sense experiences one is having, in order to have certain kinds of knowledge.

Let us modify our case, however, by supposing that whenever the machine is in one particular state (say, "state A") it prints the words "I am in state A." Then someone might grant that the machine does not in general ascertain what state it is in, but might say in the case of state A (after the machine printed "I am in state A"): "The machine ascertained that it was in state A."

Let us study this case a little more closely. First of all, we want to suppose that when it is in state A the machine prints "I am in state A" without first passing through any other states. That is, in every row of the column of the table headed "state A" there appears the instruction: *print* [10] *"I am in State A."* Secondly, by way of comparison, let us consider a human being, Jones, who say "I am in pain" (or "Ouch!", or "Something hurts") whenever he is in plain. To make the comparison as close as possible, we will have to suppose that Jones' linguistic conditioning is such that he simply says "I am in pain" "without thinking," i.e., without passing through any introspectible mental states other than the pain itself. In Wittgenstein's terminology, Jones simply *evinces* his pain by saying "I am in pain"—he does not first reflect on it (or heed it, or note it, etc.) and then consciously describe it. (Note that this simple possibility of uttering the "proposition," "I am in pain" without first performing any mental "act of judgment" was overlooked by traditional epistemologists from Hume to Russell!) Now we may consider the parallel questions "Does the machine 'ascertain' that it is in state A?" and "Does Jones 'know' that he is in pain?" and their consequences.

Philosophers interested in semantical questions have, as one might expect, paid a good deal of attention to the verb "know." Traditionally, three elements have been distinguished: (1) "X knows that p" implies that p is *true* (we may call this the *truth* element); (2) "X knows that p" implies that X believes that p (philosophers have quarreled about the word, some contending that it should be 'X is *confident* that p,' or 'X *is in a position to assert* that p'; I shall call this element the *confidence* element); (3) "X knows that p" implies that X has evidence that p (here I think the word "evidence" is definitely wrong,[11] but it will not matter for present purposes; I shall call this the *evidential* element). Moreover, it is part of the meaning of the word "evidence" that nothing can be literally evidence for itself: if X is evidence for Y, then X and Y must be different things.

In view of such analyses, disputes have arisen over the propriety of saying (in cases like the one we are considering) "Jones knows that he is in pain." On the one hand, philosophers who take the common-sense view ("When I have a pain I *know* I have a pain") argue somewhat as follows: It would be clearly false to say Jones does *not* know he has a pain; but either Jones knows or he does not; hence, Jones knows he has a pain. Against these philosophers, one might argue as follows: "Jones does not know X" implies Jones is not in a position to assert that X; hence, it is certainly wrong to say "Jones does not know he has a pain." But the above use of the Law of the Excluded Middle was fallacious: words in English have *significance ranges,* and what is contended is that it is not semantically correct to say *either* "Jones knows that he has a pain" *or* "Jones does not know he has a pain" (although the former sentence is certainly less misleading than the latter, since *one* at least of the conditions involved is knowing is met—Jones is in a position to assert he has a pain. (In fact the *truth* and *confidence* elements are both present; it is the evidential element that occasions the difficulty.)

I do not wish to argue this question here;[12] the present concern is rather with the similarities between our two questions. For example, one might decide to accept (as "non-deviant," "logically in order," "nonselfcontradictory," etc.) the two statements:

(a) The machine ascertained that it was in state A,

(b) Jones knew that he had a pain,

or one might reject both. If one rejects (a) and (b), then one can find alternative formulations which are certainly semantically acceptable: e.g., [for (a)] "The machine was in state A, and this caused it to print: 'I am in state A;' " [for (b)] "Jones was in pain, and this caused him to say 'I am in pain' " (or, "Jones was in pain, and he evinced this by saying 'I am in pain' ").

On the other hand, if one accepts (a) and (b), then one must face the questions (a¹) "*How* did the machine ascertain that it was in state A?", and (b¹) "*How* did Jones know that he had a pain?"

And if one regards these questions as having answers at all, then they will be degenerate answers—e.g., "By being in state A" and "By having the pain."

At this point it is, I believe, very clear that the difficulty has in both cases the same cause. Namely, the difficulty is occasioned by the fact that the "verbal report" ("I am in state A," or "I am in pain") issues directly from the state it "reports": no "computation" or additional "evidence" is needed to arrive at the "answer." And the philosophic disagreements over "how to talk" are at bottom concerned with finding a terminology for describing cognitive processes in general that is not misleading in this particular case. [Note that the traditional epistemological answer to (b[1])—namely, "by introspection"—is false to the facts of this case, since it cleary implies the occurrence of a mental event (the "act" of introspection) distinct from the feeling of pain.]

Finally, let us suppose that the machine is equipped to "scan" its neighbor machine T[1]. Then we can see that the question "How does T ascertain that T[1] is in state A?" may be a perfectly sensible question, as much so as "How does T ascertain that the 3000th. digit of π is so-and-so?" In both cases the answer will involve describing a whole "program" (plus explaining the *rationale* of the program, if necessary). Moreover, it will be necessary to say something about the physical context linking T and T[1] (arrangement of sense organs, etc.), and not just to describe the internal states of T: this is so becasue T is now answering an *empirical* and not a mathematical question. In the same way "How did Sherlock Holmes know that Jones was in pain?" may be a perfectly sensible question, and may have quite a complicated answer.

3. "Mental" states and "logical" states

Consider the two questions:

(1) How does Jones know he has a pain?

(2) How does Jones know he has a fever?

The first question is, as we saw in the preceding section, a somewhat peculiar one. The second question may be quite sensible. In fact, if Jones says "I have a pain" no one will retort "You are mistaken." (One *might* retort "You have made a slip of the tongue" or "You are lying," but not "You are *mistaken.*") On the other hand, if Jones says "I have a fever," the doctor who has just taken Jones' temperature may quite conceivably retort "You are mistaken." And the doctor need not mean that Jones made a linguistic error, or was lying, or confused.

It might be thought that, whereas the difference between statements about one's own state and statements about the state of others has an analogue in the case of machines, the difference, just touched upon, between statements about one's "mental" state and statements about one's "physical" state, in traditional parlance, does not have any analogue. But this is not so. Just what the analogue is will now be developed.

First of all, we have to go back to the notion of a Turing machine. When a Turing machine is described by means of a "machine table," it is described as something having a tape, a printing device, a "scanning" device (this may be no more than a point of the machine which at any given time is aligned with just one square of the tape), and a finite set (A,B,C, etc.) of "states." (In what follows, these will be referred to at times as *logical states* to distinguish them from certain other states to be introduced shortly.) Beyond this it is described only by giving the deterministic rules which determine the order in which the states succeed each other and what is printed when.

In particular, the "logical description" of a Turing machine does not include any specification of the *physical nature* of these "states"—or indeed, of the physical nature of the whole machine. (Shall it consist of electornic relays, of cardboard, of human clerks sitting at desks, or what?) In other words, a given "Turing machine" is an *abstract* machine which may be physically realized in an almost infinite number of different ways

As soon as a Turing machine is physically realized, however, something interesting happens. Although the machine has from the logician's point of view only the states A,B,C, etc., it has from the engineer's point of view an almost infinite number of additional "states" (though not in the same sense of "state"— we shall call these *structural states*). For instance, if the machine consists of vacuum tubes, one of the things that may happen is that one of its vacuum tubes may fail—this puts the machine in what is from the physicist's if not the logician's point of view a different "state." Again, if the machine is a manually operated one built of cardboard, one of its possible "non-logical" or "structural" states is obviously that its cardboard may buckle. And so on.

A physically realized Turing machine may have no way of ascertaining its own structural state, just as a human being may have no way of ascertaining the condition of his appendix at a given time. However, it is extremely convenient to give a machine electronic "sense organs" which enable it to scan itself and to detect minor malfunctions. These "sense organs" may be visualized as causing certain symbols to be printed on an "input tape" which the machine "examines" from time to time. (One minor difficulty is that the "report" of a sense organ might occupy a number of squares of tape, whereas the machine only "scans" one square at a time—however this is unimportant, since it is well known that the effect of "reading" any finite number of squares can be obtained using a program which only requires one square to be scanned at a time.)

(By way of a digression, let me remark that the first actually constructed digital computers did not have any devices of the kind just envisaged. On the other hand, they *did* have over 3000 vacuum tubes, some of which were failing at any given time! The need for "routines" for self-checking therefore quickly became evident.)[13]

A machine which is able to detect at least some of its own structural states is in a position very analogous to that of a human being, who can detect some but not all of the malfunctions of his own body, and with varying degrees of reliability. Thus, suppose the machine "prints out": "Vacuum tube 312 has failed." The question "How did the machine ascertain that vacuum tube 312 failed?" is a perfectly sensible question. And the answer may involve a reference to both the physical structure of the machine ("sense organs," etc.) and the "logical structure" (program for "reading" and "interpreting" the input tape).

If the machine prints: "Vacuum tube 312 has failed" when vacuum tube 312 is in fact functioning, the mistake may be due to a miscomputation (in the course of "reading" and "interpreting" the input tape) or to an incorrect signal from a sense organ. On the other hand, if the machine prints: "I am in state A," and it does this simply because its machine table contains the instruction: *Print: "I am in state A when in state A,"* then the question of a miscomputation cannot arise. Even if some accident causes the printing mechanism to print: "I am in state A" when the machine is *not* in state A, there was not a "miscomputation" (only, so to speak, a "verbal slip").

It is interesting to note that just as there are two possible descriptions of the behavior or a Turing machine—the engineer's structural blueprint and the logician's "machine table" —so there are two possible descriptions of human psychology. The "behavioristic" approach (including in this category theories which employ "hypothetical constructs," including "constructs" taken from physiology) aims at eventually providing a complete physicalistic[14] description of human behavior, in terms which link up with chemistry and physics.

This corresponds to the engineer's or physicist's description of a physically realized Turing machine. But it would also be possible to seek a more abstract description of human mental processes, in terms of "mental states" (physical realization, if any, unspecified) and "impressions" (these play the role of symbols on the machine's tapes)—a description which would specify the laws controlling the order in which the states succeeded one another, and the relation to verbalization (or, at any rate, verbalized thought). This description, which would be the analogue of a "machine table," it was in fact the program of classical psychology to provide! Classical psychology is often thought to have failed for *methodological* reasons; I would suggest, in the light of this analogy, that it failed rather for *empirical* reasons—the mental states and "impressions" of human beings do not form a causally closed system to the extent to which the "configurations" of a Turing machine do.

The analogy which has been presented between logical states of a Turing machine and mental states of a human being, on the one hand, and structural states of a Turing machine and psysical states of a human being, on the other, is one that I find very suggestive. In particular, further exploration of this analogy may make it possible to further clarify the notion of a "mental state" that we have been discussing. This "further exploration" has not yet been undertaken, at any rate by me, but I should like to put down, for those who may be interested, a few of the features that seem to distinguish logical and mental states respectively from structural and physical ones:

(1) The functional organization (problem solving, thinking) of the human being or machine can be described in terms of the sequences of mental or logical states respectively (and the accompanying verbalizations), without reference to the nature of the "physical realization" of these states.

(2) The states seem intimately connected with *verbalization*.

(3) In the case of rational thought (or computing), the "program" which determines which states follow which, etc., is open to rational criticism.

4. Mind-body "identity"

The last area in which we have to compare human beings and machines involves the question of *identifying* mental states with the corresponding physical states (or logical states with the corresponding structural states). As indicated at the beginning of this paper, all of the arguments for and against such identification can perfectly well be discussed in terms of Turing machines.

For example, in the 1930's Wittgenstein used the following argument: If I observe an after-image, and observe at the same time my brain state (with the aid of a suitable instrument) I observe *two* things, not one. (Presumably this is one argument *against* identification.) But we can perfectly well imagine a "clever" Turing machine "reasoning" as follows: "When I print 'I am in state A,' I do not have to use my 'sense organs.' When I do use my 'sense organs' and compare the occasions upon which I am in state A with the occasions upon which flip-flop 36 is on, I am comparing *two* things and not one." And I do not think that we would find the argument of this mechanical Wittgenstein very convincing!

By contrast, Russell once carried the "identity" view to the absurd extreme of maintaining that all we ever *see* is portions of our own brains. Analogously, a mechanical Russell might "argue" that "all I ever observe is my own vacuum tubes." Both "Russells" are wrong—the human being observes events in the outside world, and the process of "observation" involves events in his brain. But we are not therefore forced to say that he "really" observes his brain. Similarly, the machine T may "observe," say, cans of tomato soup (if the machine's job is sorting cans of soup), and the process of "observation" involves the functioning of vacuum tubes. But we are not forced to say that the machine "really" observes its own vacuum tubes.

But let us consider more serious arguments on this topic. At the beginning of this paper, I pointed out that the *synthetic* character of the statement (1) "I am in pain if, and only if, my C-fibers are stimulated" has been used as an argument for the view that the "properties" (or "events" or "states") "having C-fibers stimulated" and "being in pain" cannot be the same. There are at least two reasons why this is not a very good argument: (A) the "analytic-synthetic" distinction is not as sharp as that, especially where scientific laws are concerned; and (B) the criterion employed here for identifying "properties" (or "events" or "states") is a very questionable one.

With respect to point (A): I have argued elsewhere [15] that fundamental scientific laws cannot be happily classified as either "analytic" or "synthetic." Consider, for example, the kind of conceptual shift that was involved in the transition from Euclidean to non-Euclidean geometry, or that would be involved if the law of the conservation of energy were to be abandoned. It is a distortion to say that the laws of Euclidean geometry (during their tenure of office) were "analytic," and that Einstein merely "changed the meaning of the words." Indeed, it was precisely because Einstein did *not* change the meaning of the words, because he was really talking about shortest paths in the space in which we live and move and have our being, that General Relativity seemed so incomprehensible when it was first proposed. To be told that one could come back to the same place by moving in one direction on a straight line! Adopting General Relativity was indeed adopting a whole new system of concepts—but that is not to say "adopting a new system of verbal labels."

But if it is a distortion to assimilate the revision of fundamental scientific laws to the adoption of new linguistic conventions, it is equally a mistake to follow conventional philosophers of science, and assimilate the conceptual change that Einstein inaugurated to the kind of change that arises when we discover a black swan (whereas we had previously assumed all swans to be white)! Fundamental laws are like principles of pure mathematics (as Quine has emphasized), in that they cannot be overthrown by isolated experiments: we can always hold on to the laws, and explain the experiments in various more or less *ad hoc* ways. And—in spite of the pejorative flavor of "ad hoc"—it is even *rational* to do this, in the case of important scientific theories, *as long as no acceptable alternative theory exists*. This is why it took a century of concept formation—and not just some experiments—to overthrow Euclidean geometry. And similarly, this is why we cannot today describe *any* experiments which would *by themselves* overthrow the law of the conservation of energy—although that law is not "analytic," and might be abandoned if a new Einstein were to suggest good *theoretical* reasons for abandoning it, plus supporting experiments.

As Hanson has put it,[16] our concepts have theories "built into" them—thus, to abandon a major scientific theory without providing an alternative would be to "let our concepts crumble." By contrast, although we *could* have held on to "all swans are white" in the face of conflicting evidence, there would have been no *point* in doing so—the concepts involved did not *rest* on the acceptance of this or some rival principle in the way that geometrical concepts rest on the acceptance, not necessarily of Euclidean geometry, but of *some* geometry.

I do not deny that *today* any newly-discovered "correlation" of the form: "One is in mental state ψ if, and only if, one is in brain state Φ" would *at first* be a *mere* correlation, a pure "empirical generalization. But I maintain that the interesting case is the case that would arise if we had a worked out and theoretically elaborated *system* of such "correlations." In such a case, scientific talk would be very different. Scientists would begin to say: "It is impossible *in principle* to be in mental state ψ without being in brain state Φ." And it could very well be that the "impossibility in principle" would amount to what Hanson rightly calls a *conceptual* [17] impossibility: scientists could not *conceive* (barring a new Einstein) of someone's being in mental state ψ without being in brain state Φ. In particular, no experiment could *by itself* overthrow psychophysical laws which had acquired this kind of status.[18] Is it clear that in this kind of scientific situation it would not be correct to say that Φ and ψ are the *same* state?

Morevoer, the criteria for identifying "events" or "states" or "properties" are by no means so clear. An example of a law with the sort of status we have been discussing is the following: Light passes through an aperture if, and only if, electromagnetic radiation (of such-and-such wavelengths) passes through the aperture.

This law is quite clearly *not* an "analytic" statement. Yet it would be perfectly good scientific parlance to say that: (i) light passing through an aperture and (ii) electromagnetic radiation (of such-and-such wavelengths) passing through an aperture are two descriptions of the same event. (Indeed, in "ordinary language" not only are descriptions of the same event not required to be equivalent: one may even speak of *incompatible* descriptions of the same event!)

It might be held, however, that *properties* (as opposed to events) cannot be described by different nonequivalent descriptions. Indeed, Frege, Lewis, and Carnap have *identified* properties and "meanings" (so that *by definition* if two expressions have different meanings then they "signify" different properties). This seems to me very dubious. But suppose it were correct. What would follow? One would have to admit that, e.g., being in pain and having C-fibers stimulated were different properties. But, in the language of the "theory-constructing" Turing machine described at the beginning of this paper, one would equally have to admit that "being in state

A" and "having flip-flop 36 on" were different properties. Indeed the sentences (i) "I am in state A" and (ii) "Flip-flop 36 is on" are clearly nonsynonymous in the machine's language by any test (they have different syntactical properties and also different "conditions of utterance"—e.g., the machine has to use different "methods of verification"). Anyone who wishes, then, to argue on this basis for the existence of the soul will have to be prepared to hug the souls of Turing machines to his philosophic bosom!

5. A "linguistic" argument

The last argument I shall consider on the subject of mind-body identity is a widely used "linguistic" argument—it was, for example, used by Max Black against Herbert Feigl at the Conference which inspired this volume. Consider the sentence:

(1) Pain *is identical with* stimulation of C-fibers.

The sentence is deviant (so the argument runs, though not in this terminology): there is no statement that it could be used to make in a normal context. Therefore, if a philosopher advances it as a thesis he must be giving th words a new meaning, rather than expressing any sort of discovery. For exemple (Max Black argued) one might begin to say "I have stimulated C-fibers" instead of "I have a pain," etc. But then one would *merely* be giving the expression "has stimulated C-fibers" the new meaning "is in pain." The contention is that as long as the words keep their present meanings, (1) is unintelligible.

I agree that the sentence (1) is a "deviant" sentence in present-day English. I do *not* agree that (1) can never become a normal, non-deviant sentence unless the words change their present meanings.

The point, in a nutshell, is that what is "deviant" depends very much upon context, including the state of our knowledge, and with the development of new scientific theories it is constantly occurring that sentences that did not previously "have a use," that were previously "deviant," acquire a use—not because the words acquire *new* meanings, but because the old meanings as fixed by the core of stock uses, *determine* a new use given the new context.

There is nothing wrong with trying to bring linguistic theory to bear on this issue, but one must have a sufficiently sophisticated linguistic theory to bring to bear. The real question is not a question on *synchronic* linguistics but one on *dia-*

chronic [19] linguistics, not "Is (1) *now* a deviant sentence?", but "If a change in scientific knowledge (e.g., the development of an integrated network of psychophysical laws of high "priority" in our over-all scientific world view) were to lead to (1)'s becoming a *non*-deviant sentence, would a change in the meaning of a word necessarily have taken place?"—and this is not so simple a question.

Although this is not the time or the place to attempt the job of elaborating a semantical theory,[20] I should like to risk a few remarks on this question.

In the first place, it is easy to show that the mere uttering of a sentence which no one has ever uttered before does not neccessarily constitute the introduction of a "new use." If I say "There is a purple Gila monster on this desk," I am very likely uttering a sentence that no English-speaker has uttered before me: but I am not in any way changing the meaning of any word.

In the second place, even if a sentence which was formerly deviant begins to acquire a standard use, no change in the *meaning* of any word need have taken place. Thus the sentence "I am a thousand miles away from you," or its translation into ancient Greek, was undoubtedly a deviant sentence prior to the invention of *writing,* but acquired (was not "given," but *acquired*) a normal use with the invention of writing and the ensuing possibility of long-distance interpersonal address.

Note the reasons that we would not say that any word (e.g., "I," "you," "thousand") in this sentence changed its meaning: (A) the new use was not *arbitrary,* was not the product of *stipulation,* but represented an automatic projection [21] from the existing stock uses of the several words making up the sentence, given the new context; (B) the meaning of a sentence is in general a function of the meanings of the individual words making it up (in fact this principle underlies the whole notion of word meaning)—thus, if we said that the *sentence* had changed its meaning, we should have to face the question "*Which word* changed its meaning?" But this would pretty clearly be an embarrassing question in this case.

The case just described was one in which the new context was the product of new technology, but new theoretical knowledge may have a similar impact on the language. (For example, "he went all the way around the world" would be a deviant sentence in a culture which did not know that the earth was round!) A case of this kind was discussed by Malcolm:

We are beginning to have the means available for telling, on the basis of various physiological indicators (electro-encephalograms, eye movements during sleep, blood pressure disturbances, etc.), when dreams begin and end. The sentence "He is halfway through his dream" may, therefore, someday acquire a standard use. Malcolm's comment on this was that the words would in that case have been *given* a use. Malcolm is clearly mistaken, I believe; this case, in which a sentence acquires a use *because* of what the words mean is poles apart from the case in which words are literally *given* a use (i.e., in which meanings are stipulated for expressions). The "realistic" account of this case is, I think, obviously correct: the sentence did not previously have a use because we had no way of telling when dreams start and stop. Now we are beginning to have ways of telling, and so we are beginning to find occasions upon which it is natural to employ this sentence. (Note that in Malcolm's account there is no explanation of the fact that we give *this* sentence *this* use).

Now, someone may grant that change in meaning should not be confused with change in distribution,[22] and that scientific and technological advances frequently produce changes in the latter that are not properly regarded as changed in the former. But one might argue that whereas one could have envisaged beforehand the circumstances under which the sentence "He went all the way around the world" would become non-deviant, one cannot now envisage any circumstances under which[23] "mental state ψ is identical with brain state Φ" would be non-deviant. But this is not a very good objection. In the first place, it might very well have been impossible for primitive people to envisage a spherical earth (the people on the "underside" would abviously fall off). Even forty years ago, it might have been difficult if not impossible to envisage circumstances under which "he is halfway through his dream" would be non-deviant. And in the second place, I believe that one *can* describe in general terms circumstances under which "mental state ψ is identical with brain state Φ" would become non-deviant.

In order to do this, it is necessary to talk about one important kind of "is"—the *"is" of theoretical identification*. The use of "is" in question is exemplified in the following sentences:

(2) Light is electromagnetic radiation (of such-and-such wavelengths).

(3) Water is H_2O.

What was involved in the scientific acceptance of, for instance, (2) was very roughly this: prior to the identification there were two distinct bodies of theory—optical theory (whose character Toulmin has very well described in his book on philosophy of science), and electromagnetic theory (as represented by Maxwell's equations). The decision to *define* light as "electromagnetic radiation of such-and-such wavelengths" was scientifically justified by the following sorts of considerations (as has often been pointed out):

(1) It made possible the *derivation* of the laws of optics (up to first approximation) from more "basic" physical laws. Thus, even if it had accomplished nothing else, this theoretical identification would have been a move toward simplifying the structure of scientific laws.

(2) It made possible the derivation of *new* predictions in the "reduced" discipline (i.e., optics). In particular, it was now possible to predict that in certain cases the laws of geometrical optics would *not* hold. (Cf. Duhem's famous comments on the reduction of Kepler's laws to Newton's.)

Now let us try to envisage the circumstances under which a theoretical identification of mental states with physiological states might be in accordance with good scientific procedure. In general terms, what is necessary is that we should have not *mere* "correlates" for subjective states, but something much more elaborate—e.g., that we should know of physical states (say micro-states of the central processes) on the basis of which we could not merely *predict* human behavior, but causally explain it.

In order to avoid "category mistakes," it is necessary to restrict this notion, "explain human behavior," very carefully. Suppose a man says "I feel bad." His behavior, described in one set of categories, is: "stating that he feels bad." And the explanation may be "He said that he felt bad because he was hungry and had a headache." I do not wish to suggest that the event "Jones *stating* that he feels bad" can be explained in terms of the laws of *physics*. But there is *another* event which is very relevant, namely "Jones' body producing such-and-such sound waves." From one point of view this is a "different event" from Jones' stating that he feels bad. But (to adapt a remark of Hanson's) there would be no point in remarking that these are different events if there were not a sense in which they were the *same* event. And it is the sense in which these are the "same event" and not the sense in which these are "different events" that is relevant here.

In fine, all I mean when I speak of "causally explaining human behavior" is: causally explaining certain physical events (notions of bodies, productions of sound waves, etc.) which are in the sense just referred to the "same" as the events which make up human behavior. And no amount of "Ryle-ism" can succeed in arguing away [24] what is obviously a possibility: that physical science might succeed in doing this much.

If this much were a reality, then theoretically identifying "mental states" with their "correlates" would have the following two advantages:

(1) It would be possible (again up to "first approximation") to derive from physical theory the classical laws (or low-level generalizations) of common-sense "mentalistic" psychology, such as: "People tend to avoid things with which they have had painful experiences."

(2) It would be possible to predict the cases (and they are legion) in which common-sense "mentalistic" psychology fails.

Advantage (2) could, of course, be obtained without "identification" (by using correlation laws). But advantage (2) could equally have been obtained in the case of optics without identification (by assuming that light *accompanies* electromagnetic radiation, but is not *identical* with it.) But the *combined* effect of eliminating certain laws altogether (in favor of theoretical definitions) *and* increasing the explanatory power of the theory could not be obtained in any other way in either case. The point worth noticing is that *every* argument for *and against* identification would apply equally in the mind-body case and in the light-electromagnetism case. (Even the "ordinary language" argument could have been advanced against the identification of light with electromagnetic radiation.)

Two small points: (i) When I call "light is electromagnetic radiation (of such-and-such wavelengths)" a definition, I do not mean that the statement is "analytic." But then "definitions," *properly so called,* in theoretical science virtually *never* are analytic.[25] (Quine remarked once that he could think of at least nine good senses of "definition," none of which had anything to do with analyticity.) Of course a philosopher might then object to the whole *rationale* of theoretical identification on the ground that it is no gain to eliminate "laws" in favor of "definitions" if both are *synthetic* statements. The fact that the scientist does not feel at all the same way is another illustration of how unhelpful it is to look at science from the standpoint of the question "Analytic or synthetic?" (ii) Accepting a theoretical identification, e.g., "Pain *is* stimulation of C-fibers," does not commit one to *interchanging* the terms "pain" and "stimulation of C-fibers" in idiomatic talk, as Black suggested. For instance, the identification of "water" with "H_2O" is by now a very well-known one, but no one says "Bring me a glass of H_2O," except as a joke.

I believe that the account just presented is able (a) to explain the fact that sentences such as "Mental state ψ is identical with brain state Φ" are deviant in present-day English, while (b) making it clear how these same sentences might become *non-deviant* given a suitable increase in our scientific insight into the physical nature and causes of human behavior. The sentences in question cannot today be used to express a theoretical identification, because no such identification has been made. The act of theoretical identification is not an act that can be performed "at will"; there are *preconditions* for its performance, as there are for many acts, and these preconditions are not satisfied today. On the other hand, if the sort of scientific theory described above should materialize, then the preconditions for theoretical identification would be met, as they were met in the light-electromagnetism case, and sentences of the type in question would then *automatically* require a use—namely, to express the appropriate theoretical identifications. Once again, what makes this way of *acquiring* a use different from being *given* a use (and from "change of meaning" properly so called) is that the "new use" is an automatic *projection* from existing uses, and does not involve arbitrary stipulation (except insofar as some element of "stipulation" may be present in the acceptance of *any* scientific hypothesis, including "The earth is round").

So far we have considered only sentences of the form[26] "mental state ψ is identical with brain state Φ." But what of the sentence:

(3) Mental states are micro-states of the brain?

This sentence does not, so to speak, "give" any *particular* theoretical identification: it only says that unspecified theoretical identifications are possible. This is the sort of assertion that Feigl might make. And Black[27] might reply that in uttering (3) Feigl had uttered an odd set of words (i.e., a deviant sentence). It is possible that Black is right. Perhaps (3) is deviant in present-day English. But it is also possible that our descendants in two or three hundred years will feel that Feigl was making perfectly good sense, and that the linguistic objections to (3) were quite silly. And they too may be right.

6. Machine linguistics

Let us consider the linguistic question that we have just discussed from the standpoint of the analogy between man and Turing machine that we have been presenting in this paper. It will be seen that our Turing machine will probably not be able, if it lacks suitable "sense organs," to construct a correct theory of its own constitution. On the other hand "I am in state A" will be a sentence with a definite pattern of occurrence in the machine's "language." If the machine's "language" is sufficiently complex, it may be possible to analyze it syntactically in terms of a finite set of basic building blocks (morphemes) and rules for constructing a potentially infinite set of "sentences" from these. In particular, it will be possible to distinguish *grammatical* [28] from *ungrammatical sentences* in the machine's "language." Similiary, it may be possible to associate regularities with sentence occurrences (or, "describe sentence uses," in the Oxford jargon), and to assign "meanings" to the finite set of morphemes and the finite set of forms of composition, in such a way that the "uses" of the various sentences can be effectively projected from the meanings of the individual morphemes and forms of composition. In this case, one could distinguish not only "grammatical" and "ungrammatical" sentences in the "machine language," but also "deviant" and "non-deviant" ones.

Chisholm would insist that it is improper to speak of machines as employing a language, and I agree. This is the reason for my occasionally enclosing the words "language," "meaning," etc., in "raised-eyebrow" quotes — to emphasize, where necessary, that these words are being used in an extended sense. On the other hand, it is important to recognize that machine performances may be wholly *analogous* to language, so much so that the whole of linguistic theory can be applied to them. If the reader wishes to check this, he may go through a work life Chomsky's *Syntactic Structures* carefully, and note that *at no place is the assumption employed that the corpus of utterances studied by the linguist was produced by a conscious organism.* Then he may turn to such pioneer work in empirical semantics as Ziff's *Semantical Analysis* and observe that the same thing holds true for *semantical* theory.

Two further remarks in this connection: (i) Since I am contending that the mind-body problem is *strictly analogous* to the problem of the relation between structural and logical states, not that the two problems are *identical,* a suitable *analogy* between machine "language" and human language is all that is needed here.

(ii) Chisholm might contend that a "behavioristic" semantics of the kind attempted by Ziff (i.e., one that does not take "intentionality" as a primitive notion) is impossible. But even if this were true, it would not be relevant. For if *any* semantical theory can fit human language, it has to be shown why a completely *analogous* theory would not fit the language of a suitable machine. For instance, if "intentionality" plays a role as a primitive notion in a *scientific* explanation of human language, then a theoretical construct with similar *formal* relations to the corresponding "observables" will have the *same* explanatory power in he case of machine "language."

Of course, the objection to "behavioristic" linguistics might *really* be an objection to all attempts at *scientific* linguistics. But this possibility I feel justified in dismissing.

Now suppose we equip our "theory-constructing" Turing machine with "sense organs" so that it can obtain the empirical data necessary for the construction of a theory of its own nature.

Then it may introduce into its "theoretical language" noun phrases that can be "translated" by the English expression "flip-flop 36," and sentences that can be translated by "Flip-flop 36 is on." These expressions will have a meaning and use quite distinct from the meaning and use of "I am in state A" in the machine language.

If any "linguistic" argument really shows that the sentence "Pain is identical with stimulation of C-fibers" is deviant, in English, the same argument must show that "State A is identical with flip-flop 36 being on" is deviant in the machine language. If any argument shows that "Pain is identical with stimulation of C-fibers" could not become non-deviant (viewing English now *diachronically*) unless the words first altered their meanings, the same argument, applied to the "diachronic linguistics of machine language," would show that the sentence "State A is identical with flip-flop 36 being on" could not become non-deviant in machine language unless the words first changed their meanings. In short, every philosophic argument that has ever been employed in connection with the mind-body problem, from the oldest and most naïve (e.g., "states of consciousness can just be *seen* to be different from physical states") to the most sophisticated, has its exact counterpart in the case of the "problem" of logical states and structural states in Turing machines.

7. Conclusion

The moral, I believe, is quite clear: it is no longer possible to believe that the mind-body problem is a genuine theoretical problem, or that a "solution" to it would shed the slightest light on the world in which we live. For it is quite clear that no grown man in his right mind would take the problem of the "identity" or "non-identity" of logical and structural states in a machine at all seriously—not because the answer is obvious, but because it is obviously of no importance *what* the answer is. But if the so-called "mind-body problem" is nothing but a different realization of the same set of logical and linguistic issues, then it must be just as empty and just as verbal.

It is often an important insight that two problems with distinct subject matter are the same in all their logical and methodological aspects. In this case, the insight carries in its train the realization that any conclusion that might be reached in the case of the mind-body problem would have to be reached, *and for the same reasons,* in the Turing machine case. But if it is clear (as it obviously is) that, for example, the conclusion that the logical states of Turing machines are hopelessly different from their structural states, even if correct, could represent only a purely *verbal* discovey, then the same conclusion *reached by the same arguments* in the human case must likewise represent a purely verbal discovery. To put it differently, if the mind-body problem is identified with any problem of more than purely conceptual interest (e.g., with the question of whether or not human beings have "souls"), then *either* it must be that (a) no argument *ever* used by a philosopher sheds the *slightest* light on it (and this independently of the way the argument tends), or (b) that some philosophic argument for mechanism is correct, or (c) that some dualistic argument does show that *both* human beings *and* Turing machines have souls! I leave it to the reader to decide which of the three alternatives is at all plausible.

NOTES

1. By a "deviant" utterance is here meant one that deviates from a semantical regularity (in the appropriate natural language). The term is taken from (14).

2. Cf. (1), (2). This model of a scientific theory is too oversimplified to be of much general utility, in my opinion: however, the oversimplifications do not affect the present argument.

3. This point was made by Quine in (9).

4. Cf. Ziff's paper (13) and the reply (10) by Smart. Ziff has informed me that by a "robot" he did not have in mind a "learning machine" of the kind envisaged by Smart, and he would agree that the considerations brought forward in his paper would not necessarily apply to such a machine (if it can properly be classed as a "machine" at all). On the question of whether "this machine thinks (feels, etc.)" is *deviant* or not, it is necessary to keep in mind both the point raised by Ziff (that the important question is not whether or not the utterance is deviant, but whether or not it is deviant for non-trivial reasons), and also the "diachronic-synchronic" distinction discussed in section 5 of the present paper.

5. In particular, I am sympathetic with the general standpoint taken by Smart in (11) and (12). However, see the linguistic considerations in section 5.

6. For further details, cf. (4) and (6).

7. This terminology is taken from (6) and differs from that of Davis and Turing.

8. This generalization is made in (4), where it is employed in defining relative recursiveness.

9. This statement is a form of *Church's thesis* (that recursiveness equals effective computability).

10. Here it is necessary to suppose that the entire sentence "I am in state A" counts as a single symbol in the machine's alphabet.

11. For example, I know that the sun is 93 million miles from the earth, but I have no *evidence* that this is so. In fact, I do not even remember where I learned this.

12. In fact, it would be impossible to decide whether "Jones knows he has a pain" is deviant or not without first reformulating the evidential condition so as to avoid the objection in note 11 (if it can be reformulated so as to save anything of the condition at all). However the discussion above will indicate, I believe, why one might *want* to find that this sentence is deviant.

13. Actually, it was not necessary to add any "sense organs"; existing computers check themselves by "performing crucial experiments with themselves" (i.e., carrying out certain test computations and comparing the results with the correct results which have been given).

14. In the sense of (7); not in the "epistemological" sense associated with Carnap's writings on "physicalism."

15. In (8).

16. In (5).

17. Cf. (5).

18. Cf. the discussion of geometry in (8).

19. Diachronic linguistics studies the language as it changes through time; synchronic linguistics seeks only to describe the language at one particular time.

20. For a detailed discussion, cf. (14). I am extremely indebted to Ziff, both for making this work available to me and for personal communications on these matters. Section 5 of the present paper

represents partly Ziff's influence (especially the use of the "synchronic-diachronic" distinction), and partly the application of some of the ideas of (8) to the present topic.

21. The term is taken from (14).

22. The *distribution* of a word = the set of sentences in which it occurs.

23. Here "Mental state Ψ is identical with brain state φ" is used as a surrogate for such sentences as "Pain is identical with stimulation of C-fibers."

24. As one young philosopher attempted to do in a recent article in the *British Journal for the Philosophy of Science*.

25. This is argued in (8).

26. By sentences of this *form* I do not literally mean *substitution instances* of "mental state Ψ is identical with brain state φ." Cf. note 23.

27. I have, with hesitation, ascribed this position to Black on the basis of his remarks at the Conference. But, of course, I realize that he cannot justly be held responsible for remarks made on the spur of the moment.

28. This term is used in the sense of (3), not in the traditional sense.

BIBLIOGRAPHY

(1) Carnap, Rudolf. "The Interpretation of Physics." Reprinted in H. Feigl & M. Brodbeck, *Readings in the Philosophy of Science*. New York: Appleton-Century-Crofts, 1953, pp. 309-18.

(2) ———. "The Methodological Character of Theoretical Concepts," in *Minnesota Studies in the Philosophy of Science*, I, 38-76. Minneapolis: Univ. of Minnesota, 1956.

(3) Chomsky, Noam. *Syntactic Structures*. The Hague: Mouton & Co., 1957.

(4) Davis, Martin. *Computability and Unsolvability*. New York: McGraw-Hill Book Co., 1958.

(5) Hanson, Norwood Russell. *Patterns of Discovery*. Cambridge: Cambridge Univ. Press, 1958.

(6) Kleene, Stephen Cole. *Introduction to Metamathematics*. New York: Von Nostrand, 1952.

(7) Oppenheim, Paul, and Putnam, Hilary. "Unity of Science as a Working Hypothesis," in H. Feigl, G. Maxwell, and M. Scriven (eds.), *Concepts, Theories, and the Mind-Body Problem* (Minnesota Studies in the Philosophy of Science, Vol. II). Minneapolis: Univ. of Minnesota, 1958.

(8) Putnam, Hilary. "The Analytic and the Synthetic," to appear in Minnesota Studies in the Philosophy of Science (Vol. III). Minneapolis: Univ. of Minnesota, 1960.

(9) Quine, Willard Van Ormand. "The Scope and Language of Science," *British Journal for the Philosophy of Science*, VIII (1957).

(10) Smart, J. J. C. "Professor Ziff on Robots," *Analysis*, XIX (1959), 117-18.

(11) ———. "Incompatible Colors," *Philosophical Studies*, X (1959), 39-42.

(12) ———. "Sensations and Brain Processes," *Philosophical Review*, LXVIII (1959), 141-56.

(13) Ziff, Paul. "The Feelings of Robots," *Analysis*, XIX (1959), 64-68.

(14) ———. *Semantical Analysis*. Ithaca: Cornell University Press (forthcoming).

Chapter 16

On Consciousness in Machines

Arthur C. Danto, *Columbia University*

SUPPOSE ALL THE physical discrepancies between the human brain and the currently most highly developed servomechanisms were someday overcome, and that the machine turned out to be conscious. What then would happen with the old quarrel between dualists and anti-dualists regarding the mind-body problem? I venture to say that nothing would happen with that quarrel: partisans of each position would doubtless applaud the great feat in technology, but the machine would nonetheless leave the basic philosophical disagreements where it found them. For, by hypothesis, the machine will have been brought to an order of functional complexity comparable with that of the human brain, and the quarrel has all along been concerned with relations, one term of which consists in mechanisms of just this order of complexity. And since the problems have always arisen in connection with human beings, the more the machines can be changed to resemble human beings, the more, philosophically, *c'est la même chose*. So the empirical crux of the controversy, if it exists at all, is not be breached in this manner. The best that might be shown would be a certain correlation between consciousness and mechanisms of a certain order of complexity, independent of the causal provenance of the latter. But the empirical hypothesis thus confirmed is compatible with all main positions on the mind-body problem.

But what about my initial supposition regarding the construction of a conscious machine: is this a sheer exercise in science fiction or a wild anticipation of the shape of things to come? This is not for me to answer, but I do wish to distinguish two different questions which the supposition raises: (a) can machines be brought to this required degree of complexity, and (b) would they then be conscious? It lies outside the competence of the philosopher to pronounce on (a): the answer to it is wholly a matter of the progress of science, and has to do with the correctness of neurone theory, of proposed analogies between nerve-cells and switches, and on the solution to a host of intricate problems concerning circuitry, cooling, and the like. But about (b) the philosopher may say a word or two. Is the proposition "A machine M becomes conscious when it reaches a point p of complexity" of the same kind as "Water boils at 100° C"? If so, the only answer to (b) is: *wait and see*. But philosophers might temporize, on the grounds that while we are reasonably clear about the predicate "is boiling" we are far from clear on "is conscious," so that until a bit of philosophical lexicography has been done, we will hardly know what to look for when M has been brought to p. This would be my response to (b). But other philosophers have a readier answer: there is no point in waiting and seeing, for there will be nothing to look for. We are indeed not clear on the predicate "is conscious," but we *are* clear on the entities to which it appropriately applies when it applies at all. And the predicate does not apply to machines. Some such premise as this seemed to underlie the remarks of a number of persons at our conference, their statements being enthymenmatic conclusions to a near-relative of a Paradigm Case Argument. But this short way with (b) seems to me to raise problems of its own, if not about machines at least about language, and I would like to spell some of these out.

I.

Dr. Scriven, in the course of his talk, was concerned to specify a set of crucial properties of the human brain, properties such that if mechanical brains lacked them, we would be obliged to concede that mechanical brains belong to an order essentialy different from human brains. Consciousness was one such property, perhaps the critical one. Now it can be argued that even human brains are not conscious: *persons* are, and persons have brains. But this only calls for rephrasing on Scriven's part. It has become a natural idiom to speak of certain machines as "brains" (e.g., "giant brains"), but we could as easily speak of them as having brains, the question being whether machines are conscious the way persons are in virtue of their mutual possession of comparable brains. Scriven went on to sketch an experiment, the positive outcome of which would yield an affirmative answer to this query. We construct a machine (of a kind I shall henceforward refer to as a Scriven Machine) which (1) is programmed in such wise as to have command of the full resources of the English language and (2) furnishes only true answers to questions asked it when it can furnish any answer at all. Now we simply ask the machine whether it is conscious or, perhaps, whether it feels when we send through an unduly high number of volts. If the answer is affirmative, we can conclude from (1) that the answer is linguistically correct and from (2) that it is true, and that *Scriven* Machines, at least, are conscious.

But if the "short way" with (b) rests on a sound argument, we can readily predict the outcome of the experiment without going to the trouble and expense of building a Scriven Machine. For given the conventions of English which the argument invokes, and given that these conventions are built into the machine in accordance with (1), it immediately follows that the Scriven Machine must answer "No" to the critical question. And the reason it would give (if it could give reasons) would be "I am a machine and machines are not conscious." The programming of it in accordance with (1) has made the machine an unwitting master of Paradigm Case analysis. But I begin to feel just here that (1) conflicts with (2), except in the sense that in view of (1) the truth in question is so trivial as to eliminate the value of the experiment. Adherence to the presumed conventions of English disqualifies the Scriven Machine from giving a non-trivial answer to the question, just in the same way that the conventions of some Eastern European country in the old days, which ruled that peasants have no feelings, disqualifies a non-trivial answer to the question "Did that hurt?" asked of a peasant under the knout.

The question I would ask then, consistently with my view on (b), is when and at what point would we be prepared to *change* the conventions and so allow the Scriven Machine at least the option of a non-trivial answer to questions regarding its inner states? But in fact, I contend, the very existence of a Scriven Machine would force *some* change in language whether we liked it or not. Thus, to refuse to make a change at one point would automatically be to allow a change elsewhere (I take my cue here from some comments of Professor Hilary Putnam). Not to change our language would be perforce to change our language. The Scriven Machine, indeed, is so designed as to force a change in the rules governing its own construction. Here is another instance of mechanical treachery of the sort to which Prof. Wiener likes to call to our attention.

II.

For, notice that, given (1), the Scriven Machine would be

obliged to give a negative answer to any question Q which made essential use of any predicate f which, in ordinary usage, is not correctly applied to machines. As a special case, the machine would have to refuse self-application of any predicate f, application of which presupposes correct application of the predicate "is conscious." In particular, "is thinking," "is feeling," "is wanting to," etc. For consciousness, as defined in the OED, is "The state of fact of being conscious, as a condition and concomitant of all thought, feeling, and volition." All such predicates I shall tern non-M. From remarks made in our discussion, I gather "gets the meaning of Q" (where Q is a question) is non-M. So while it is true that we can ask and get answers to questions from the Scriven Machine, we cannot say the machine gets the meaning of the questions we ask. With this restriction in mind, I want to construct a dialogue between the Scriven Machine and a human interlocutor.

I: Here are some rather complicated instructions. I am going to ask you a question Q, but before you give me an answer to Q, I want you first to give answers to a series of other questions. Then give me an answer to Q. Now, Q is: how much is three times four? The first thing I want you to answer is: do you get the meaning of Q?

M: No.

I: Do you know the answer to Q?

M: No.

I: Do you recall what Q asked?

M: No.

I: Fine. Now what is the answer to Q?

M: Twelve.

I: Do you believe that to be the correct answer?

M: No.

I: *Is* it the correct answer?

M: Yes.

I: Then why don't you believe it's the correct answer?

M: I'm a machine, and machines don't have beliefs. So I don't have beliefs.

I: I suppose that's why you answered "No" when I asked whether you got the meaning, knew the answer, and recalled the question?

M: That's right.

I: Suppose you weren't a machine: how would you answer those questions?

M: That's a counterfactual, I'm afraid.

It is hard to make out from this dialogue whether greater violence is being done to English or to truth, quite apart from the matter of injustice to the Scriven Machine—as though it were being denied the *right* to apply predicates to itself which we would have thought descriptive but which turn out also to be honorific. And one begins to feel that in fairness both to truth and the Scriven Machine, we had better relax some conventions of language.

For in fact some conventions of language have already been relaxed. As Moore recognized, one cannot say and disbelieve a proposition, one cannot correctly use "I don't believe *p*" together with "*p* is correct." One might get out of this by insisting that neither "believes *p*" nor "does not believe *p*" applies to machines. But this way out is at best prompted by a certain prejudice, and still leaves us with the fact that, in ordinary English, to answer at $t + \Delta t$ a question Q asked at t is to recall Q. And I should think that it follows from the fact that something is recalled by x that x is conscious. So either we must allow that the Scriven Machine is conscious, or change the meaning of certain important mental terms. Of course, one can always avail oneself of Duhem-Quine maneuvers, and make changes "elsewhere in the system." I should like to consider another alternative myself. We might (A) decide that Scriven Machines are human and (B) persist in saying that non-M predicates are to be withheld from application to machines. But (A) reflects the sort of mentality which finds it congenial to deny that black swans are swans, to retain empirical generalizations only at the price of making them analytic and hence no longer empirical generalizations. And it continues to solve the problem of consciousness in machines by such trivial devices as insisting that whenever something is conscious it is not a machine. (B), meanwhile, imposes upon us the task of finding other terms which will do the work non-M predicates would do if non-M predicates could be applied to machines. For the whole language of action must go by the board: as Prof. Toulmin pointed out, we could not even speak of machines playing checkers.

So let us construct a special language, L_m to be exclusively applied to machines. We might save ourselves a great deal of labor by just affixing subscripts to the appropriate English words, e.g., "recalls$_m$" or "plays$_m$ checkers." But the subscripted terms of L_m must designate movements of mechanical parts, or dispositions of mechanical parts to move in certain ways, or functions of integrated motions of mechanical parts. But just which movements, dispositions or functions are to be designated with "recalls$_m$"? Surely those which are related to whatever machines do which corresponds to what humans do when "recalls" is true of humans. Otherwise why use "recalls$_m$" and not just some arbitrary word? But even arbitrary terms in L_m require translation into English if the machines are to be used in any significant way. So, (1) L_m is parasitic on English roughly as sense-datum language is parasitic on physical-object language; (2) we are still left with a problem whether to include a term "conscious$_m$" in L_m, and a further problem as to what "conscious$_m$" would designate if it *were* included in L_m—since, after all, we are not clear on what properties "conscious" connotes in English; finally, (3) there would be cold comfort in saying that machines are conscious$_m$ but not conscious, since there is a major problem as yet to be seriously faced in our discussion— namely, how are we to distinguish between the class of entities to be spoken of with "m" subscripts and humans? Granted that L_m applies exclusively to machines, the question remains how machines are to be distinguished from human beings. And this, I gather, is far less easy to make clear than once it was thought to be. Indeed, it is likely to grow more difficult in the future. And how strange it would be to insist that machines are not conscious, and yet be unable to single out machines.

Well, we could try another experiment. We could program the Scriven Machine with the full resources of English *and* L_m, but refuse to tell it which language is appropriate to itself. And when we asked it to find out, which comes to asking it "Are you a machine?", I don't know what the answer would be: perhaps the Scriven Machine would produce answers in un-subscripted English, and what would we say then? After all, the language it employs is bound to reflect whatever vaguenesses exist in our language, and it would have the same problems in the face of indefinite criteria which all of us have. So in the end it is up to us to decide. The Scriven Machine has only our conventions to work with.

III.

But suppose we just *decided* that Scriven Machines are conscious! Would this really make its answer to the critical question any less trivially predictable than it now is—i.e., "I am a Scriven Machine, and Scriven Machines are conscious. So I am conscious"? I say it all depends on what basis the decision was made. If it was simply a *fiat* on our part, or perhaps just a trouble-saving reaction to the linguistic tensions the Scriven Machine precipitates, then the issue remains trivialized and there is no special gain. If it was made on the basis of differential behavioral criteria, then it depends upon whether the Scriven Machine satisfied these. "But which behavioral criteria?" I do not know. And that is why I gave a temporizing answer to (b).

But someone is apt to be discontented with this. "Satisfaction of differential behavioral criteria doesn't *prove* that something is conscious. At best it still reflects a decision you have made concerning when and when not to bestow the predicate 'is conscious.' Whether or not something is conscious, however, is a matter independent of your tests. So just because something has passed all the tests doesn't guarantee that it is conscious. Even if Scriven Machines *are* conscious, other machines might not be and still pass all the tests!" True. But this is a problem we face amongst ourselves. René Descartes, that arch-doubter, would cheerfully have taken you and me to be automata, differential behavioral criteria notwithstanding. So let's not ask the impossible.

Chapter 17

Machines, Brains, and Models

Roy Lachman, *University of Hawaii*

CYBERNETICS HAS PROPOSED that the human brain functions in the manner of a stable control system of servomechanisms. Procedures of control and communications in physical systems are said to parallel in certain fashions the working of the human nervous system. Various functions of living organisms appear to contain digital and analogue features of automata.

It has been proposed that the art of automata construction and the theory of their functioning may provide scientific models for the brain and the various behaviors that are mediated by the brain. Brain models based on the theory of modern machines may be applied at two levels. Empirical elements and relationships which constitute the neurological phenomena are thought about in the new and unusual fashion prescribed by the computer or telecommunication models. Attributes and meanings concerning the working of machines are transferred from their initial context of usage to the phenomena of neurophysiology. Thus, if the brain is regarded as if it were a computing or control machine, then to some determinable degree the nervous system should be capable of analysis in accordance with the laws describing the operations of automata.

The second type of application of machine models for the brain may be described as theoretical. Models based on automata may provide novel modes for conceiving and constructing the hypothetical ideas or postulates of a theory (a so-called conceptual nervous system) from which laws describing functionings of the brain may be derived. Here any individual property or combination of properties of automata may be assigned to the theoretical constructs employed to organize and derive relationships operating within the nervous system. Either type of application for models based on automata may some day contribute to the understanding of the nervous system and the behavior of organisms.

It so happens that both levels of application of machine models for the brain are largely ignored by those engaged in active research into the nervous system. This may be due less to the mathematical barrier than to the conviction that the most efficient method for exploring the nervous system is to study the nervous system. A number of advances that have occurred at various stages of science suggest that this viewpoint might be rather narrow.

While many investigators have ignored the development of ever more subtle machines, their colleagues with a propensity for speculation have not done so. In the past few years, debates have raged on such topics as "Do machines think?" Although this question was mercifully avoided during the conference that produced this book, an equally fanciful problem was considered: When may we attribute consciousness to a machine? At first this appeared to be something of a good joke. However, the extensive comments that were elicited suggest that a new debate may be germinating. As one theologian has remarked, this problem will concern him only when the machines start worrying that their parts might be wearing out.

Utilizing Dr. Toulmin's notion of the deployment of a model, the question of consciousness for automata is an example of reverse deployment: attributing to a model properties which are meaningful only for the phenomena the model was supposed to explain.

Chapter 18

On Computers and Semantical Rules

R. M. Martin, *University of Texas*

WITHOUT STRETCHING THE ordinary usage of the term too far, we may say that a computer *speaks* a language, more specifically, a language-system with a specified primitive vocabulary, axioms, and rules of inference. *Algol,* under current study by the British Computer Society, and IBM's *Vortran,* for example, are presumably such systems or could be reformulated as such. Systems of this kind are usually regarded as *object-languages.*

Professors Wiener and Scriven have in effect raised the question concerning the extent to which computers can speak *metalinguistically.* Professor Wiener has pointed out that in view of the Gödel arithmetization, a computer can in effect handle a good deal of its own syntax. Perhaps also its syntax could be handled more directly in the manner of Tarski's concatenation theory. The question now arises as to what extent or in what way (if any) a computer can handle its own *semantics.* In other words, we may query the status of *semantical rules* for the computer language.

Let us think of semantical rules in the simplest sense as stating merely that certain expressions *denote* such and such objects, or that an expression denotes an object x if and only if ———x——— (where '———x———' is some suitable sentential function of the one variable 'x'). If the computer language contains no symbol for denotation in this sense (or for a suitable alternative notion or notions), it should then presumably best be regarded as an object-language. It is then *we,* the *users* of the machine, who must supply the semantical rules. And of course we may do this in many different ways gaining many different interpretations, some of these being normal or standard, others not. Such variety in the number and types of interpretations is to be expected, and indeed is desirable, if the computer is to be of service for different types of purposes. But in these cases it is we who supply the semantical rules, not the computer.

Suppose now the computer language C either contains its

own syntax in some way or other or is augmented so that it does. And then suppose a notion for denotation or designation is added so that semantical rules of the kind described can be handled. This extended computer language, call it *SC*, could accommodate the semantics of the original language *C*, but could not presumably handle the semantics of itself. It would be in effect a semantical metalanguage of the usual kind for *C*. Again, it is *we* who would supply the semantical rules for *SC*, but *SC* would supply them for *C*.

Professor Scriven has raised the point that, in view of the Löwenheim-Skolem theorem, another interpretation for the computer language *C* is always forthcoming in the domain of the natural numbers (assuming of course that *C* exhibits the necessary logical structure). Of course, *we* are free to supply alternative sets of semantical rules if we wish, and some of these may provide an interpretation within a denumerable domain. On the other hand, if the computer language is augmented in the way described to constitute an *SC*, the interpretation and semantical rules of *C* relative to *SC* are fixed. Of course we may reinterpret *SC* ad libitum, and the Löwenheim-Skolem may stipulate the existence of a non-normal interpretation. But if the interpretation of *SC* has been fixed once and for all, then *SC* supplies one and only one interpretation for *C*.

More interesting than languages such as *SC* would be languages capable of *comparing* several object-languages and their interpretations. But very little work has been done by logicians to date in analyzing the structure of such comparative semantical metalanguages.

There have been attempts to construct weaker types of semantics which can in a sense handle their own semantical rules, e.g., a system of Fitch and non-translational semantics. It would be interesting to investigate whether such systems could be handled by a computer and whether or in what way they might prove to be genuinely serviceable.

Note that nothing has been said here concerning semantical rules in the sense of an intensionalist semantics, i.e., rules which purport to give the *meaning* or *intension* of an expression. It is not clear that such rules are ever needed. At any event computers are surely not designed to deal with a host of mysterious new entities such as meanings or intensions. Intensionalist semantics does not appear needed in empirical or theoretical linguistics nor for the logical analysis of science. Nor is it clear that such a semantics is needed in analytic philosophy. The analysis of the use or usage of expressions, and of how they function in pragmatic contexts, presumably takes its place. For such analyses a systematic, and indeed even a quantitative, pragmatics is needed. And this should have the kind of simplicity and sparse ontology that a computer language has.

Chapter 19

Love in a Machine Age

Paul Weiss, *Yale University*

THE PARTICIPANTS IN this symposium all suppose, without question or examination, that one never knows other minds— or, to put it better, other selves with their minds, wills, emotions, etc.—directly. They resolutely put aside the suggestion that there may be an immediate intuition, sympathy, love, or other way of penetrating beyond the outward forms men exhibit. They take it for granted that no one can even reach the edge of another's privacy, that one cannot possibly get below his surface. Most of them speak as if there were no "below"; they are phenomenalists, differeing amongst themselves as to whether or not they want to stress language, behavior, perception, process, or some other horizontally-structured way of dealing with the world. One need remark only that there are other reputable philosophic positions besides phenomenalism—metaphysical theories which insist that there are substances, existentialisms with their acknowledgment of radical privacies, and the like—to know that the common position of these symposiasts is open to question. It is surely unwarranted. I think it is mistaken.

For the moment let us put that matter aside. The question then before us would seem to be fourfold:

1. Do or can machines act in ways which in principle duplicate all the acts of men?
2. If machines could not duplicate all men's actions, would such behavior testify to the presence in men of some inward nature or power?
3. If machines could duplicate all men's actions, would that testify to the presence in the machines of some inward nature or power?
4. Would the incapacity to distinguish the behavior of men from that of machines show that men were indistinguishable from machines?

1. Behavior occurs in space and time. There is no path or rhythm which one can antecedently claim is closed to some machine or other. It seems clear, then, that the behavior of men can in principle be duplicated by machines.

2. Were a man to behave in ways machines could not, this would show only that he was more flexible, had a wider range, than those artifacts had. It would not necessarily show that he had a private nature, mind, or will, and that the machines did not.

3. Were a machine to behave just as men do, it would have to be credited with a mind, if minds are accredited to men; or the men must be denied to have minds, if this is denied to the machine.

4. When I see others I see them from the outside. If this is the only source of my knowledge of them I cannot know whether or not they have minds. Attending only to *other* men, and observing only their behaviors, I cannot find a way of distinguishing them in principle from all possible machines. But if there be another source of knowledge regarding at least one man, which is not grounded on observable public behavior, then men and machines can be distinguished, despite a lack of difference in their behaviors.

I know myself not only from the outside but from within. Others may not know that I have a mind. Since I can see in the mirror, and in other ways, that I behave somewhat like other men, I conclude that they have minds similar to mine, or that I, being alone in having a mind, am a distinct type of being. And if I cannot distinguish men from machines, I must go on to say that the machines too have minds, or that once again I am distinct in type from them.

To say that I am a distinct type of being is to make an ontological claim. To say that I am like others but have a source of information regarding myself which they do not have, is, in contrast, to make an epistemological claim. The former insists on a difference in natures despite all publicly available evidence that can be produced to the contrary. It goes beyond what the facts warrant. The fact that others are not sure that I have a mind does not make me conclude that I do not have one. Rather, I conclude that they are not privy to all my sources of information. (I am glad to find myself in agreement with Dr. Watanabe, particularly in his reply to Dr. Scriven.) The only warranted conclusion to be drawn is the epistemological one that though I am of the same type as they are, as evidenced by our behavior, I have a source of evidence they do not have regarding the existence of my own mind. Since behaviorally they are of the same type as I am, I must credit each of them with a mind as well, and with the capacity to draw on direct evidence showing that he has one.

When machines behave as men do, I ought to say of those artifacts what I now say of those men: that they too have minds. Furthermore, I ought to say that they have wills as well, that they have private selves, secret feelings, a damning conscience, foolish hopes, good and bad intensions, justified and unjustified beliefs. I ought to grant that they have aesthetic sensitivity, the power to speculate, and that they may even have a religious faith. I ought to say of them, as I say of myself, that they are responsible, they are guilty, they are human—all too human. In short, I ought to say that the kind of mind I know I have, must be attributed to all beings which behave as I do, no matter what their origin or appearance— providing behavior is the only criterion for determining whether or not beings are of the same type.

If we now withdraw the supposition shared by the symposiasts and affirm that through love and sympathy we can penetrate beneath the forms men exhibit in public, and can therefore directly reach their private beings, we will still be able to say that, on the basis of bodily behavior alone, we rightly can attribute minds, wills, feelings, etc., to machines, as well as to other men. But we will also be able to say that we cannot love those machines. There will perhaps be some men we will not love, and some machines to which we will become attached. If we find a being which looks and behaves like other men and is beyond our capacity ever to love, we must say of it that it is only a machine, to be placed outside the society where only men can be. Should we find a machine which we can love, we must say of it that it has a human nature and human powers. We will, in short, divide beings, all of whom behave in the same way, into two classes, calling "men" those which are in principle within our powers to love, and calling "machines" those which we cannot possibly love.

Alternatively, I may find that I am unable to love what other men or even machines may report that they can love. If I cannot show that they are in error, I must conclude that they are superior to me. If it is the case that I not only do not, but cannot possibly, love Nazis, or Israelis, or Japanese, or whatever, while others, whether they be machines or men, *can* love them, it is *I* who must be said not to be human. I preserve my humanity only so far as I am one who is intrinsically able to love whatever can be loved.

Both what cannot be loved by one who can love, and what cannot love what can be loved, are less than human, no matter how much they look like and behave like men. Machines fail on both counts. They are not on a footing with me. They are, in short, not human, and thus cannot be said to have selves or minds, rights or responsibilities. The conclusion is not surprising, for we all know that a machine is an artifact whose parts are united so as to enable them to act together, whereas a man is a unity in which the whole governs the behavior of the parts. Only such a unity has a self, with feelings, mind, will, and the rest.

Phenomenalism may reach the point where men and machines are indistinguishable. It must then conclude that machines, like men, have minds, or conversely, that men, like machines, have no minds. The results are equivalent. But love and pity, hate and contempt, will then show how limited phenomenalism is.

Phenomenalism may—inded must—stop short with behavior. It may fail to see but cannot make nonexistent what love discerns. In a machine age, as in any other, it is love that marks the man.

Chapter 20

On the Reduction of Sentiment

Fritz Heider, *University of Kansas*

I WANT TO make a remark that refers in a general way to the mind-body problem. However, I like to avoid getting involved in a consideration of "raw feels" or phenomenal qualities. I shall use as example of a mentalistic concept one taken from the psychology of interpersonal relations. If one studies this field one soon comes to the conviction that it is profitable to conceive of it as being autonomous to a certain degree and not to try to reduce it to terms of a lower level. In many cases we can make sense of interactions between people, and we can find more or less lawful relations concerning these interactions if we use such molar concepts as: one person, A, induces another person, B, to act, A perceives B, A benefits or harms B, A likes B, A thinks B ought to do something, etc. For instance, there seems to be a relation between A's belief concerning B's sentiment toward him, and A's sentiment toward B. If A believes B likes him, he will be inclined to like B.

However, in spite of this heuristically useful assumption of the autonomy of interpersonal phenomena, we cannot help wondering how the terms of this level can be connected with other levels of description, especially with the level of physicalistic description. There seem to be two ways in which this might be done. The first has to do with physicalistic definitions and also with perception; the second has to do with the mind-body problem.

I suppose everybody will agree that the sentence "A likes B" refers to a mental state or disposition. It refers to a sentiment that belongs to person A and is directed toward person B. If we try to define this concept physicalistically we get into all the difficulties that are often connected with such attempts. We can point to a number of effects, consequences, or manifestations to which "A likes B" can lead under certain conditions. For instance, if A likes B, A will be likely to help B, to try to seek B's company, to be bothered by disagreement with B, and so on. But none of these manifestations seem to be co-ordinated to "A likes B" in a one-one way, they will appear only if certain other conditions hold. Furthermore, these manifestations themselves are not defined in terms of a physicalistic language. They cannot easily be identified with specific overt motions of the body. For instance, a great number of such motions, all different from each other, could be described by the statement "A helps B."

Thus, we are confronted with a dilemma: on the one hand we are somehow convinced that "sentiment" is a useful concept, on the other hand we get into trouble when we want to specify the conditions of its application in a simple way.

Essentially the same problem exists in regard to the "perception" of the sentiment of another person. If we take for granted that in many cases it is possible to "perceive" or "cognize" the sentiments of other persons veridically, then we have to assume that the stimuli which mediate this cognition are in some way co-ordinated to the sentiment. But again we seem to be hard put to point to simple cues which would be co-ordinated in a one-one way to the sentiment. Even if we include stimulus patterns in our search we do not succeed. As soon as these patterns are defined as spatio-temporal physical events we lose the correlation to the mental phenomenon.

This leads us to the conclusion that though we have to assume some co-ordination between construct and indices, or between percept and stimulus patterns, this co-ordination is of a peculiar nature. To one construct or percept belong many different patterns of indices or stimuli which cannot be defined physically in a unified way. One might say that the more percepts or judgments are elicited by specific restricted stimulus patterns, the more they are apt to be non-veridical. A person will often go wrong if he always interprets the wrinkling of a forehead as thinking. Veridical perception is anchored in the stimuli in a very complicated way, probably by means of a hierarchical organization of successive classifications.

The second possibility of connecting such a construct as "sentiment" with the level of physicalistic description is to correlate it with processes or structures in the brain. We might guess that again it is very unlikely that we ever will be able to coordinate to a positive sentiment of one person to another a certain process in the brain which is identifiable in physico-chemical terms. There certainly will be found many relations between "A likes B" and locally circumscribed brain processes. But this is a far cry from co-ordinating events of the two levels in a one-one way. It may be that one will find such co-ordinations if one considers configurations, or the role of processes in a wide network of relations. But even that seems to be unlikely at least at present.

Maybe Nicolai Hartmann is right when he says that each level has its own categories and laws. There is no dependency "from above," only one from "below" — that is, while the lower levels are independent of the higher ones, these latter depend to a certain extent on the lower levels. But this dependency is never complete, since there are many events possible in the higher level which cannot be described in terms of the lower one. (See Nicolai Hartmann, *Das Problem des geistigen Seins* [Berlin: de Gruyter, 1933], pp. 15-16.)

For the concept of sentiment, that would, I suppose, mean for instance, that the physical processes co-ordinated to the relations "A likes B because he perceived that B likes him" could never, as general statement, be covered by a description in physical terms. It is true that when we consider a concrete case of this relation we could describe all the manifold processes involved, and describe them in terms of the lower level without leaving any gaps which would have to be filled by the assumption of a non-physical causation. But all the lower-level processes which are co-ordinated to different instances of the molar relation cannot be described in a unified way, they cannot be integrated into the framework of lower-level concepts. And it is unlikely that the thought model of probability which works with correlating higher and lower levels in thermodynamics is very useful when more complicated structures are involved. Of course, that does not mean that one should give up trying to find connections between the levels.

Chapter 21

A Pragmatic Note

Sidney Hook, *New York University*

ALTHOUGH I DO not believe that an account of how concepts are acquired in infancy and early youth is necessarily required in order to understand their meaning and use in subsequent life, there are some gross facts about the way we come to learn about persons, things, and machines which may suggest some fruitful distinctions.

It seems to me significant that all human beings in the first years of their life regard, or behave toward, all identifiable things in their environment as if they possessed human, or—generically speaking—animal, traits. They react to their environment in terms of their own needs and wants and gradually sort out the objects and things which affect them on the basis of differential responses made to their activities. They learn that some objects do not respond like mothers and nurses or whoever it is that attends to their needs. They act as if the block that hurts, the toy that cuts, and the very floor on which they fall have something of the apparent intent which they sense and note in the behavior of the persons who respond to their cries. They gradually learn that some agencies which they took to be human are play*things,* or machines. Sometimes this learning is unduly prolonged when their guardians, to pacify their "disillusion" with untoward behavior, personify objects and machines. But every normal child in time learns the difference.

As the child grows older it applies its concepts to anything which possesses some of the conspicuous traits of the objects that the concept originally denoted. Every man is "Daddy"; every four-legged animal is "Doggy." A large bear and a small bear is a "mother bear and baby bear"; a large tank and a small tank nestling on top of it or beside it is a "mother tank" and a "baby tank."

Children learn the differences between parents and other adults, between human beings and animals, and between both of the latter and machines only through the different consequences which ensue in response to their anticipations of their behavior toward them. A little girl may start out loving her mechanical doll even more than her baby brother but she soon comes to learn that the doll is a machine even if she still loves it more than, or prefers it to, her brother. Some people love their cats and dogs, even their possessions, more than they do their neighbors, although they are perfectly cognizant of the differences between them. Indeed, beyond a certain point the inability to distinguish between them would be a sign of stupidity or insanity.

Another interesting fact or series of facts is bound up with the tendency of children to refer to themselves with the pronoun "me" before they use "I." Everyone will admit that in a certain sense children become "more human" or "more like a person" as they acquire the capacity to react with finer discrimination to the things and persons around them in relation to the achievement of their goals. This is the only way we mark the presence and growth of "awareness."

All this suggests that we do not infer by analogy that other human bodies feel the way we do on the basis of their physical resemblance to us. Long before we are ever in a position to make such comparisons, we are already convinced that humans feel because on the basis of our own feelings toward them we get an answering response which is appropriate—either by way of fulfilling or frustrating—to its quality and object. Dewey maintains that the chief constituent in knowledge of ourselves and others is knowledge of emotions.

At the present time we can easily distinguish between machines and human beings because of their differences in appearance and differences in their response to us. We call some human beings "mechanical" or "machinelike," we say they lack "feeling" or "compassion," because in certain situations they do not make the appropriate response to the things we have undertaken in expectation that their conduct will be influenced by ours. But let us assume that machines will be manufactured of ever greater complexity and ever closer resemblance to human beings. At what point if ever would we regard them as human beings? It seems to me that if they are made to look like human beings, and can act within the range of behavior open to human beings at any time, we would accept them as human beings if they responded the way other human beings do when we set out to determine whether they have "feelings" or "pains" or "*weltschmerz*." The situation would be exactly the same as with James's illustration of "a mechanical sweetheart" which (who) would behave in every respect, including speech, like a natural one.

One might object that a mechanical sweetheart would be different, she would not have feelings. But we would never say that she had no feelings if we did not know she was mechanical. What we really mean is that *our* feelings and actions would be different if we believed she was mechanical, just as they might be if we believed she was Minerva masquerading as a human being. Knowledge of origins often makes a difference—but only to some people. The difference it makes is to them. It is not relevant to the question of whether the thing or person whose origin has been discovered has any particular trait or quality. Some people who see sewage converted into chemically pure water before their eyes will not drink it even when the latter passes all the tests for pure water. Others will. Unless we are to make having a natural origin part of our conception of what it means to be a human being, the question of origin is not relevant. Children learn to distinguish between human beings and machines long before they learn that human beings have a natural origin.

Imagine a situation like this: suppose a kidney made out of plastic could replace a diseased kidney in the body of a friend; suppose in time every organ of his body were replaced by some manufactured part, just as teeth and hair are sometimes replaced today. If his conversation showed he remembered past events, if his actions were congruent with ours or even if he now systematically frustrated what we attempted to do, would we regard him or even refer to him as a "machine"? I doubt it. Reactions to knowledge of origins, independent of current behavior, are evidence only about the individual reacting. There are some bigots who would receive word of an individual's mechanical origin with equanimity, without excluding him from the community of human beings, who would deny human status to those whose racial or religious origins are objectionable to them.

Consider two cases. Someone returns from war to take his place in the community. One day his friends receive word he is an "impostor," that the man he is supposed to be has been killed and his physical double trained and assigned to take his place. How would we find out that the man is an impostor? If the man could pass every test that our neighbors could pass if we tested them for *their* identity, we would accept him as authentic even though it would not be inconceivable that he might still be an impostor and that we might someday discover it.

Suppose now we are told that someone we know is an "impostor," that he is not a human being but a robot sent from outer space. We would dismiss the whole notion as a fantasy. There could be no way of distinguishing him from the rest of us.

Our conclusion that machines have feelings—indeed, that any nonhuman thing in our environment has feelings — depends upon precisely the same set of considerations which lead us to the belief that other human beings have feelings. The exact point at which we conclude that objects hitherto regarded as nonhuman and treated as devoid of feelings have acquired them depends upon complex considerations, all reducible in the end to weather they look like and behave *like* other people we know. A situation described by the Czech dramatist Karel Capek in his *R.U.R.* may someday come to pass.

My own feelings can sometimes be known to others although they cannot experience or have them. Sometimes I may have feelings which I myself do not know or understand. There are situations in which on the basis of all the revelant evidence I am warranted in saying that someone died of fright in his sleep in consequence of a nightmare, or that a man who committed suicide repented of his act at the last moment. The conclusion, right or wrong, is logically of the same order as my assertion that, on the evidence, a man died of thirst in the desert. In no case can I have certain knowledge. If we approach particular problems in the specific contexts in which we are *genuinely puzzled* as to whether a person has feelings (say, a child who does not shrink when his body comes in contact with a burning substance) we can always devise some kind of test which will make one conclusion rather than another more probable. If I am in doubt whether X is really friendly to me, I can observe his actions and examine his words more carefully. If I observe his actions and examine his words to the very end of his days and in all circumstances he has acted in a friendly way, then to doubt whether he really has friendly feelings would either betoken a peculiar use of the word "friendly" or indicate I was the victim of a doubting-mania. *A general theory of the relation of mind and body has no bearing upon any specific problem that arises in the communication of human beings with each other or in their transactions with things in their environment.* No theory can call the existence of my feelings or consciousness into question or lead me to conclude that other human beings are devoid of them, if, to make sense of the occasion, object, and meaning of my own grief or anguish, I must take note of theirs. "To assert," says John Dewey, "that *conscious* behavior is a fiction is to draw a logical deduction from a premise, not to observe a fact. And since the fact of conscious behavior, of observing, analyzing, noting, reasoning, is involved in the whole undertaking, the absurdity of the conclusion shows the falsity of the premise."

The problem of the existence of other minds in general— as distinct from whether this or that person or machine "has" a mind or feeling—is no more intelligible than is the problem of the existence of an external world, as distinct from whether this or that thing exists within it.

PART THREE

Concept-Formation

Chapter 22

Concept-Formation in Philosophy and Psychology

Stephen Toulmin, *University of Leeds*

FROM THE TIME of Socrates, philosophers have been recurrently concerned with the analysis of concepts, notions, or the meanings and uses of linguistic expressions. At some periods, this inquiry has been closely associated with contemporary ideas about psychology: one thinks, for instance, of Aristotle's *De Anima* and of such men as Locke, Hume, and Hartley. But in recent years, since the development of theoretical psychology as a discipline nominally (at any rate) independent of philosophy, philosophers and psychologists have for the most part gone their separate ways. The philosophical analysis of concepts has, in particular, been vigorously separated from the study of their acquisition, and learning-theory (to say nothing of other branches of psychology) has been held to be irrelevant to an understanding of our concepts in their adult forms.

The chief purpose of the present paper is to suggest that this separation has been too complete. Even for strictly philosophical ends (I shall argue) it is worth studying the manner in which our concepts develop; such a study can often bring to light a certain 'logical stratification' within our concepts, notions, or language-uses, which is essential to their proper understanding; and a recognition of this stratification has possible morals for psychology as well as philosophy.

I

In what follows, I shall first trace out the manner in which one sample family of concepts develops, so as to draw attention to their internal stratification; next, I shall discuss the bearing of this analysis-in-depth on some long-standing philosophical issues; and finally, in the light of this example, I shall hint briefly at the terms on which relations between philosophical analysis and psychological theory might be reestablished.

Let me begin with a word about my procedure. It has been customary for analytical philosophers to characterize concepts by citing contexts in which they would, or would not naturally be at home. Meaning what they do, our words will appear congruous in certain linguistic collocations, incongruous in others: we know what it is for a man to "learn something gradually," but not for him to "know it gradually," and the latter incongruity shows something about the concept of knowledge (the meaning of the verb 'to know'). This method of philosophizing was clearly advocated as early as Plato's *Sophist,* and it has recently acquired the dignity of a title: Gilbert Ryle calls it the method of 'sentence-frames.' It raises, however, three difficulties. In the first place, it leaves open the question why (as opposed to whether) we find any particular collocation of words congruous or incongruous; secondly, it provides no way, other than forcible reiteration, of arguing with a man who professes to find congruous some expression (e.g., "He knows his multiplication table gradually") which we find incongruous or vice versa; and thirdly, it explicates any interesting concept only by collecting the aggregate of sentence-frames in which the corresponding words can or cannot figure, and does not explain the nature of the relationship between these congruities and incongruities.

Ludwig Wittgenstein's method of 'language-games' has (as I see it) the virtue of avoiding these difficulties. To characterize a specific language-use was, for him, to place it not just in a linguistic context but in a behavioral one: to show the pattern of conduct against the background of which the concept has to be understood. Congruities and incongruities are to be explained in terms of the *point* of the behavior-pattern in question: seeing them against this behavioral background enables one to understand, and so to agree on them. And finally, what is most relevant to my present purpose—it turns out to be necessary to characterize all philosophically-interesting concepts in terms not of one single language-game but of whole sequences of them. We acquire such concepts as knowledge, intention, number, probability, and the good by stages, and the logical character of the mature concepts is in certain important respects the product of these sequences of stages.

But surely, some may ask at once, nothing logical could be dependent on mere facts about learning and child-psychology? This is not what I shall be claiming: rather, it is that the internal logical complexities of a concept can in certain respects prescribe the order in which the learning-process must be gone through, if we are to be satisfied that the learner has got the concept in question. Certain later stages in the sequence can be gone through only by someone who has already passed through the earlier, the learning of the more sophisticated language-games presuppose an undertaking of the simpler. It is in this sense that I shall be speaking of our concepts as having a 'logical stratification.'

For purposes of illustration, I shall take the family of terms: 'want,' 'wish,' 'desire,' 'choose,' 'prefer.' (There is no special virtue in choosing terms which themselves have psychological associations and relevance: the same points could be made about other families of concepts. But one can perhaps illustrate the central issues quite neatly by taking this example.) We can begin by isolating one deliberately simplified situation in which such terms are used; and then gradually introduce complexities absent in the first situation, so as to show how distinctions originally without an application come to acquire a sense.

(A) Suppose, then, that two of us are seated in a restaurant, and the waitress comes up to our table bearing a tray on which there arc six cups each of tea and coffee. She asks me: "Which do you want, tea or coffee?" and I reply: "I want coffee." Several things now need to be remarked on: (a) in this situation, I will interpret the waitress' question as an invitation to make a choice, and she will understand my answer as the expression of a choice; (b) there will accordingly be no place for her to ask: "How do you *know* that you want coffee?" for I could only reply: "What do you mean? You asked me to choose and I chose"; (c) since the situation is one in which it is (for all that has been indicated) quite indifferent which I choose, there will also be no obvious occasion for her to ask: "Do you *really* want coffee?"—this question would imply some ground for disregarding my choice, of a sort we have not yet allowed for; and (d) if, instead of answering at once, I hesitated and vacillated and ended by saying: "Tea—coffee—tea—coffee—I don't know which I want," this would be put down as a weakness, not in my powers of observation or interpretation, so much as in my powers of decision.

These four point are all connected with the essentially *executive* character of this particular example. The first-person present indicative "I want . . ." can function like "I choose . . ." as a straight act of choice, selection, or request, as the linguistic counterpart of pointing, taking, or otherwise indicating the object or item in question. In this respect, of course, other tenses and persons of the verb differ from the first-person present indicative: "I wanted coffee" does not mean the same as "I chose coffee," nor "He wants coffee" as "He is choosing coffee." Yet one might perhaps hint already that there is some essential connection between the ideas of wanting and choosing: at any rate, to the extent of saying that "I wanted coffee" entails "I would have chosen coffee, if the occasion had arisen and everything else had been equal," and "He wants coffee" entails "He would choose coffee, given the opportunity and no other consideration."

(B) Our first example leaves no occasion for distinguishing between expressed and unexpressed wishes. Yet there is clearly one sense in which the *esse* of a choice is *exprimi* and another in which it makes sense to speak of making a choice but leaving it unexpressed, e.g., through deferring the moment of expression. If children are picking up sides for a game of baseball, each captain will take it in turns to choose (name his choices) and for one of them to say: "I had already chosen Billy, but I hadn't shown or said so" will not be understood: unless the choice was indicated *somehow,* there was no choice. Yet a child who understands 'choosing' in this sense may be introduced to a new sense of the term, by being shown a tray of objects and given the instruction: "Choose one, but don't say or show in any way which you choose." Although this instruction may be self-contradictory in terms of the previous sense of the word 'choose,' he will soon grasp what is meant, viz., that he is required, say, to decide now and indicate his decision later. But notice: the two senses are not entirely on a par. We would expect a child to catch on to the notion of 'unexpressed choice' only if we were already satisfied that he knew what it was to make a choice in the simpler and more basic sense.

With this reflection in mind, suppose the waitress in our restaurant holds out the tray to us as before and says: "Make up your mind which you want, and I'll come back for your order in a minute." Now the idea of a wish or desire becomes associated, not just with simple acts of choice, but also with unexpressed choices, preferences, and selections, and so the connection comes to be made between "I want coffee" in the executive sense of our first example, "I want coffee, though I'm not going to tell her yet," and "I wanted coffee, even though I didn't say so." Notice two things however: (a) with wishes, as with choices, the distinction between unexpressed and expressed wishes is logically dependent on the simpler idea of a wish as something we utter, show, or otherwise indicate; (b) so far, we have introduced only the distinction between expressed and unexpressed wishes: to introduce the distinction between sincere and simulated wishes requires a further step.

(C) To see how this further step is taken, modify the initial example again. Suppose now, for instance, that instead of there being six cups each of tea and coffee, there are six of tea and only one of coffee. The waitress asks: "Which do you want?" and I reply: "I want tea." In the new context, my answer can be queried in a novel way: whereas to begin with we supposed the situation to be one in which (for all that was indicated) it was quite indifferent which I chose, now there is one clear respect in which everything is *not* equal, so that my choice is not between two quite indifferent alternatives. If someone now asks me, "Did you *really* want tea?" the question will accordingly have a point: it will naturally be understood as referring to the respect in which things were not after all indifferent—"Would you have chosen tea, if everything else had been equal, or did you do so only out of politeness, so as not to take the last cup of coffee?" There may, of course, be other reasons why my choice is not entirely equal —e.g., I may believe that coffee is more fattening than tea, even though I would prefer coffee on grounds of taste alone. All this is essential for my argument is this: that to question the sincerity of my expressed wish is to imply that in *some* respect the situation is not entirely equal, and that as a result my choice is not what it would otherwise have been.

Now, simulating a desire is a comparatively sophisticated activity, which presupposes the ability to express straightforward desires or wishes. This being so, the distinction between real and simulated desires, like that between expressed and unexpressed ones, is a derivative one. A man might understand what it was to have and express straightforward wishes or desires without knowing what it was to put on a pretense of them, but to be able to simulate desires one must understand what the straightforward expression of a desire is. The distinction between real and simulated desires is, logically speaking, on a higher stratum than the idea of simple wishes.

(D) This analysis of the internal stratification of the ideas of wishing/wanting/choosing/desiring/preferring could be carried further. Proceeding in the direction of further complexity, one could consider how the additional step is taken by which we come to distinguish between 'conscious' and 'unconscious desires.' It scarcely needs emphasizing that, in terms of the example considered so far, the idea of 'unconscious' desire involves as much of a prima facie contradiction as that of an 'unexpressed choice' in terms of the primary sense of 'choose': yet in this case, too, the step on to understanding the point of the puzzling phrase is easily taken, once the phenomenon of 'repression' (with the associated displacement of one's desires) is recognized for what it is. It may however be worth remarking that, on this analysis, the doctrine that there can be no unconscious desire without a previous repression would become a truth of definition: it would be a result of our criterion for distinguishing between actions springing from drives and impulses that had never been a part of one's overt, voluntary behavior, and compulsive actions associated with desires which were now unconscious, because repressed.

Alternatively, one might ask whether our first example was really simple enough to be the starting-point. Surely (it may be said) we can express desires even without yet being able to exercise the power of choice. So perhaps we should take, as a simpler case, the child who is offered a drink on a take-it-or-leave-it basis—"Do you want a drink?" as the cup is held out: "Answer Yes or No." And even simpler, it might said, is the case of the child who cannot yet talk or even gesture, yet of whom we might readily say, using the third-person, that *he* wanted a drink. Yet, is this last case really simpler? It is arguable that it is logically a derivative one, and that in so speaking we are interpreting the situation in the light of the analogy with the case of an articulate agent—"If the child were grown-up enough to talk or gesture, it would ask for a drink." Only if 'want' is taken as equivalent to 'need' instead of 'wish for' or 'desire' will there be a simple sense in which we can talk of an infant's 'wanting' a drink: of course 'want' does have both these aspects, and this makes its possible to slide without thinking between 'needing a drink' and 'wishing for a drink.'

One last point should be made about these examples, before we go on to consider their wider relevance. I have tried to show that, in the philosophical analysis of concepts, it is worth while arranging one's examples in order, so as to show relations between cases of different degree of complexity, and bring out the ways in which one sense or use of a term may be logically dependent, or parasitic on a simpler sense or use: this may help to show why some locutions are congruous, other incongruous, and on what conditions a distinction comes to have a sense in some situations that it would lack in others. But I have *not* been arguing that there is a unique sequence of examples, or types of situation, through which we must proceed in order, if we are to acquire any particular concept or family of concepts. There will presumably be parallel but related sequences of situations/usages/language-games/examples which we master in coming to grasp the full meaning of most concepts or concept-families; the logical stratification that I have tried to establish will be found within each sequence, and the fully-developed concept will be, as it were, a tree, with a limited number of primitive types of situation and language-game developing into a much larger range of uses, as a result of successive branching at each logical level.

II

The picture that I have here attempted to sketch, of the manner in which concepts develop ontogenetically, suggests lines of attack on a number of philosophical problems that are resistant to more conventional sorts of philosophical analysis. In this section let us consider, first, the general implications of this view, and secondly, some problems that arise particularly in the case of psychological concepts.

To begin with the general point: In many branches of philosophy the disputes have turned on the comparative merits of different views about goodness, truth, knowledge, probability, intentions, or whatever, and these views have been considered to be necessarily rivals and in opposition to one another. Is 'probability' a matter of relative frequencies or of states of belief—indeed, is it essentially a mathematical notion or not? Does 'goodness' express fitness for a purpose, an attitude of approval, or the universalizability of a motive? Are one's desires, intentions, sensations, pains, and the like of the nature of dispositions or private introspectables? In each case it is possible to get into rigidly-entrenched positions in defense of views to which some examples appear to give unquestionable support while other examples appear to be equally fatal.

What requires to be made clearer in such a situation is the mutual relations of the examples by which the seemingly rival views are backed up. So long as they are considered 'in the flat,' so to say, there seems no way of reconciling the rival theories short of hitting on some exceedingly ingenious and hitherto unnoticed 'philosophical hypothesis' of the sort Professor C. D. Broad is always hoping to find. But perhaps the very appearance of rivalry between the theories can now be removed. For if the concepts around which philosophical disputes have raged are as complex as I have supposed, they should not be thought of as having *single* functions, capable of being completely characterized in a simple formula or doctrine: rather we should expect their functions to be manifold, corresponding to the various trunks and branches of the ontogenetic 'tree.'

One can illustrate this point in the case of the term 'probability.' Here we have, on the one hand, a multitude of practical activities in which there figures the family of concrete terms 'probable,' 'probably,' 'probability,' 'chance,' 'likelihood' and so on; and on the other, a number of rival philosophical theories which explicate probability in terms either of frequencies or of partial entailments or of degrees of belief. At best, it is suggested, we can avoid the conflicts between these theories by distinguishing different senses of the terms in question, and recognizing that they harbor unsuspected ambiguities.

That is surely not the best we can do in this case. For to speak of 'ambiguities' here is to ignore the organic connections between the multitude of uses to which our family of probability-terms is put. Rather, one needs to follow out the development of these concepts from their elementary beginnings up to their most sophisticated and complex uses in statistical and physical theory, so as to see how the different uses branch off from one another, and how much of the logical character of the terms at one level is carried over to the higher levels. This will mean conducting one's analysis in the reverse order from that which is sometimes considered appropriate: instead of concentrating on mathematical and scientific uses and ignoring as crude and irrelevant approximations the 'prescientific' uses of probability-language, we shall have to isolate for a start examples which will illustrate the logical germ or seedling from which the more complex uses in due course branch off at higher levels, and present the example on which the rival philosophical doctrines have traded as subsequent development in different directions of the same seminal notions. This is the justification for paying attention to something that might otherwise appear philosophically trifling—the uses of the adverb 'probably': what saves such a study from being footling is the possibility of displaying other more complex uses of our probability-concepts as organic developments from this common seminal beginning. Cut off from this root, talk about frequencies, say, would be irrelevant to questions about probabilities: if probabilities become in some contexts a matter for mathematical calculation, that is because statistical theory and combinatorial analysis have been given applications to the measurement and estimation of probabilities—have been grafted, so to speak, on the tree whose logical beginnings can be studied by looking at the adverb 'probably.'

To turn next to another family of concepts, more closely connected with our earlier analysis. The ambition to characterize knowledge, sensations, desires, intentions, or other psychological terms by simple formulate is bound to lead to 'aporia'—as it led Socrates in the *Theaetetus*—if each term in practice lends itself to a variety of stratified applications and its logical character changes in essential respects as one passes from one level to another. The term 'choice,' as we saw, may refer to an essentially public action (the first sense above), or it may be used, in an alternative way, in cases where either either there is no public action, or the action is deferred. That being so, it can hardly be helpful to define 'choosing' in such a way as to require this to be either a public physical action or a 'mental act'—either definition will rule out some possible and legitimate application of the term. And 'choice' is a comparatively simple term: when we pass on to 'wish,' 'want,' and 'desire' and consider the variety of cases in which these terms are employable, it will become even more misleading to produce simple definitions or characterizations. A wish may be an essentially public expression, like a choice of the first kind, or it may be something we leave unexpressed, or express insincerely, or out of politeness, or "against our real wishes." A want may be something we diagnose in others regardless of their actual expressions of desire. Yet again, unless there is some feature we can point to in the situation to justify our disregarding an expressly declared wish or want, the declaration must have a certain primacy and authority, just because it is each man's own business to announce his own plans and intentions—the executive character of our seminal example is not entirely canceled out as a result of the complexities subsequently superimposed on it.

Least of all can one hope to find a simple term with which we can characterize the essential nature of *all* psychological concepts, or produce a general solution applicable to all such concepts of the epistemological problems they raise. The term 'disposition,' for instance, may serve us well when explaining what it means to call a man 'irritable' or 'equable,' and it may be extended usefully for some purposes to cover also skills, habits, and character. Certainly in all these classes of case it can be said that we know about ourselves in the same way as we do about other people. Whether a man is unusually clever or equable or considerate is something about which he is in no privileged position to speak: he must decide in the light of the evidence of his own performances and behavior, and indeed his own estimates are likely, if anything, to be *less* reliable than other people's. On the other hand, there are undoubtedly many terms over which the epistemological situation is different. Whether I have pains in my joints, spots before my eyes, or a green patch in my visual field, or whether I enjoy contemporary jazz, want a drink of water, or intend to visit Salt Lake City, these are things about which what I say carries special weight and has special authority.

Even these examples, however, are not all alike. In the case of pains and sensations a strong case can be made out for saying that the special authority each man has to speak for himself springs from the fact that he alone has access to the private introspectables—the pains and sensations—which are in question. Yet over wishes and intentions, I shall argue, our special authority has a different source. The doctrine of 'privileged access' interprets this authority as the authority of an *expert:* suppose I had captured on an uninhabited island the only known specimen of a species of green macaw and kept it in a secret room which I alone ever entered, all questions about the habits, plumage, and anatomy of the bird would have to be referred to me—I would be 'the authority,' as being the only person having access to the crucial evidence. Yet there is another kind of authority beside that of the expert, viz., the authority of the *official.* For certain legal purposes, a document will not have any effect unless it carries, say the state Governor's signature. If he writes on the document the words: "I approve, N. Rockefeller," he does so in virtue, and as an exercise, of his authority. He has the authority to perform this executive act, so what he says, goes.

Now our own study of 'wants' and 'desires' brought to light at the very beginning of the development of these concepts a similar executive element. To say what you want was, in our simplest case, to make a choice: to make use of the opportunity to choose which is given you by the question "Which do you want?" Since you have been given the choice, it is your business to make it, and what you name or point to thereupon becomes irrefutably your choice. And as to his own wishes, desires, plans, and intentions, it is, I should be prepared to argue, each man's business to speak *for his own part:* in speaking authoritatively about our own wishes or plans we are exercising our rights rather than posing as experts. Suppose a mother and her teenage daughter are in the restaurant, as before, and the mother says to the waitress: "My daughter wants milk." What the daughter will complain of in this case is not her mother's bad guesswork, but rather the usurpation of her right to speak on her own behalf.

There is room accordingly, for some first-person present-indicative psychological statements to have special authority, without any references to introspectables or privileged access being necessary. To say this is not to imply that we *never* make up our minds what we want, say, in ways that involve some element of introspection. But it *is* to say that we can have and express wishes, desires, and even wants, without needing to refer to inner introspectable pangs of the sort which sometimes accompany, say, hunger. To know your own mind, to know what you want, is essentially to be able to take effective decisions, rather than to introspect skillfully—the effectiveness of the decision being measured by its power to satisfy the desire concerned for the time being.

III

The central point of this paper has been to establish the existence of a 'logical stratification' within many of our concepts. This claim would be refuted if it could be shown that it was actually quite indifferent in what order one was introduced to the various aspects of one concept. The indifference in question is, of course, a logical indifference. Suppose a child were taught to say (out of politeness) "I want tea," whenever there was only one cup of the alternative available, *before* learning to use the rubric "I want ———" as the expression of a straightforward desire; the result, I am arguing, would be that he had acquired a stylized behavior-pattern, rather than learning under what circumstances to avoid expressing his desires. No doubt it *makes sense* to suppose that he might learn at one stroke both how to express, and when to avoid expressing, the same straightforward wish; but it would be highly surprising if he in fact did so, and we should require some other demonstration that he now understood what a straightforward wish was before believing that he had. To that extent, the logical stratification would still hold: we could accept that he understood the more complex notion of 'simulated wishes' only on the assumption that he understood the simpler practice of expressing one's wishes quite straightforwardly.

With this idea of 'logical stratification' in mind, let us reconsider what relevance philosophical analysis and psychological theory have to each other. So long as philosophers concerned themselves only with our fully-developed concepts, they could afford to ignore the psychologists' inquiries: using a concept was one thing, acquiring it was something quite different. If, however, the process of development of our concepts—the sequence of language-games by which we acquire them—has a bearing on their final character, we shall not be able to keep up so watertight a barrier between philosophical analysis and learning-theory. Though in one sense the *manner* in which we acquire our concepts may be irrelevant to philosophy (whether we learn this or that aspect quickly or slowly, at the age of four or six) *what it is* that we learn will now be part of the common stock of psychological theory and analytical philosophy. For instance, if 'wishes' are indeed such that the simple expression of a wish is more a fundamental idea than that of an unexpressed or simulated wish, this fact will now be relevant both for the philosophical characterization of the concept and when planning a study of the relevant learning-processes. The psychology of the intellect will be inseparable from the analysis of our concepts.

One can perhaps go further. For there is something to be learned from considering what the consequences are of being introduced to a concept in a way which runs counter to its normal stratification: this will provide us with a means of recognizing certain characteristic kinds of *mis*conception. We asked, for instance, what would be the natural thing to say of someone in whom the capacity to 'simulate wishes' was inculcated either before, or to such an extent as to suppress, the spontaneous expression of straightforward wishes. Such a person will, in one important sense, *not know* what it is to 'want' things in a straightforward way—will always be looking in every situation for social cues indicating what to choose, and will know what to say he 'wants' only when he finds some such clue. Carried to extremes, such a state of mind can become positively neurotic: this lends point to the suggestion made earlier, about the way in which the notion of 'unconscious desires' is related to that of normal desires and wishes. It also shows the justice of regarding neuroses as eventually involving misconceptions about one's personal relations, as some quite orthodox psychoanalysts (such as Money-Kyrle) have recently suggested. At a certain level, therefore, conceptual analysis, learning theory and psychoanalytic theory may even converge.

Chapter 23

Concept-Formation in Philosophy and Psychology

B. F. Skinner, *Harvard University*

THE RELEVANCE OF Toulmin's analysis to "philosophical ends" is of less interest to a psychologist than the methods he uses. Like Bertrand Russell in *An Inquiry into Meaning and Truth* and the later Wittgenstein, Toulmin sees the need to go beyond verbal context to the situation "in which a term is used." In so doing he finds himself, as they did, in psychology. The terms, principles, and formulation he uses are therefore subject to scrutiny from the point of view of psychological, rather than logical, method.

(1) Terms

Toulmin does not go very far toward reducing linguistic activity to verbal behavior. He describes a few instances of verbal behavior in casual terms. This constitutes a useful subject matter to the extent that any two readers would infer important features of these episodes with consistency. But he is not concerned with relating verbal responses as such to identifiable aspects of situations. The terms he has chosen to analyze (*want, wish, desire, choose,* and *prefer*) are also part of his own psychological vocabulary, as are such expressions as *sincere* (or *simulated*) *wish, conscious* (or *unconscious*) *desire, intention, meaning, hesitation, vacillation, powers of observation,* and so on. These are not part of an agreed-upon psychological repertoire, and no matter how readily they may seem to suggest basic psychological states or processes, they are not necessarily the terms most suitable for a description of behavior. In *Verbal Behavior* I have suggested how the same subject matter may be reduced to terms and principles derived from an experimental analysis of behavior, where the formulation can be rigorously tested in actual prediction and control, but this is not the place to re-write Toulmin's paper in such terms.

(2) Principles

Psychologists themselves may well be responsible for Toulmin's overemphasis on the *acquisition* of behavior. It is often important to ask whether a particular feature of a stimulus is important to an organism, or more important than some other feature. Until recently, the almost inevitable procedure was to follow the course of the process through which an organism came to make a distinction between features. Speed of acquiring a discrimination or a concept was taken as a measure of the importance or significance of defining properties. But the external conditions which bring learning about do not become inactive when learning has been completed. A pattern or feature continues to be significant in controlling behavior, and techniques are now readily available for analyzing the extent of the control, quite apart from the acquisition of a concept.

Since the *genetic* element is present only in one phase of the control exerted by a stimulus, the stratification, possibly of logical significance, that Toulmin demonstrates in the process of acquisition is of doubtful value. As he himself indicates, it is not necessary that a complex concept be approached along any one channel, but he seems to insist that way stations in any channel are nevertheless logically simple versions or components of the ultimate concept. But logical complexities of the concept need not prescribe the genetic order, and there is no necessary relation among various kinds of genetic order. Linguists have often traced the *historical* development of a complex concept, but an individual at a particular epoch does not by any means climb the family tree. The more or less *accidental* sequences of events through which a child acquires a working concept of "inertia," for example, need not follow the sequence traceable in the history of mechanics, and there is no particular point in duplicating either the historical or the accidental order in constructing an expeditious *tutorial* sequence to be used in teaching the concept.

(3) Formulation

Two points may be mentioned. Toulmin does not distinguish clearly between the development of a given form of behavior and the development of the description of that behavior by the behaver himself. The five terms he examines are basically self-descriptive. Saying "I want a drink of water" is more than a request, even though under common circumstances it functions as such. It reports not an act but a probability of a class of acts. "I choose" describes an act but specifically in a situation involving at least two responses. The difficulties which Toulmin encounters in changing tenses or speakers disappear when the distinction between behavior and self-description of behavior is made clear.

As a second difficulty, Toulmin's vocabulary makes it impossible for him to achieve an effective empirical analysis of verbal behavior in which an act, verbal or otherwise, is related to the circumstances under which it occurs and to its consequences. In one of his examples the verbal response "Tea, please" may have two consequences: it may produce a cup of tea for the speaker and may injure a friend by depriving him of the chance to ask for tea. These are separate consequences, having different effects on the probability that the response "Tea, please" will be emitted. Under better conditions we could demonstrate this in a simple way. Insofar as the response is strong because it produces a cup of tea, we can alter its probability by making tea more or less reinforcing. Thus, by depriving the speaker of tea we can increase the probability that the response will occur, or by giving him a large quantity of tea before he speaks we can reduce the probability of the response. Insofar as the response has the effect of injuring a friend, we can alter its strength by altering the speaker's tendency to work injury. If we can persuade the friend to insult the speaker, for example, or in some other way increase the latter's tendency to take revenge, the probability of saying "Tea, please" will rise.

Interpretations of this sort are easily misunderstood. We have not, indeed, actually deprived or satiated the speaker with tea or altered his attitude toward an acquaintance, and we have no quantitative measure of his tendency to say "Tea, please." But the analysis is not therefore meaningless or spuriously scientific. In discussing an example of this sort we are not interested in predicting or controlling an instance of behavior, but merely in treating it as if we were. This is what the physicist does when he offers a casual explanation of some occurrence in daily life. If the handle of a tea cup has been satisfactorily mended when the cup was cold but breaks easily when the cup is full of tea, a physicist may hazard the suggestion that different rates of thermal expansion on the two sides of the joint, or between cup and cement, are responsible for separating the cement from the cup. A captious critic might object that he has not measured the temperature on the two sides of the joint, probably knows little or nothing about the coefficients of expansion of the materials of which the cup and cement are constructed, is only guessing about the adhesive properties of the cement, and so on. Nevertheless we accept the explanation as plausible and possibly as useful in affecting some future course of action because we know the physicist is speaking against an experimental background in which surfaces in contact have indeed been studied under various changes of temperature, in which the binding properties of adhesives have been studied, and so on. He will admit that he has not told us very much about this particular instance, and logicians and psychologists alike ought to admit, similarly, that nothing much of importance *can* be said about an episode in which a waitress offers a customer a choice of tea or coffee. These are not rigorously prescribed circumstances and we must not expect to do very much with them with rigor. The test of an adequate analysis of verbal behavior must be made under other circumstances. Meanwhile, interpretation of a casual instance in the light of such an analysis has its value in estimating the extent to which current terms and techniques are adequate. Toulmin's comments have neither the sanction nor support of a careful test under better conditions.

Chapter 24

Psychology and the Analysis of Concepts in Use

Ernest Nagel, *Columbia University*

MR. TOULMIN'S EXPLICITLY stated aim in his paper is to show that by studying the way in which our concepts are acquired, light can often be thrown on various "logical stratifications" within them which are essential to their proper understanding. He believes, moreover, that such a psychological-historical approach can answer fundamental questions about the logical structure of concepts which cannot be resolved by the currently fashionable purely linguistic mode of analysis. Although I share Mr. Toulmin's sense of the importance of familiarity with the behavioral (and not simply the linguistic) contexts in which linguistic expressions acquire their use, I nevertheless do not think he has made any case for his central contention.

Mr. Toulmin's argument in the first part of his paper, dealing with the stratifications of certain psychological concepts, seems to me both puzzling and utterly unconvincing. For example, he presents the order in which the notion of wanting something (as expressed in overtly adopting one of several given alternatives) and the notion of having an unexpressed wish *might* be learned, notes that the second of these is logically more complex than the first, and apparently thinks he has thereby shown that the first notion *must* be acquired before the second can be understood. But it is obscure to me how a purely speculative reconstruction of a possible learning-process constitutes pertinent evidence for the presumably *factual thesis* Mr. Toulmin is aiming to establish. His apparent answer to this query is that no one would be convinced that a person has acquired the notion of an unexpressed wish unless the individual already understood (and had therefore previously learned) the notion of an expressed want. However, why *could* not an individual grow up in a society in which this temporal order of learning is reversed? Perhaps the answer is that such a conjecture is logically impossible. I am not concerned to dispute the correctness of this answer; but if it is the one Mr. Toulmin would advance (and I can think of no alternative to it compatible with his principal thesis), two points become clear: (a) Mr. Toulmin is employing the outcome of a purely logical analysis (as distinct from a professed psychological-historical one) of the assumed meanings of certain expressions to prescribe the temporal order in which the uses of those expressions must presumably be learned, and not vice versa; (b) accordingly, since the "light" which a study of the way concepts are acquired supposedly sheds on the logical stratification of the concepts under discussion is thus entirely spurious, the sole function in Mr. Toulmin's discussion of his speculative reconstruction of a learning-process is at best the *pedagogic* one of providing a temporal model for certain logical relations between concepts, with a view to an easier recognition of those relations.

It is too well known to require illustration, moreover, that many concepts can be analyzed in several alternate ways, so that the particular "logical stratification" attributed to such concepts depends on which other concepts are taken as primitive in the analysis. Is one analysis in this case to be counted as inherently better or sounder than another, if the hierarchy of subordinate notions in the first but not in the second corresponds to the temporal order in which the corresponding subordinate notions have been acquired? To assent to this would be to court absurdities, utterly remote from Mr. Toulmin's thought. But what if each of the alternative heirarchies in such variant analyses of a concept were to correspond to alternate ways in which the concept has actually been acquired? Mr. Toulmin explicitly denies that "there is a unique sequence of examples, or types of situation, through which we must proceed in order, if we are to acquire any particular concept or family of concepts." However, if he is correct in this denial, as I believe he is, nothing in his central thesis seems to me to be left standing.

Nevertheless, Mr. Toulmin recommends his approach as a way of assessing, if not resolving, various philosophical disputes. In particular, he thinks it is insufficient to outflank the frequently futile debates over the proper analysis of probability by merely recognizing, as many students suggest, that the word "probable" has several distinct meanings, since to do no more than that is to ignore the "organic connections" between various meanings of the term. He recommends that we ought to trace out the evolution of these concepts "from their elementary beginnings to their most sophisticated and complex uses in statistical and physical theory," in order to show how they have branched off from a common logical germ and "how much of the logical character of the terms at one level is carried over to the higher levels."

The value of such a historico-analytic study of probability-terms seems to be beyond dispute. For among other things such a study can present a range of different but historically important uses of those terms, and it can supply indispensable data for explaining how and why the terms became associated with divergent uses. Nevertheless, there are limits to what such a study can accomplish. It cannot legislate the senses in which the terms are to be currently employed in the contexts in which they currently occur, nor can it establish just what is the logical stratification of any of these current senses. It may indeed be the case, as Mr. Toulmin appears to hold, that the "logical germ" of the notion of probability embedded in some contemporary statistical research may be found in prescientific uses of the term—conceivably in the ways children use the term in kindergarten or perhaps even earlier. But surely there is no necessity that this is the case, or that, more generally, every current technical use of "probable" must be a "graft" upon a more primitive one occurring in some temporally prior experience of those now employing the term in a special technical sense. To vary the illustration, it would certainly result in nothing but serious misconceptions if one sought to construe the meaning of the expression "curvature of space" in current physical cosmology as a "graft" upon the meaning most of us acquired first when we learned to associate the word "curvature" with certain characteristics of lines and surfaces—even though as a matter of actual history the notion of the curvature of space was developed in anology to the previously acquired notion of the curvature of a surface.

In short, an account of the historical development of a term is no substitute for an analysis of its current uses or functions, and throws no light upon the logical stratifications of those uses. In my opinion, Mr. Toulmin has misstated what I think is an excellent case for the importance of studying concepts in terms of their functions in behavioral settings, by confounding the question of how concepts are learned with the very different question of how concepts are used.

Chapter 25

The Stratification of Concepts

N. R. Hanson, *Indiana University*

TWO INTERPRETATIONS OF Toulmin's thesis are possible. He might be articulating a bland truism that no scholar of maturity would dream of denying. On the other hand he may be advancing a shockingly unique thesis, one which, if true, would be profoundly important for philosophy. Consider these interpretations more fully.

What *could* Toulmin mean? He might only be reminding us that (1) facts about the genesis and the growth of a concept could be relevant to a fuller understanding of that concept; or he might mean that (2) from an examination of the genesis and the growth of a concept one can *infer* to the present logical structure of that concept.

Now, as already intimated, (1) is true. It is incontestable. Anyone who claimed that knowledge of the history of an event contributes *nothing* to our understanding of that event would be adopting a most bizarre position. So (1), presumably, cannot be Toulmin's thesis, since no thinking man would propose the antithesis. If it were his thesis, it would be neither novel nor interesting; and we have learned to expect novel and interesting things from Mr. Toulmin.

Position (2) must be the one Toulmin is advancing. And if he is correct in doing so, a lot of rethinking about the nature of philosophy in our times will be in order.

However, (2) raises difficulties far greater than any that are resolved by Toulmin's analysis.

Any inquiry into the growth and genesis of a concept will be a contingent inquiry. Propositions which purport to describe the history of an idea are such that their negations, if false at all, are but contingently false. These negations may fail to square with the facts, but they will be logically consistent. Historical statements are always synthetic.

But a claim as to what is or is not the logical structure of a concept—if such a claim be true at all—could not but be true. The logician, or the analytic philosopher, is not doing natural history when he describes the internal logic of a concept. He is, rather, concerned with argument, with form, with the question of what would follow from assuming that the logical structure was *this* way rather than *that*. A statement which purports to set out the stratification or structure of a concept is such that its negation is logically *inconsistent*—or it as least conceptually quite untenable. It would be an elementary mistake to suppose that the historian's comments on the genesis of an idea were logically of the same type as the logician's comments on the stratification of an idea.

Toulmin's thesis, therefore, if it is meant to be the bold and interesting one I suspect he has in mind and not the featureless truism which was set out in interpretation (1), must consist in the claim that one might legitimately *infer* from a statement whose negation is consistent, to a statement whose negation is inconsistent—or is at least conceptually untenable. In other words, Toulmin is arguing for the legitimacy of an inference across logical types, from a merely contingent proposition to a necessary proposition. (A necessary proposition here can either be one whose negation is demonstrably self-contradictory, or one whose negation, although not self-contradictory, is conceptually untenable. Thus, 'No surface is both red and green at *t*' is necessary in the last sense.)

The plausibility of Professor Toulmin's position rests on his unquestioned acceptance of the possibility of such a trans-type inference. Yet precisely this is most dubious. It is dubious in itself and it is dubious when one considers the philosophical consequences of allowing such an inference into our logical warehouse.

But there is no alternative for Toulmin. His argument must proceed across types. For if his conclusions about the logical stratification of a concept were meant to be *merely* contingent they would be of but marginal philosophical interest. In this day of grace it should be unnecessary to point out that the philosophical enterprise is not primarily contingent on matters of fact. On the other hand, if Toulmin's premises concerning the *de facto* genesis and growth of concepts were taken to be necessary, his references to this history of ideas would be scarcely intelligible. For what could one be doing if one sought both to describe how a particular idea did in fact grow up and also claim that this particular development was inevitable? Statements about the history of a concept must be contingent; statements about a concept's logical structure must be necessary. So Toulmin's argument *must* proceed trans-type in order for it to be suitable for our attention at all.

But *can* it do so? Are there really trans-type inferences?

Toulmin does not say. He certainly does not argue for their existence. But he does make it clear that *if* there are trans-type inferences then his program of approaching the present logical stratification of an idea by digging into the idea's past would be a reasonable one. But in the total absence of one unassailable example of a trans-type inference, is Toulmin's program even reasonable?

Chapter 26

A Comment on Toulmin

Sidney Morgenbesser, *Columbia University*

I

IN ATTEMPTING TO relate the issues of philosophy to those of psychology, Mr. Toulmin runs the risk of committing the reputed Lockean error of identifying a thesis in psychology with a theory in epistemology. But, whatever its dangers, Mr. Toulmin's program cannot be dismissed on the grounds that it conflicts with the currently entrenched thesis that philosophers qua philosophers only analyze concepts, for that thesis is either vague or dubious. It is vague if no meaning is assigned to 'analysis'; it is dubious if it rests upon a contrast between the analysis of concepts and the support of factual claims—a contrast which in turn rests upon, and is as questionable as, the one between analytic and synthetic sentences in ordinary language.[1]

Nothing clearly established in analytic meta-philosophy excludes Mr. Toulmin's program, and much in British philosophical practice suggests it. Recently some philosophers of ordinary language have intertwined logical and factual issues,[2] especially when appealing to theories of learning and teaching in order to depict the logical behavior of terms. Mr. Toulmin's innovation is twofold. He recognizes that many of the relevant considerations are scientific ones, and invites the professional psychologist to handle them. And unless we believe that philosophers have a priori knowledge about the means for the acquisition of language and other skills, Mr. Toulmin's invitation must be viewed as a simple, even if rare, act of philosophical humility.

Clearly the analyticity or nonanalyticity, the compatibility or incompatibility of a philosophical thesis with a metaphysical one is of less importance than its acceptability, which in turn is a function of the conceptual scheme adopted by a philosopher. Conversely, unless a philosopher at least indicates his ontology, his acceptable stock of predicates, and his criteria for knowledge and acceptable explanations—and I shall mean all three by a complete philosophical conceptual scheme

Notes to this paper begin on page 221.

—it is difficult to know why he considers certain predicates unclear, some sentences unacceptable, and a given system suspect. It is on these grounds that I find Mr. Toulmin an unhelpful guide. He never indicates any general reason for thinking that mental or psychological predicates give rise to any special philosophical problems.

Conceptual schemes are not adopted and then mechanically applied. They are both tested and revised in the light of instances which we presystematically accept. Confirmed sentences may therefore be of importance if some widely acceptable philosophical scheme cannot account for them. Conceptual schemes once adopted need not be elaborated. Since Kant, much of the best work in epistemology has consisted of a depiction of the structure of those scientific systems or theories which, for the most part, are compatible with, and at times cause us to revise, our criteria of knowledge. Mr. Toulmin may therefore indicate his problem by example, or contribute to our philosophical understanding by examining some system of scientific psychology.

But none of Mr. Toulmin's illustrations suggest that he feels like a fly caught in a bottle, and none of his statements about the psychological sciences indicate that he finds anything striking about their structure. His references to privacy reveal that he does not discover any epistemological puzzles loitering around sentences containing mental predicates.[3] He countenances mental states and entities as well as physical bodies, abstract entities as well as individuals, and challenges neither behavioristic learning-theories nor psychoanalytic ones. I doubt whether Mr. Toulmin is happy about everything he seems prepared to bless. In the light of his acceptance of epistemological privacy he must find behaviorism restricted, and his well-known empiricism must make him sceptical of various psychoanalytic claims to knowledge about the behavior of ids, egos, and super-egos. But Mr. Toulmin never indicates any of these concerns, and I doubt whether he could develop them without adumbrating his conceptual scheme.

The preceding remarks do not imply that Mr. Toulmin fails to touch upon many traditional theses in the philosophy of mind. He does—primarily to dismiss them. His tolerance on epistemological issues and his silence on ontological ones, conjoined with his explication of the variety of ways in which such terms as 'choice,' 'desire,' etc., are employed in ordinary language leave him with a pluralistic position in philosophical psychology. He eschews any simple formula that would attempt to summarize the role or function of mental predicates. Some psychological terms are dispositional, others are not; some sentences containing mental predicates are epistemologically private, others are not, etc.

Note, however, that Mr. Toulmin does not offer any criterion for picking out mental or psychological predicates, but simply assumes that the terms 'does choose,' 'does desire,' etc., are mental ones, and are such in all their usages. Given this approach it is doubtful whether any important philosopher would have disagreed with Mr. Toulmin. Ryle, whom everyone seems intent upon refuting, never suggests that all the mental concepts he discussed are dispositional ones; a Cartesian would insist that predicates like 'does choose' are not mental ones, or at least not mental in all their employments. Moreover, the Cartesian would suggest that some of the terms Mr. Toulmin does explicate commit him to a dualism, and that therefore Mr. Toulmin must face the problem of the interconnection between the mind and body, even if it is raised only by some predicates, or only by some predicates in some of their usages. But, of course, we do not know whether Mr. Toumin does consider the mind-body problem a problem.

II

To develop a conceptual scheme is to develop a language; to examine alternative conceptual schemes is to examine alternative languages. And since no formalized and uninterpreted language can be understood unless it is related to ordinary language, an examination of the latter is of importance for the understanding and testing of rival conceptual schemes. Patently this is not the only reason for studying terms in ordinary language, but at least it indicates one way of connecting the study of ordinary language with the philosophical enterprise.

Mr. Toulmin's explication of the logic of mental terms and his emphasis on the notion of stratification is therefore of importance even for those who do not think philosophy both begins and ends with the investigation of natural languages. Unfortunately there are unclarities hovering over Mr. Toulmin's elucidation of 'stratification.'

To indicate the conditions under which a concept is stratified Mr. Toulmin employs the relational phrase "is on a higher stratum than'—a phrase that presumably applies between senses or usages of a term or concept. 'Is on a higher stratum than' is in turn explicated in two ways, the indicative and the modal. A concept is stratified indicatively if it has at least two senses one of which is learned or understood before the other; a concept is stratified modally if one of its senses must be learned or understood before the other.[4] That the stratification relation may also be defined to apply between concepts is apparent; the logic of stratification when a concept has more than two senses is not. I presume that Mr. Toulmin thinks that the stratification relation is asymmetrical, transitive, and not connected in the class of senses of a given term. But if that is the case it does not follow, as he seems to think it does, that there is always one sense which must be the one upon which all other senses depend.[5] However, these problems are not handled explicitly by Mr. Toulmin and we shall therefore restrict our attention to concepts with two senses.

The indicative sense of stratification can be relativized. There may be some who learn sense A of concept C before they learn sense B, and others who learn sense B first. The only prima facie interesting case would therefore be a concept which is unconditionally stratified—for example, a concept C whose sense A is learned by all before they learn sense B. Modally stratified concepts are unconditionally so, but the converse need not hold.

It is difficult to know which sense of 'stratification' is employed by Mr. Toulmin and at times he seems to vacillate between them. At the beginning of the paper he implies that there is one sense of 'choice' which is on a lower stratum than others and which must be understood before other senses of choice are mastered; and at times he speculates about the psychological difficulties experienced by those who do not learn to employ 'I choose' in the normal sequence. Despite these possible unclarities, much of Mr. Toulmin's paper reads as a defense of the thesis that many of our psychological concepts are modally stratified, and some of it can be viewed as a presentation of criteria to distinguish between stratified and unstratified concepts. But none of these criteria are satisfactory.

Mr. Toulmin informs us that stratified concepts are complex. But unless we believe in ultimate simples, all concepts are complex. Relative to a base we may distinguish between simple and complex predicates, and we might think that Mr. Toulmin presents us with a base. Given a concept C whose sense A must be learned before sense B, A is the base and B more complex than A. Presumably B is defined in terms of A but not vice versa. However, while this procedure at best allows us to compare the complexity values of the senses of a term, it does not allow us to contrast the complexity of different terms. Moreover, we are still not afforded any reason for thinking that A must be the base, and it would be evasive to suggest that it must be since 'B is on a higher stratum than A.'

The problem reappears with Mr. Toulmin's examples. Even if he shows that everyone up to a given time has defined sense B of 'choice' in terms of sense A, it does not follow that he has established that 'choice' is either unconditionally or modally stratified. Someone, perhaps a philosopher, may think of a new way of defining sense A in terms of sense B, or of defining sense A independently of sense B, and may even teach his children in a new manner.

Related difficulties surround Mr. Toulmin's appeal to various quasi-logical locutions—for example, 'presuppositions.' A can be said to presuppose B if B is necessary condition for A. A can be said to logically presuppose B if 'B > A' is analytic or a logical truth. The appeal to presuppositions therefor places us in the onerous position of having to discover a criterion for analyticity. But even on Mr. Toulmin's grounds he must be able to prove the analyticity of some sentences, and do so without appealing to 'stratification'—and this I suggest he cannot do. I think he wants to say that the sentence 'A must be learned or understood before B' is analytic, but this is merely proving that 'A is on a lower stratum than B' is analytic.

I fail to see that Mr. Toulmin has presented us with any theoretical clues for distinguishing between stratified and unstratified concepts. And despite some of Mr. Toulmin's insinuations, the availability of such clues or even of a well-developed theory would not provide psychologists with hypotheses for confirmation. Given a proof that a concept is stratified there is nothing left for the psychologist to confirm.

Since I doubt that we can prove that some concepts are modally stratified by appealing to such over-employed terms as 'presuppose' and 'analytic' or 'complex,' or by speculating about the processes of learning or teaching, I would suggest that the interconnections between Mr. Toulmin's analysis and psychology are even more intimate than he thinks. It is not the case that philosophers can discover which concepts are stratified and then hand the results over to a psychologist; psychological theories are required *ab initio*. Even his invitation may be a tardy one.

III

When it is applied to mental predicates or sentences like 'I choose,' new difficulties emerge with Mr. Toulmin's doctrine. He himself notes that if we first teach a child to employ 'I choose' when he is actually picking something, and to use 'I choose' not to denote but to be the act of choice, it may be self-contradictory to tell the child: 'Choose, but tell us later what you choose.' Confidence in his position leads Mr. Toulmin to conclude that the child will in a short while catch on to what we mean. Unfortunately Mr. Toulmin does not inform us how the child catches on, nor why the child is less puzzled with locutions like 'Choose but inform us later' than with directives like 'Walk but don't move your legs or any part of your body.'

I suspect that we must supplement Mr. Toulmin's approach in the following way. When we teach a child to use 'I choose,' we do so if, and only if, we assume that other predicates which are not defined in terms of choice are true of that child. Thus, we may think that the child is able to anticipate outcomes, remember the differences between pleasurable and unpleasurable experiences, recollect that he has frequently reached out and has then been permitted to manipulate the things he picked, etc. The terms denoting these other factors, though not defined in terms of choice, will be systematically related to it, and the new sense of choice can be introduced in terms of these relations.

My remarks about choice are inconclusive, but they are intended to support two points. Proof that a given term denotes or applies to a stretch of publicly observable behavior does not in itself show that mentalistic predicates (in the traditional sense) are not systematically related to it. The behavioristic predicate may never be applied unless it is assumed that some non-behavioristic predicate is also true of the person to which it is applied. And if some of these non-behavioristic predicates apply either to the necessary or the sufficient, or to part of the necessary or part of the sufficient, conditions for the behavior to which the behavioristic predicate applies, the latter may be partially defined in terms of, or reduced to, non-behavioristic ones.

Secondly, I suggest that some of Mr. Toulmin's difficulties are in part due to his incomplete break with some recent trends in British philosophy. Though, most likely, they do not want to equate 'meaning' with 'application,' some British philosophers restrict their attention to application and some even seem to say that to know the meaning of a term is to know the paradigm cases to which it applies, or to know the paradigm situations in which it is appropriate to employ the term. Mr. Toulmin's emphasis is more sophisticated and at least calls for an awareness of the paradigm cases to which the term applies in a number of senses and focuses attention on the interconnections between the various senses of a given term.

The concentration on application has had the salutary effect of blocking the search for such vague entities as intentions and meanings. Moreover, there is little doubt that application can function as a negative test. If a man does not know how to apply a term, then we may say that he does not understand it, or does not know what it means. Nevertheless, no one, I suspect, is ready to equate 'meaning' with 'application,' and few have clarified the distinction between 'use,' 'usage,' and 'application.'

Perhaps—and what follows is no more than a suggestion— to know the meaning of a term does not merely require that we know how to apply it, but also requires that we know the connections between that term and the other terms that appear in the theories in which the original term occurs.[7] To know the meaning of 'acid,' for example, we need know not merely to which liquids, etc., it applies, but also the interconnections between 'acid,' 'base,' 'ion,' etc. The emphasis on the theory will frequently be important to explain shifts in application, and in some cases might be relevant to explain why we say that we have shifted the application of a term in order to hold the meaning constant.

In specifying the meaning or a meaning of a term 'A' we rarely mention all the other terms to which 'A' is systematically connected. If 'A' is systematically related to 'C,' 'D,' 'E,' etc.,[8] and we think that 'B' is a good index of 'C,' 'D,' 'E,' etc., we may simply say that 'A' means 'B,' or that 'A' and 'B' are similar in meaning, or that 'A' is definable in terms of 'B.' The systematic connections are taken for granted fi we think that 'B' is a good index, and explicitly discussed if we think that it is not. The term 'index' requires elucidation and the term 'theory' replacement when we deal with terms in ordinary language. But though these problems remain to be solved, I think that the task of explicating the meaning or a meaning of a term merges into the task of portraying the structure of the theories in which the term appears, and cannot simply be handled by noting the cases in which the term is applied. Analysis of psychological and mental predicates require examination of psychological theories or beliefs. And it is both by noting the connections between psychological terms and beliefs, and by challenging these beliefs that philosophers like Dewey, Ryle, and Wittgenstein have been helpful. Otherwise the distinction between philosophy and informal linguistics vanishes.

NOTES

1. These strictures, with modification, apply even to those who do not identify philosophy with the analysis of concepts, but with the analysis of terms or sentences or even larger language units. I hope it is realized that I am not maintaining that philosophical disputes are purely factual ones and factual in the same sense in which scientific ones are factual.

2. Also Ryle, Wittgenstein, and Geach in *Mental Acts*.

3. I think he is misleading on this point. To say that 'S' is epistemologically private to T is, I think, to say that 'S' is about T and that T is in the only position to confirm 'S.' To say that T is privileged in respect to 'S' at time t, is to say that T at time t is in a unique position to exhaustively confirm 'S.' 'Privilege' and 'privacy' are different, and the former may apply, if it applies at all, to sentences containing mental predicates.

4. These definitions, though not explicitly Mr. Toulmin's, are, I hope, not at variance with his intent.

5. Assume that term 'T' has six senses and that the stratification relation holds between sense A and B, B and C, and also between D and E, E and F, and not between A and D, or D and A, or B and E, etc. Mr. Toulmin's appeal to alternate routes suggests that we might learn 'T' either by way of A-B-C, in that order, or by way of D-E-F, in that order. No sense is especially privileged. Here Mr. Toulmin's animadversion about the philosophical disregard of the root sense of 'probability' may be without substance.

6. I hope the reader will forgive the blurring of the distinction between a sentence and a sentence schema.

7. Or, if one wishes, the systematic interconnections between the entities to which the predicate in the theory apply. Note, however, that we must restrict our attention to those relations specified in the theory.

8. If term 'T' appears in a set of laws of the form 'if T then L,' 'if T then B,' 'if T and Y then G,' 'if T and K then j,' etc., we can say that 'T' is systematically connected with all the other terms that appear in the laws. Frequently, instead of dealing with the term 'T' and a family of laws, we must discover that all T's have a property L, and we can then, via theories, deduce many of the laws in which the term 'T' appears. On such occasions we might say that 'L' is a good index of 'B,' 'G,' 'K,' and 'L' and that 'L' means 'T.'

Chapter 27

Are Complex, Considered Preferences Only "Simulated"?

H. Van Rensselaer Wilson, *Brooklyn College*

PROFESSOR TOULMIN PROPOSES that we look for connections between two kinds of stratification within families of concepts, viz., the temporal stratification involved in the time-order in which we first acquire the concepts, and the logical stratification in terms of which the concepts can be arranged in an order of increasing complexity. He concludes with the suggestion that some of our misconceptions may be a consequence of our having learned the concept (or, rather, its various phases) in a time-order which "ran counter to its normal stratification."

These suggestions are interesting and well worth further exploration. My disagreement is not with his main contention, but with a secondary aspect whose amendment would probably not affect the general tenor of his paper. But I do feel that certain expressions which he uses have unfortunate connotations to which attention should be called.

Professor Toulmin contrasts a comparatively complex, comparatively sophisticated activity which he calls "simulated" preference (or "pretended" or "insincere" preference) with a presupposed, relatively simple activity which he calls "sincere" preference (or "straightforward" or "real" preference). I suggest that instead of calling the simple peference "sincere," or "straightforward," or "real," it would be better to call it "impulsive" or "short-run" or "unconsidered," with the more sophisticated peference described as 'considered," or "long-run," or "contextual," rather than as "simulated," or "pretended," or "insincere."

This is not merely a matter of terminology, I think, but of ethical orientation. It strikes me as objectionable to cry "Insincere!" when there is a valid, considered subordinating of a less important short-run preference to a more important long-run preference—unless one is prepared to accept the notion that *all* considered moral judgments are "insincere" or "simulated." In Toulmin's illustration, the question of course is: "All things considered, *in the existing context,* do you prefer tea or coffee?" Supposing that *ceteris paribus* I like coffee better but there is only one cup of coffee left and plenty of tea, the question becomes: "Do you prefer, all things considered, to take the second-best beverage and be polite, or do you prefer to be impolite and take the beverage you like better?" My *considered* preference in this context may well be to prefer ("really" prefer) politeness-and-tea to rudenes-and-coffee, even though I would have preferred politeness-and-coffee had that been one of the available alternatives. But it was not. I am not asked what I *would* have preferred in a different context; I am presented with a context for my choice along with the request that I choose.

No considered choice can be contextless. And every *moral* choice is a considered choice. The very core of ethical judgment lies in substituting long-run, considered, context-mindful choices for naïve, impulsive, short-run, unconsidered (and inconsiderate), "blind" choices. Neither kind of choice, I suggest, deserves to be labeled "insincere," "pretended," or "simulated." If one rather than the other is to be deemed a person's "real" preference, I would suppose it to be the considered, second-thought preference, mindful of remote as well as immediate consequences and arising out of a hierarchy of values in which one deliberately subordinates the less important to the more important considerations in case there is conflict. Such preferences are my "real" preferences because they are the preferences of my "real" self, i.e., of my relatively mature, intelligent, civilized "better" self, the self which *on due reflection* I accept as "me." The casual, naïve, impulsive, childish self is the one which, on due reflection, I tend to reject as *not* really me, certainly not the me that I really intend to be. To imply that the mature self is only simulated and its preferences only pretended and insincere hardly squares with usual ethical discourse on these matters.

In any case, to be sure, there remains the "stratification" which Toulmin was illustrating—a contrast between the relatively simple "impulsive" or "unconsidered" preference (as I should call it), and the more complex "considered" or "contextually modified" preference. The greater logical complexity of the latter would appear to lie in the fact that *more than one* consideration is relevant to the preference. With only *one* relevant consideration there is choice *"simpliciter,"* whereas the complex situation presupposes our being familiar with the process of *simpliciter* choosing (one consideration at a time) but being now called upon to apply at least two such processes simultaneously, with the added complication of needing to decide which consideration is to take precedence over the other in case they result in opposite preferences when taken singly. It is only thus that one can discover what one "really" prefers in the particular circumstances—certainly not by saying "I shall *pretend* to prefer something that I don't really prefer, when I make a considered choice that varies from the impulsive choice I would otherwise have made." When the college student who faces a philosophy test tomorrow decides to stay home and study instead of going to the movies (as he would have done in the absence of the prospective test), I see no reason to accuse him of only "pretending" to prefer studying. He *does* prefer studying under those circumstances, although in different circumstances he would prefer the movies. If the mark of intelligence is to take appropriate account of relevant modifying circumstances, then instead of calling such choices "insincere" or "simulated," we ought to call them "intelligent" choices.

One further comment. The notion of choosing or prefering does not arise in connection with wanting or wishing until the "but-not-both" relation of contrariety or incompatibility is added. "I want that *and* that *and* that *and* . . ." does not entail choice. It is at least debatable, I think, whether there is any logically "normal" time-order for (1) learning that things in general are occasionally incompatible, and (2) learning what it means to want something. Are not these concepts basically independent? How early in a child's development does he learn (or should he learn) that when he wants to eat his piece of cake and at the same time wants to have it, his two wants are incompatible? Perhaps it is not really anomalous at all for people to learn *from the beginning* to want in a context, aware that gratifying one wish may entail denying some other wish. Perhaps one *should* know what to say one 'wants' only after having given some thought to what *other* (and perhaps more important) goods would be precluded by one's obtaining what one "thought one wanted" prior to such consideration. "Carried to extremes" this could become neurotic, as Professor Toulmin remarks; but *not* carried to extremes, it would seem to be ordinary intelligent behavior, whose basic principles young children can begin to learn earlier, perhaps, than we sometimes suppose.

Chapter 28

Wishing Won't—But Wanting Will

Gertrude Ezorsky, *Hunter College*

I

ACCORDING TO MR. Toulmin, we have special authority to speak about our own wants and desires. This authority is not epistemic, for it does not derive from privileged access to private introspectables like the "expert authority" we exercise in speaking about our pains. Authority for expressing our wants derives rather from the right we all have to make our own choices. In the act of choosing we find the root concept of wanting. To learn wanting in its more complex uses we must first learn its seminal identity with choosing. Our right to choose carries over as an "executive element" into more complex declarations of wants. We are therefore required to grant each man's expressly-declared wish or want a certain primacy and authority, unless some special features of the situation point to our disregarding it.

The root choosing use of "I want" is illustrated by Mr. Toulmin in a situation in which I am asked by a waitress to choose tea or coffee from a tray. There is nothing "unequal" in this situation to influence my choice. There is not, for example, only one cup of tea left. I respond by saying "I want tea." Here "the first-person present indicative "I want . . ." like "I choose . . ." can function as a straight act of choice, selection, or request, as the linguistic counterpart of pointing, taking, or otherwise indicating the object or item in question."

Mr. Toulmin is correct when he describes the utterance of "I choose————" as the *act* of choosing. For the executive "I choose————" belongs to that class of expressions, different from assertions, which Mr. Austin has tagged "performatory" (See J. L. Austin, "Other Minds," *Logic and Language,* Second Series [Oxford: Basil Blackwell, 1955] and J. L. Austin, "Truth," *Aristotelian Society Supplementary Volume XXIV,* [London: Harrison and Sons, Ltd., 1930]). If "I want————" were a performatory expression, like "I choose————," then it would be very plain that "I want————" asserts nothing about introspectables; for a performatory expression asserts nothing at all—nothing which is true or false.

An assertion is either true or false. Thus, if I assert something which I believe to be false I am lying. A performatory enunciation, however, is not either true or false. When I say "I choose————" I cannot be lying, for by saying "I choose————" I do choose. This applies only to the first-person indicative. "I chose————," "She chose————," "she is choosing————" are assertions which are true or false. They report or describe an act. When I say "I choose————" I am not reporting or describing an act but performing it. This also applies to Mr. Toulmin's other example of the exercise of executive authority, the state Governor writing on a document: "I approve, N. Rockefeller." Mr. Rockefeller, as Governor, is not asserting his approval of the document, but officially approving it. He may personally disapprove of the document, but no one would thereby accuse him of writing a false statement. "I approve, N. Rockefeller," written by the state Governor on an official document is a performatory expression.

"I want————," however, is not a performatory expression. When I say "I want————" I may be lying, I may be asserting something which is either true or false and which I believe to be false. "I want————" then is not an executive expression.

If we are to accept Mr. Toulmin's contention that the authority for "I want————" does not rest on privileged access, then a complex use of "I want————" should not be accorded any special authority. He describes a complex use as one in which an executive element carries over from the right to choose, giving such a declaration—like one of our plans and intentions—a certain primacy and authority, unless some special feature of the situation points to our disregarding it.

When I grant the right to choice I am granting a right or authority for a certain act, but when I grant special primacy or authority to a person's *assertion* that he wants X, I am conceding a different kind of authority—epistemic authority. If I grant him such authority I must have some reason for believing that he is in a better position to *know* that his assertions are true than I am. His authority with respect to these assertions must be epistemic, and the act of choice is not an exercise of epistemic authority. Mr. Toulmin's analysis suggests that in complex instances "I want X" entails "I would choose X" (everything else being equal). This does not remedy the situation. For "I would choose X" (everything else being equal) is an assertion, and to grant such a declaration special authority is to grant that the one who makes it is in a special position to know *that* he would choose X (everything else being equal). "You don't know that you would choose X" (everything else being equal) is a usurpation of authority only if the person being addressed is in a special position to know what he would choose. And conceding his special position to know is conceding, to some extent, the doctrine of privileged access, which Mr. Toulmin finds dispensable as a basis for the "special primacy and authority" we should give to each man's declaration of his wants.

The objection may be made that in distinguishing between "I want————" and "I choose————" I have not accounted for the fact that, in a situation where I am asked to choose, I may choose by saying "I want————." The reason I can use "I want ————" in this way is as follows. "I want X" may be interpreted as a propensity to choose and in other ways secure X. The expression for propensity to choose X is of a logically different order from the one for choosing X. For the first is dispositional and the second is an act. But because a disposition is manifested by acts and occurrences we sometimes use the dispositional expression for the act. Because dispositions and acts are intimately related, the function of the expression for one may rub off on the other. For example, suppose doubt has been expressed about Jones' word that something has happened. Jones may ask me: "Do you take my word for it?" I may reply: "I believe in your honesty." This last may be interpreted as assertion of a fixed disposition to accept the word of Jones. But the dispositional "I believe in your honesty" functions here like the performatory "I accept your statement," although the two expressions are of a logically different order. Similarly, "I want X," which asserts a propensity to choose and in other ways secure X, may function in a choice situation like "I choose X" although they are of a logically different order, the first being a dispositional expression, the second a performatory utterance. Thus "I choose X because I want X" is at once a significant and trivial declaration, its significance deriving from the logical difference between "I choose X" and "I want X," its triviality deriving from the fact that wanting X entails the disposition to choose X.

II

Can a person ever claim that he has unique or special authority with respect to the declaration of his wants? What does this claim involve? It cannot mean merely that at the moment there is no way of testing his declaration that he wants X because X is not presently available. For if the test for wanting X is really a test, then he is in the same position we are in—his claim remains untested. He may support his claim with past efforts to secure X, but this kind of evidence is not *uniquely* available to him. His past efforts to secure X are open to public examination. The claim to special authority does not rest on the contingent matter that one has more information about one's past behavior. It rests on the alleged authority for knowledge of our own wants because they are private—given in private consciousness and in the nature of the case, uniquely known by the self. Are there occasions on which I make this claim?

If I am serious when I say "I want X," I can make no claim to unique authority, although I may be counted on to secure what I say I want. If I am not serious then the authority is all mine, although I may be counted on never to claim what I say I want. If I am not serious when I say that I want X then I merely *wish* for X, and to merely wish for something implies nothing about securing it. I may wish and keep my wish to myself. I am in a privileged position with respect to my wishes. I can keep them from the public. But if I really want what I say I want—if I am serious—then I show it in my behavior. Behaviorism is a call to seriousness.

This difference between wants and wishes is reflected in the behavior of "I want———" and "I wish———" in sentences. Because our wants are manifested in our acts we never say "I want X" when X is clearly impossible of attainment. When I am late, I do not say "I want to have gotten up earlier," for there is nothing I can ever do now about my oversleeping this morning. I might say, however, "I wish that I had gotten up earlier." For the objects of my wishes are unbounded. I may wish for the moon. "I wish———" unlike "I want———," can be contrary to fact, as is indicated grammatically by the use of the subjunctive conditional, "I wish that S were P." We never say "I want that S were P." "I want———" never points back to the past, for we cannot undo the past. We can only say "I wish that something had not happened." We are supposed to be serious when we say "I want———." For if I mean what I say when I say that I want X, then I should do something about securing it. But to say I want something and do nothing about getting it is not to mean what I say, not to really want it, but merely to wish for it. The employer who says "If you really wanted to keep this job you'd come in on time" is correctly basing his employee's seriousness ("reality of his want") on behavior, and correctly refusing to grant primacy and authority to his employee's assertion that he wants his job. The trouble with Marie Antoinette was that she gave primacy and authority to the declaration by the French people that they wanted bread. She did not realize that they really meant it.

Thus wishes may be "idle," "products of fancy," "silly," "unrealistic," "fleeting." They go with birthday cakes, candles, parlor games, and magic. They are frivolous, as is our thinking when it is wishful. A fairy godmother grants our wishes; our wants are up to us. Thus wishes are comparatively passive, they "come true," "are granted," "are fulfilled." But we may struggle, fight, demand, and even die for what we really want. No one dies for a wish. "I want————" or "I wish————" may function as a request, but the former suggests formality, unhurriedness and minimizing of the importance of the request, while the latter is plain, direct, and blunt.

When a person confuses a real want with a wish, he confuses what he really wants with what he thinks he wants, with what it may appear to him that he wants. To the man who says "I want to study medicine" and never opens a book, we accord only the wish and deny that he really wants what he says he wants. We deny that he *knows* what he wants. Now if "I want————" reported a private datum then we could not properly deny the reality of his want, for it would not be accessible to us. We could not claim that we know that he does not really want to study medicine. But the fact that we do deny someone's declaration of his wants in a way that would be irrelevant to, say, his "seeing an after-image," indicates that "I want————" is not a report of a private experience.

We give special authority to a person's declaration of his wishes, but his real wants can be diagnosed by others. Our wishes may be private. We are in a special position to conceal and deceive with respect to our wishes. We have merely to be silent. But a great deal of activity is required to cover up our wants. A person may wish that he were dead by enjoying an image of himself in a coffin, surrounded by weeping relatives, but to really want to die involves more radical measures. We may wish for what we really do not want, but we cannot say "I wish that I had X, but I really don't want X," for part of the game of wishing is forgetting what we really want. "I want————" belongs to the language of commitment, but "I wish————" implies no responsibility. Can these lapses into irresponsibility give us special knowledge?

I can conceal my wishes from the public, keep them for myself. Thus I may have special authority with respect to my wishes, for I am in a privileged position to know them. But the fact that I am in a privileged position *to know* what my wishes are does not mean that I *do know* what my wishes are. A man may be in a privileged position to know what is in a Latin text if he owns the only existing copy, but he cannot take advantage of his privileged position unless he takes the trouble to learn how to read Latin. To know what my wishes are is not the same as to be in a privileged position to know what they are. To know what my wishes are involves being able to distinguish between wishing and what wishing is not— really wanting, for example—and this is not as easy a matter as wishing is. The man who insists that he really wants to study medicine but never does it is someone who does not know what his wishes are, for he erroneously includes them where they do not belong—with his real wants. If he does not know how to distinguish his wishes from what they are not, he cannot be said to know what they are, for he thinks they are what they are not. And even if one knows the difference between a real want and a wish, one may not be rational enough at the moment to apply it. ("I never want to see you again" may turn out the next day to have been a momentary wish. But did I know this when I said it?)

It does not follow then that privileged access to our wishes gives us special knowledge. And special knowledge is surely the significant claim of the philosophical doctrine of Privileged Access. Mr. Toulmin's attempt to undercut this doctrine by substituting "executive authority" for privileged access does not, as I have argued, stand up. Besides, it is unnecessary. We may accept the fact that we have privileged access to our wishes and reject the central philosophical claim of the doctrine of Privileged Access—that privileged access makes experts of us all.

Chapter 29

A Spade Is a Spade, So Mind Your Language

Raziel Abelson, *New York University*

IN THE FOLLOWING commentary on the papers read and discussed at the third annual conference of the New York University Philosophical Institute, my general purpose is to defend the long-neglected practice of calling a spade a spade, even in philosophical discussions. I have in mind three particular entities which I think should, despite what many philosophers say, continue to be called by their right names. I shall argue for the continued propriety of (1) calling wanting "wanting" and not "choosing," (2) calling mechanical computing "mechanical computing" and not "thinking," and (3) calling the mind "the mind" and not "the brain." If this defense of the perfectly obvious should seem truistic, it is indeed truistic. But I am confident that to many it will seem totally wrong, in which case it will, at least, neither seem nor be truistic.

(1) "I want" and "I choose"

I wish first to take issue with two points in Stephen Toulmin's suggestive discussion of concept stratification: (a) his analysis of the so-called "family" of words, "choose," "desire," "want," and "wish"—words which seem to me to form a family only by a marriage of Toulmin's convenience; and (b) the dubious character of Toulmin's match-making efforts on a general level, when he attempts to wed philosophical analysis to genetic psychology.

While I agree generally with Toulmin's theory of levels of concept use, according to which phrases like "I want" and "I choose" have various senses that can be arranged in order of increasing logical complexity, I would question his choice of the lowest or "primary" level for terms such as "want" and "wish." I do not think that the primary use of these expressions is, as Toulmin claims, the executive use. Just as the early positivists recognized nothing but indicative or ostensive

Notes to this paper begin on page 242.

use of words, and the pragmatists found evaluative use at the bottom of everything, linguistic analysts are now discovering performatory, recommendatory, and executive uses under every linguistic bed. But I would like to row against the current here, and put in a word for the good old-fashioned kind of use that served our philosophical grandfathers so well, namely, the descriptive use.

Toulmin equates the primary use of "I want" with that of "I choose," and explains this so-called "executive use" of both expressions as the employment of language to announce, and in announcing to make, a decision. As support for this interpretation, he claims that the executive use of "choose," "want," and "wish" is the first kind one learns, although he does not make it clear whether he means that one is logically compelled to learn it first, or whether one just always happens to learn it first. But it does not much matter which claim Toulmin means to make, because he would be wrong, I believe, in either case. It is logically possible to learn to use a word in any way at all, so it cannot be logically necessary to learn it in Toulmin's way. Nor does Toulmin cite any statistical or experimental evidence to show that everyone—or even that anyone—does, in fact, learn to use "I want" in an executive way first. What is more to the point, any children who did learn to use it in this way would be poorly instructed, because to use "I want" in place of "I choose" is frequently a *mis*use. For example, in selecting a weapon from a brace of duelling pistols, the well-bred duellist might say "I choose this one." But it would be very bad form for him to say "I want this one." The point is that wanting always has a motive, so that to *want* one of the pistols is to imply that it contains some hidden and unfair advantage. Moreover, as Skinner observed in his comments on Toulmin's paper, "I choose" implies the existence of alternatives, whereas "I want" does not.

I suspect that Toulmin is misled into equating "I want" with "I choose" on a primary level by a use of "I want" that has a strong resemblance to the executive use, but differs in a rather important way, namely, the imperative use. Jean Piaget has shown, in his studies of child behavior, that children often learn to say "I want" as a command or a request, before they learn to use it as a description of their psychic state.[1] Nevertheless, a command or a request is not the same as a choice, and lumping all three under the category "executive use" conceals important differences. In this regard, Toulmin's illustration of purely executive use of language in saying "I want coffee" when offered coffee or tea is misleading, since "I want coffee" can mean *either* "Please give me coffee" *or* "I choose coffee," and it more frequently means the first.

Not only is it a mistake to identify the imperative use of "I want" with the executive use of "I choose," but it is also wrong, I think, to regard even the imperative use as logically primary. Granted that the imperative use is often the first to be learned, this only goes to show that the order of learning need not be a logical order, and that linguistic analysis has nothing in common with genetic psychology. Consider two cases of a child learning to use "I want":

(1) Irritable and somewhat authoritarian parents have a small child. The father comes home from work, sits down with a newspaper and, annoyed by the child who is crying for attention, thunders: "I want peace and quiet in this house!" The mother then gives an order to the child: "I want you to go to bed."[2] Whereupon the child leaves the room, muttering to himself: "Wait till I grow up and I'll tell everybody what *I* want!"

(2) Now imagine a more permissive and democratic family, i.e., one in which people tend to consider each other's wants. The mother asks her child, "Do you want that toy in the window?" The child says yes, gets it, and promptly throws it away. Whereupon the mother protests: "You didn't really want it. I won't buy you another one." This child learns to say "I want x" as a prediction that he will preserve, use, fondle— in a word, *enjoy* the object x. This use of "I want' 'is primarily predictively descriptive, although it can acquire imperative or supplicatory overtones.

Thus the meaning of an expression like "I want" varies with the personality and traning of the person who uses it. "I want x" is impolite when spoken in an aggressive tone of voice, but merely plaintive when said in a soft and hesitant tone. In the aggressive tone, it means "I order you to give me x," while in the softer tone it means "I would enjoy x and I trust you will be considerate enough to give me what I enjoy"—as when Oliver Twist held out his plate and whispered "Please, I want some more."

Yet even when "I want" is used imperatively it presupposes the descriptive use, for it implies that the speaker is accustomed to getting what he desires and enjoys. Thus the literary effectivenes of "Your wish is my command" is due to the fact that a wish (or a want) is not *usually* a command. For the same reason, the purely descriptive phrase "I would very much like x" is more polite than even the softly spoken "I want x," since the conditional verb ("would like") expresses considerable doubt about getting x. The point of all this is that while either the imperative use or the descriptive use which is logically primary and, for the sake both of logic and of good manners, *should* be learned first.

Incidentally, following Toulmin's lead in accounting for irresolvable controversies in terms of levels of concept use, it is tempting to speculate on the fact that, in ethical theory, German philosophers tend to be Kantians and stress the imperative use of ethical terms, while American philosophers tend to be pragmatists and stress the descriptive-predictive use. Perhaps philosophical differences such as this are due to differences in the type of family and social structure in which one first learns to use ethical expressions. And perhaps it is for similar reasons that many British philosophers regard eithical standards as intuitively self-evident. The well-bred British child does not have to be argued into doing the right thing, nor need he deliberate about what is proper. Good form is, for him, axiomatic simply because it is automatic.

So far I have been firing away at Toulmin's reduction of "I want" to "I choose" because I believe that "I want" has primarily descriptive meaning. But at this point I would like to refill the revolver chamber and take a few shots at his analysis of "I choose," which seems to me to be seriously impaired by his assumption that the meaning of "choose" is logically simpler than the meaning of "want." In pointing to "I choose" as a case of purely executive use of language, Toulmin apparently is trying to account for the fact that there is something final and unquestionable about a person's announcement of his choice, such that no one can properly say to him: "You didn't really choose what you said you choose" (although surely one *can* say: "You didn't really want what you said you want"?). The concept of executive use performs a valuable philosophical task, in this regard, by explaining how certain utterances can be taken as unchallengeable, without abandoning the empiricistic principle that all *statements of fact* (i.e., all *descriptive* utterances) are subject to public scrutiny and possible disproof. Toulmin makes an important point in suggesting that "I choose x" sometimes functions in this unchallengeable way, without thereby qualifying as a synthetic a priori statement, and thus without giving aid and comfort to rationalistic metaphysics. It is well to follow Toulmin's lead here by granting that the authoritative and unfalsifiable character of utterances such as "I choose x" is due to a non-descriptive component of their meanings which Toulmin aptly calls, their "executive use." Nevertheless, "I choose" seems to me a poor model of *purely* executive use, even in the simplest linguistic context. A better paradigm of purely executive use would be "I take x." For the term, "choose," when properly used (i.e., thoughtfully, and with care to one's words) is rather complex in function, and conveys both descriptive *and* excutive meaning. There is a long-established philosophical tradition behind the view that choice involves both the psychic state of wanting something and the act of selective taking, a tradition beginning with Aristotle's penetrating analysis of choice in the *Nichomachean Ethics*[3] and most recently argued by P. H. Nowell-Smith in his *Ethics*.[4] There is, of course, the opposed philosophical tradition, from the sophists through Thomas Hobbes down to the Logical Positivists, a tradition which, in one way or another, maintains that the ultimate basis of choice is arbitrary assertion, backed up by force. Thus the interpretation of "I choose" has more than casual importance, and Toulmin's claim that everyone has the right to choose for himself and that no one can question another person's choice (on the primary level) tends to support the ethical skepticism that Toulmin himself took great pains to refute in his *Reason in Ethics*. The word "choose" has an ethical ring, whereas a word such as "take" does not, and where a word has ethical import we should, on Toulmin's own view of ethics, be able to find some rational grounds for its application. Expressing a choice is a very serious kind of utterance. In many situations, and perhaps in all, to say "I choose" is to accept responsibility for what one does. Thus to say "I choose x" is more than merely to announce that one is taking x, it is also to claim to have reasons to take x rather than y or z. It is more than merely to select; it is to select carefully, deliberately, and in relation to a desired end. If choice were, even in the simplest, most primitive case (such as choosing up sides in a game), merely the exercise of executive authority independent of any arguable grounds, then one could not distinguish the purely physical act of pointing to x from actually choosing x. Yet one might point at x accidentally or because one feels a gun in his ribs, in which case one has surely not *chosen* x. If merely saying "I choose x" were identical with the act of choice, as Toulmin claims, then it would make no sense for a child choosing up sides to say, afterwards; "I didn't really choose Johnny. By mistake I said

'I choose Johnny' but the one I wanted was Freddy." And yet it makes perfectly good sense.

I suggest that the expression "I choose x" has, even in the most rudimentary contexts, a highly complex meaning, involving at least three distinct components, one being the factual report of what I want, another the indication that I have grounds for selecting x from a group of possible alternaitves (for if I have no grounds for my selection, I am selecting *at random* rather than exercising choice—I am not being "choosy"). The third component (and this is where the concept of executive use applies) is the *act* of taking x, and act which is performed merely by uttering the words "I choose x," just as the act of marriage is performed by merely saying "I do" to the appropriate question put by the appropriate official.[5] When I say "I do," at the altar, I then and there *do*, even if there happens to be a shotgun at my back. But when "I choose x" is used in such a way that this executive component is the only component, i.e., when I have no reasons for my choice and no desire for what I say I am choosing, then my use of "I choose" is a poor and misleading use, just as I might thoughtlessly say "I love martinis," when all I mean to say and thus all that I *should* say is "I enjoy martinis." [6]

Generalizing from these observations, I would say, in opposition to both Toulmin and Skinner, that philosophical analysis is and should remain quite distinct from the psychology of learning. Philosophical analysis is concerned with refining and clarifying the rules of use of concepts and expressions, rather than with discovering or confirming generalizations about human behavior. Its method is logical rather than empirical, and its idiom is normative rather than descriptive. Philosophy and psychology may be (and often are) mixed together in one inquiry, but they do not fuse into a compound. I very much fear that, if philosophers follow Toulmin's daring forays into the camp of psychology, they will find themselves cut off and captured by hostile forces—something which Skinner no doubt would approve of, but Toulmin would as surely regret.

(2) Thinking and Computing

The gap between thinking and mechanical computation is bridged by Norbert Wiener and Michael Scriven, who perform another wedding ceremony—this time not between psychology and philosophy, but between psychology and engineering.

Once again, words which most of us had assumed to represent quite different things were claimed to represent pretty much the same things. Machines (at least those of the future) were said to think and even to be human—perhaps even superhuman! The upshot of Norbert Wiener's fascinating analogies between the human brain and self-regulating generators, self-programming computers, etc., and Michael Scriven's refutations of the stock distinctions between humans and even the very best machines seemed to be that the only ace man still holds is consciousness—an ace which behaviorists Wiener and Scriven then proceeded to trump on behalf of the machine. Max Black then retrumped for man, arguing that, according to the implicit rules governing the use of the word "think," it is absurd to say that something can think unless we can also say that it is human, so that it is false by definition to say that machines can think. But the flaw in this linguistic defense of the human mind against the oscillating circuit is that language habits do change, and this particular habit of predicating human attributes, such as thought, only of creatures born of woman is already falling out of fashion. The jargon of the scientists is rapidly becoming popular idiom in this science-minded age, and it is not unusual to hear machine attributes predicated of human beings—"His mind is working on all cylinders," "He took an hour off from his work for refuelling," "Your new secretary is a real dynamo," or "Last year the Yankees went into a tailspin." Conversely, discourse about machines is rapidly becoming more personalized. Saint-Exupéry wrote about his airplane as if it were his mother, describing the pilot stick as an umbilical cord, and many a man, when he says: "She's a sweetheart, she never lets me down no matter how roughly I treat her," is referring, not to his wife or mistress, but to his automobile.[7] The point is that the facts of language alone cannot protect the human ego by justifying its feeling of superiority to its manufactured products—they can only reflect that feeling while it lasts. Justification must be sought elsewhere.

Nor can the grounds of human superiority be found in introspective consciousness. For how can an introspectionist prove to a behaviorist that he (the introspectionist), unlike machines and behaviorists, feels pain, perceives images, and lives an essentially private mental life? To prove something to others, one must appeal to publicly verifiable evidence. It is therefore self-contradictory to claim to prove that one has states of awareness which can only be observed by oneself.

The issue between introspectionism and behaviorism is therefore *in principle* undecidable—or rather, it can be decided only by arbitrary dictum, in the way, for example, that Paul Weiss decides it by, in effect, exclaiming to Norbert Wiener: "Well, maybe *you* don't have consciousness, but I assure you that *I* do!"

It is an odd but characteristic feature of the philosophical defense of man against the machine that it vacillates between appealing to special properties that man has but the machine lacks, and then, when machines are found to have (or to be capable of acquiring) those properties, denying the propriety of using the same words to represent them. We tend to argue: man can do x and machines cannot. Then, when a machine is designed that can do x, we shift to the linguistic gambit and protest: "But when a machine does x, it is inappropriate to call what it does, 'x.'" (The same procedure is frequently used in mind-body and vitalist-mechanist disputes.)

While this shifty mode of defense seems sophistical, it has, I think, some basis in truth, and derives from the fact that the key words in such disputes serve a dual function, and the disputants tend to shift their attention from one function to the other. Words like "thinking," "conscious," "human," "mind" on the one hand and, on the other, "computing," "unconscious," "machine," and "body" are, to use Nowell-Smith's suggestive term, Janus-faced. They indicate properties and capacities that can be observed or inferred from observation, but they also express attitudes (favorable in the first group and unfavorable in the second) toward the things to which they are applied, and the relation between their descriptive content and their normative content, while intimate and fairly constant, is to some extent flexible. Thus, to say that something is human, we require two conditions to be fulfilled: (1) it must have a certain shape, be able to perform certain activities such as talking, laughing, etc.; and (2) its activities must be those which rank highest in our scale of values— and, more than that, we must approve of the quality of their performance. If this second element is missing, we are likely to say about a creature that looks and talks like a man: "How remarkable. That creature that looks and talks like a man!" We are not likely to say that it *is* a man. Thus the question as to whether machines can be built that will be equal or superior to man depends, for its answer, on two factors: performance, and *how we evaluate* the performance. Mechanistic behaviorists answer the question too quickly, thinking only of the operationally definable factor, performance. What they fail to consider, and what makes sense of the anti-mechanist complaint that mechanism debases man, is that words like "thinking" and "human" are honorific as well as descriptive words, medals that we pin only on things we like and admire. Thus to call a man-made creature "human" in a literal rather than metaphorical tone is to imply, not only that it looks like *homo sapiens* and acts like *homo sapiens,* but also that it has been awarded honorary membership in the species *homo sapiens.* To earn this award, it must interest us, amuse us, arouse our emotions and desires; in general, it must provoke us to *feel that it is one of us,* or, as Kant might have said, to treat it as a person. But no mechanistic behaviorist can prove to us that we *must* take such an attitude toward something we have manufactured. As long as we reject the credentials of even the very best machines, they will remain outside our club, although, if Norbert Wiener's predictions come true, we may someday beg for admission to theirs.

(3) Mind, Body, and Dispositions

Still another shotgun wedding has been performed in this book, the ill-suited couple in this case being the mind and the brain. Wolfgang Köhler's thoughtful and learned survey of psychological and physiological research bearing on the mind-body problem seems to support a parallelist theory (in a tentative way), but makes the final resolution of the problem dependent upon the completion of the studies he describes. The trouble with his approach, soundly empiricistic though it seems, is that the scientific studies in question will *never* be completed, so that, defined in such terms, the mind-body problem will never be solved. The approach of scientific empiricism to philosophical problems such as this is logically self-defeating. For the mind-body problem (if there is one) is not like the problem of whether or not heavy smoking causes lung cancer, nor like that of whether light is made up of waves or particles. It is not a problem to be settled by the discovery of new data, nor by the construction of a systematic theory that accounts for all the known facts. Even the most enterprising experimental scientist will never succeed in isolating the meeting point of mind and body in some kind of cloud chamber, nor in devising a microscope under which mind-body interaction can be observed.

The linguistic approach of Gilbert Ryle in his *The Concept of Mind* seems to me a much more promising one than that of scientific empiricism, although I shall express some reservations about it. Ryle regards the mind-body problem as a *logical* puzzle, a problem of making more clear the logical grammar of the concepts of mind and body. He argues that questions like "How does the mind affect the body?" or "Where is the mind located?" are spurious combinations of words, as pointless as the query "How high is up?", because the concepts of mind and body belong to different conceptual "categories." Mind, according to Ryle, is a dispositional concept, while body is a substantival concept, and it is bad logical grammar to combine such diverse concepts in one sentence or in one question. Thus, for Ryle, none of the traditional metaphysical positions on the mind-body makes sense—neither dualism nor materialism nor idealism nor parallelism nor identity theory.[8]

But one weakness in Ryle's analysis of mind is that, while it effectively explains why and how questions about the relation of mind and body often do not make sense, it fails to provide an explanation of why and how such questions sometimes make very good sense, yet it seems perfectly obvious that they sometimes do. When a doctor tells his patient that the main cause of his illness is mental rather than physical, or when he tells another patient that a blow on his head has affected his (the patient's) mind, the doctor conveys significant information, and yet he implies some kind of mind-body interaction. I suspect that Ryle, in his eagerness to settle the matter once and for all, overstressed the mechanistic sense of causal expressions such as "interaction," a sense (that of transference of motion from one body to another on contact) which requires that both terms of the relation be of the same conceptual type, i.e., both must be capable of occupying space. But it seems fairly obvious that causal concepts such as interaction have many and diverse senses, some of which may very well permit combinations of different categorial concepts, such as mind and body. We often say that motives (which are mental) cause bodily motions (which are physical), and I see no reason to prohibit this mode of speech so long as we avoid the temptation to picture motives as invisible engines inside our heads.

A second and more serious inadequacy in Ryle's solution is that his dispositional account of mind fails to explain the radical difference of *feel* between mental and psysical concepts. His distinction between dispositional and substantival categories is not sufficient for this job, because there are plenty of physical dispositional concepts as well as mental ones. What is it, then, which makes us classify some dispositions and activities as physical, and others as mental? The reason why Ryle does not provide the answer to this question is, I think, very similar to the reason we found for Toulmin's forced union of wanting and choosing, and Wiener's identification of thinking with computing, namely, the oversimplification of the meaning of a complex concept. The term "mind," like the terms "thinking," and "human," has both normative and descriptive meaning. If, like most philosophers including Köhler and Ryle, we search only for a difference in descriptive content—i.e., observable properties and dispositions—we are bound to fail to do justice to the depth of the mind-body chasm, and we naturally arrive at an implausible difference of mere degree of complexity. For the really basic difference lies in our value attitudes toward the mental and the *merely* physical (I use the word "merely" deliberately here). It is not only *what* a creature does—such as talking, reading, repairing a car, etc.—that manifests a mind, but also how well it does it and how highly we rate the quality of its performance. Certain activities are so generally admired that we tend, mistakenly, to assume that they always belong to the category of the mental. Memory, for instance, is assumed always to be a mental capacity. Then, when a machine performs prodigious feats of memory, we are astounded and philosophically confused. Yet we need not be, if we merely bear in mind that to classify an activity as mental is to *evaluate* it as well as to describe it. Remarkable feats of memory, even when performed by human beings, inspire in us more curiosity than admiration when they make uninteresting uses of the information remembered, and thus evidence no understanding on the part of the performer. In such cases we tend to say: "He doesn't have a good mind, he just has a photographic memory." Thus we shift what is usually classified as a mental capacity to the category of the physical, not because of any difference of observable properties, but because of our unenthusiastic response to the same properties. The point is that the difference between mind and body, like the difference between men and machines, has as much to do with the way we feel about them as with their scientificaly determinable properties.

(4) Conclusions and Afterthoughts

In each of the three discussions, above, I have argued against the tendency to overstress one component of the meaning of a complex concept, to the unwarranted exclusion of other components, and thereby to reduce the complex concept to a simpler one. I argued, in my first discussion, against Toulmin's reduction of wanting to choosing and of choosing to mere taking, in my second discussion against Wiener's and Scriven's reduction of human thought to mechanical computation, and, my third discussion against Köhler's reduction of the mind to the brain, as well as Ryle's reduction of mind to a set of bodily dispositions. In the first case, it seemed to me that the descriptive component of meaning was overlooked, while in the last two cases it was the normative component that was left out of account.

Perhaps, then, the spade metaphor with which I began this paper was misleading, since the things I have argued should be called by their right names are as complex and subtle as a spade is simple and crude. One might rather compare them to golf clubs—wooden driver, iron driver, mashie, niblick, putter, etc.—each of which, for the expert at golf, has a distinctive function to perform, but for the novice does pretty much the same job as any other. In fact, if I may stretch the analogy to the bursting point, for the duffer who digs up turf at every swing, one could just as well call each of these instruments a spade! [9] Yet who would regard the duffer as an authority on the metaphysics of golf?

NOTES AND REFERENCES

1. Piaget, J., *The Language and Thought of the Child* (New York: The Humanities Press, 1952), pp. 27 ff.

2. When I cited this example at the conference, Sidney Hook remarked that he has witnessed such scenes in many families which he would not call authoritarian. My reply was that probably, in the families he had in mind, the *child* is the authoritarian figure.

3. "Wish relates rather to the end, choice to the means. . . . It seems to be voluntary, but not all that is voluntary to be an object of choice. Is then what has been decided on by previous deliberation? At any rate choice involves a rational principle and thought." Aristotle, *Nichomachean Ethics,* trans. W. D. Ross, 1111b-1112a.

4. "A man can choose without having any reason for his choice in sheer absence of mind or from sheer force of habit. These are minimal cases that *hardly deserve the name of 'choice.'* . . . But if he did not want to do anything else . . . he could not in these

conditions be said to have *chosen* to do something else." P. H. Nowell-Smith, *Ethics* (Baltimore: Pelican Books, 1956), pp. 102 and 278. My italics.

5. Note that the appropriate question is "Do you take this woman?", not "Do you choose this woman?", and *certainly* not "Do you *want* this woman?"

6. My claim that choice presupposes wanting may seem inconsistent with my earlier illustration of the well-bred duellist who may say "I choose this weapon" but not "I want this weapon." But it is only apparent inconsistency, calling for the following qualification: we *can* use "I choose" in an arbitrarily executive way, because, as I have already pointed out, the executive sense is one component of its meaning. But while this is a possible use of "choose," it is not, as Nowell-Smith observes in the passage quoted in note 4 above, the best use. For the duellist to say "I choose this weapon" is like my saying "I love martinis," It is not likely to be misunderstood, yet neither is it a thoughtful choice of language. What the duellist really should say is: "I'll take this weapon," and, better still, he should say it with his eyes closed.

7. Such personifications of machines are, of course, metaphorical, because the descriptive component of meaning is absent. But if the machines in question looked and behaved like women, the personified language would be quite literal.

8. Ryle's view was effectively argued for at the conference by Hilary Putnam, but without the qualifications that I think must be added to make the view tenable.

9. In card games, as well as in golf, it is a most serious error, leading to most dire consequences, to confuse clubs with spades.

INDEX 2546

INDEX

Abelson, R., 231

Adrian, E. D., 35

Analytic propositions: from concept of emergence, 94-95; definitions in science as, 157; as distinct from synthetic, 139, 150-151, 214, 218; empirical generalizations as, 165; psychophysical laws as, 152

Aristotle, 191, 235, 242

Assertions: of epistemic authority, 225, 254, 256; of executive authority, 193-194, 199-201, 225-226, 230, 234-237; of expert authority, 200-201, 225, 230; of special authority, 199-201, 225-230. See also Use.

Atomic theory, 69

Austin, J. L., 225

Awareness: of brain in introspection, 92; field of, 20, 34, 62-63; growth of, 185; as indefinable, 79-80, 83; of introspective data, 50; proof of, 237; Whitehead's view of the concept of, 102

Ayer, A. J., 43

Behaviorism: inadequate for discovering reality, 136, 177-180; inadequate for mind-body problem, 37, 39, 50, 79 ff., 87, 130-131, 215, 237-240; linguistic, 33, 91, 149, 159, 171; as methodological, 17, 46, 205

Bergson, H., 40

Berkeley, G., 47, 61

Bifurcation of nature, 101-104

Biology, 22 ff.

Black, M., 153, 158, 163, 237

Bohr, N., 137

Boolian logic, 137

Brandt, R. B., 62

Brentano, F., 133

Bridgman, P. W., 78, 90

Broad, C. D., 88, 198

Brodbeck, M., 163

Butler, S., 109, 111

Carnap, R., 33, 43, 139, 152, 163

Category mistake, 88, 156

Causal relations: in emergence, 95; of mind and brain, 16, 30, 36-37, 65, 67, 80, 88-90, 149, 157, 182; in paranormal cognition, 84, 136-137; between two minds, 62; ultimate nature of, 101-102

Child phychology, 192, 201, 210, 219, 224, 232; distinction between human beings and machines based on, 184

Chisholm, R. M., 153

Choice: as behavior, 205; complex uses of concept of, 225-226, 231-232, 241-242; logical stratification of concept of, 192 ff., 204, 216, 217-219; in varied contexts, 223-224

Church, A., 162

Clairvoyance, 74-78

Concepts, analysis of, 191 ff., 208, 210, 211-212, 214, 221, 222

Consciousness: causal efficacy of, 37; definition of, 113, 144, 165 ff., 173, 237-238; gap between brain and, 33, 161; of other people, 39, 79-80; in parapsychology, 75-77; self-, 82, 91, 98-99, 136, 228

Conservation of energy, 30, 88, 151

Contextualism, 45, 48, 58-59, 94, 192, 222-223

Creativity, 118 ff., 135

Cybernetics, 172

Danto, A. C., 165

Definition: artificial, 113; explicit, 69; formal, 92; operational, 38; in ordinary language, 55; ostensive, 62, 231; in parapsychology, 77; physicalistic, 181; stipulative, 62, 113, 154, 158; theoretical, 157-158

Descartes, 35, 50, 60, 89, 100, 171, 216

Desires: conscious, 195-196, 202-204; real, 195, 199, 201-203, 222 ff.; simulated, 195, 199, 201-203, 222 ff.; unconscious, 195-196, 202-204. See also Unconscious

Determinism, 65, 116, 119